NOTTING HILL GATE 1

Herausgegeben von
Dr. phil. h. c. Christoph Edelhoff, StD a. D.,
Vorsitzender THE ENGLISH ACADEMY und
Prof. Dr. phil. Torben Schmidt, Leuphana Universität
Lüneburg, Mitglied THE ENGLISH ACADEMY

Erarbeitet von
Denise Arrandale (Neumünster), Michael Biermann
(Hamburg), Hannelore Debus (Mörfelden-Walldorf),
Phil Mothershaw-Rogalla (Volkmarsen-Külte), Semra
Siyli (Duisburg)

sowie
Otfried Börner (Hamburg), Ingrid Preedy (Dortmund),
Jürgen Wrobel (Oberursel)

Fachliche Beratung
Lieselotte Bohnsack (Essen), Rolf-Olaf Geisler
(Oberhausen), Dr. Sandra Götz (Gießen), Susanne
Quandt (Bremen), Dr. Ivo Steininger (Wetzlar)

Domenica

Diesterweg

NOTTING HILL GATE 1

Für Klasse 5 an Gesamtschulen und anderen integrierenden Schulformen

---

Zusatzmaterialien zum vorliegenden Schülerbuch

Das Textbook ist auch als Digitales Schulbuch erhältlich. Mehr Informationen unter
www.diesterweg.de/digitales-schulbuch

Materialien für Schülerinnen und Schüler

- Workbook mit Audio-CD 978-3-425-14011-7
- Workbook mit Lernsoftware und Audio-CD
  978-3-425-14021-6
- Lernsoftware mit Einzelplatzlizenz
  978-3-425-14051-3
- Vokabel-App WEB-425-14061
- Trainingsheft Besser lesen 978-3-425-14031-5
- Inklusions- und Fördermaterialien mit Audio-CD
  978-3-425-14671-3
- Zoom-App www.zoom-app.de

Fördert individuell – passt zum Schulbuch

Optimal für den Einsatz im Unterricht mit Notting Hill Gate! Stärken erkennen, Defizite beheben. Online-Lernstandsdiagnose und Auswertung auf Basis der aktuellen Bildungsstandards. Individuell zusammengestellte Fördermaterialien.

www.diesterweg.de/diagnose

Online-Diagnose

Materialien für Lehrkräfte

- Teacher's Manual 978-3-425-14801-4
- Vorschläge für Lernerfolgskontrollen mit CD-ROM 978-3-425-14841-0
- Workbook mit Lösungen und Audio-CD 978-3-425-14811-3
- Audio-CD für Lehrkräfte 978-3-425-14831-1
- DVD für Lehrkräfte 978-3-425-14821-2
- Kopiervorlagen 978-3-425-14851-9
- Materialien für projektorientierten Unterricht 978-3-425-14071-1
- Wortbildkarten 978-3-425-14901-1
- BiBox Digitale Lehrermaterialien Einzellizenz WEB-425-14891,
  Einzellizenz (auf DVD-ROM) 978-3-425-14055-1
  Kollegiumslizenz WEB-425-14889
- Interaktive Whiteboard-Software Einzellizenz 978-3-425-14871-7
- Interaktive Whiteboard-Software Schullizenz 978-3-425-14087-2
- Differenzierung & Inklusion digital 978-3-425-14861-8
- Lernsoftware Schullizenz 978-3-425-14881-6

© 2015 Bildungshaus Schulbuchverlage
Westermann Schroedel Diesterweg
Schöningh Winklers GmbH, Braunschweig
www.diesterweg.de

Druck A² / Jahr 2016
Alle Drucke der Serie A sind im Unterricht parallel verwendbar.

Redaktion: Doris Bos, Jutta Eckardt-Scheurig, Charlotte Finn, Daniel Harnett, Amy Frances Koerner und Dr. Katja Nandorf
Vokabelanhang: Doris Bos
Herstellung: Harald Thumser, Frankfurt am Main
Illustrationen: Ulf Marckwort, Kassel
Umschlaggestaltung: blum design und kommunikation GmbH, Hamburg
Umschlagfoto: Dirk Schmidt / dsphotos.de
Layoutkonzeption und Satz: tiff.any GmbH, Berlin
Druck und Bindung: westermann druck GmbH, Braunschweig

ISBN 978-3-425-14001-8

Herzlich willkommen in deinem neuen Englischbuch. Es soll dir beim Lernen helfen. Deshalb ist es wichtig, dass du dich gut darin zurechtfindest. Beantworte die Fragen und lerne dein Buch kennen. Hinter jeder Antwortmöglichkeit steht ein Buchstabe. Wenn du alle Fragen richtig beantwortet hast, erhältst du einen englischen Satz.

1 Wie heißt dein neues Englischbuch in Klasse 5?
- Notting Hill Gate (E)
- Notting Hill (A)

2 Auf den Seiten 4–8 findest du das Inhaltsverzeichnis. Mit wie vielen *Themes* kannst du dich in diesem Schuljahr beschäftigen?
- sechs (N)
- acht (M)

3 Nun schau auf die Seite 22. Hier treffen sich alle *Notting Hill Gate* Kinder und begrüßen sich. Wie viele Kinder sind es?
- sieben (P)
- sechs (G)

4 Jedes *Theme* hat ein Hauptthema. Blättere *Theme* 2 durch. Worum geht es?
- was man am Morgen macht (L)
- um Geburtstage (K)

5 Auf den *Wordbank*-Seiten findest du viele Wörter und Ausdrücke, die zu einem bestimmten Thema passen. Auf welcher Seite findest du die *Wordbank* zum Thema *Animals*?
- auf Seite 147 (I)
- auf Seite 13 (O)

6 In den Wortlisten kannst du die Wörter nachschlagen, die im Buch vorkommen. Auf welcher Seite werden die Wortlisten erklärt?
- auf Seite 229 (C)
- auf Seite 182 (S)

7 In den Land & Leute-Boxen erfährst du mehr über das Leben in Großbritannien. Worum geht es in Land & Leute 5?
- Doppeldeckerbusse (T)
- die Londoner U-Bahn (H)

8 Am Rand der Buchseiten findest du verschiedene Symbole, die dir bei der Arbeit mit dem Buch helfen, wie zum Beispiel dieses: 🔍 Worum geht es? Tipp: Schau auf Seite 9 nach.
- um Grammatik (I)
- um ein Projekt (W)

9 Finde dieses Symbol: 📖 Wohin soll dich der Verweis führen?
- zum Wörterverzeichnis (D)
- zu einer Aufgabe im Workbook (S)

10 Jedes *Theme* hat eine Wortliste, in der du die Wörter findest, die ihr gerade im Unterricht besprecht. Wo beginnt die Wortliste für *Theme* 1?
- auf Seite 191 (F)
- auf Seite 241 (O)

11 Auf den Seiten 239–261 befinden sich Wörter, die nach dem Alphabet geordnet sind. Welche Wörter kannst du hier nachschlagen?
- englische und deutsche Wörter (U)
- nur englische Wörter (G)

12 Techniken zum Englischlernen stehen auf den How to …-Seiten ab Seite 136. Wie viele davon gibt es?
- 22 Seiten (S)
- 10 Seiten (N)

Hast du die Lösungen gefunden? Prima! In deinem Englischbuch gibt es noch viel mehr zu entdecken. Blättere einmal in Ruhe durch das Buch.

Viel Spaß in diesem Schuljahr mit *Notting Hill Gate!*

Inhalt

Die Angebote in *Notting Hill Gate* sind nicht linear abzuarbeiten.
Die Auswahl richtet sich nach den Schwerpunkten des schulinternen Curriculums.
Theme 6 ist optional.

In diesem Buch gibt es folgende Symbole:

A1

Diese Aufgabe gehört zum **Basisweg**.

CD
1/1

Der Hörtext ist auf der **Audio-CD** für Lehrkräfte (CD 1, Track 1).

A7

Diese Aufgabe gehört nicht zum Basisweg und ist **fakultativ**.

CD
1

Der Hörtext ist auf der **Audio-CD** für Schülerinnen und Schüler (Track 1).

A8 Choose

Suche dir eine Aufgabe aus. Ihr könnt alleine arbeiten, zu zweit oder in einer Gruppe. Ihr könnt auch eine eigene Aufgabe finden.

DVD
1

Der Videoclip ist auf der **DVD** für Lehrkräfte (Clip 1).

WB p. 13
A1, A2

Hierzu gibt es im **Workbook** weitere Übungen.

A9 Target task

Zielaufgabe der Sequenz

p. 13
A3, A4

Hierzu gibt es Übungen in den **Inklusions- und Fördermaterialien**.

Diese Aufgabe eignet sich für Schülerinnen und Schüler mit **Förderbedarf**.

LiF p. 162
1

Hierzu gibt es eine Erklärung im Grammatikteil *Language in Focus*.

☆ leichte Aufgabe

how to p. 138
listen

Hierzu gibt es eine Erklärung in den *How to ...*-Seiten.

☾ mittelschwere Aufgabe

☀ schwierige Aufgabe

wordbank
places p. 149

In den **Wordbanks** befinden sich die wichtigsten Wörter zu einem Thema.

Diese Aufgabe eignet sich für die **kooperative Arbeit** in der Klasse mit allen Schülerinnen und Schülern.

model text

Ein *model text* ist eine Vorlage für deinen eigenen Text.

▶ Zu diesem Videoclip gibt es eine Aufgabe.

Tipp
Club kann auch Schul-AG bedeuten.

Hier bekommst du kleine **Tipps** und Hilfen.

Primary pick-up
Hier kannst du dein Wissen aus der **Grundschule** einbringen.

Berry the clown

CD 1/1

DVD 1

Listen to Berry. What do you understand?

WB p. 5
1, 2

p. 4
1, 2

My name is …

Talk about yourself.

DVD

2

- My name is **Boris**.
- I'm from **Dortmund**.
- I'm **eleven** years old.
- My favourite colour is **blue**.
- I speak **German**, **Polish** – and **English**!
- …

Ask your partner.

- What's your name?
- How old are you?
- What are your favourite animals?
- What languages do you speak?
- …
- …
- My name is …
- I'm … years old.
- My favourite animals are …
- I speak …

Ask four more classmates.

 WB p. 6
1, 2

 p. 5
1–3

Colourful clothes

CD 1/2 1 1/3 2

DVD 3,4

**Listen to the song and sing along.
Act it out.**

 Look around the circle, what colours can
   you see?
Get ready if you're wearing **blue**. One,
   two, three.
Stand up, stand up and turn around.
Point at your **blue** then sit back down.

Look around the circle, what colours can
   you see?
Get ready if you're wearing …

 red

 green

 blue

 yellow

 orange

white

 brown

black

 purple

Talk about Lily's clothes.

She has got …

There are …

There is …

*Lily has got a **blue cap** in her wardrobe.*

WB p. 7
1–4

p. 6
1

Animals

Do you know the animals in the picture?

 DVD
5

Which animals can you find on a farm?

Which animals can you find in a zoo?

Which animals can be pets?

 WB p. 8
1–3

 p. 7
1–3

Numbers

CD
1/6 3
1/7 4

DVD
6

Listen to the number rap.

Number rap

1 – 2 – 3,
this is fun, do you agree?

4 – 5 – 6 and 7,
a rap in English, I'm in heaven!

It's time for 8 and then for 9,
up till now we're doing fine!

Next is 10, yes 10 is next.
We are the champions,
we are the best!

Now what about 11?
That's 2 and 2 and 7.

Hey, 12 at last
and we're rapping, rapping,
rapping, rapping very fast!

12 – 11 – 10 – 9 – 8.
We like to rap with Notting Hill
Gate.

7 – 6 – 5 – 4 – 3 – 2 – 1.
Let's start again! This rap is fun.

Now it is your turn.

Talk to your partner.

22 93 06

What's your phone number?

It's two two nine three oh six.

Tipp
Die Zahl „0"
heißt bei
Telefon-
nummern „oh".

And what's your mobile phone number?

...

WB p. 9 **Write your partner's phone number down.**
1–4

p. 8
1, 2

Weather

CD
1/9

DVD
7,8

spring — *I like spring and I like rain.* — *I can jump into big puddles.*

summer — *I like summer. Hot weather – no clouds …* — *I can sit in the sun and eat ice cream.*

autumn — *I like autumn. I like the wind.* — *On a windy day I can fly my kite.*

winter — *I like winter. I love snow.* — *Then I can build a snowman.*

Collect weather words.
What can you do on a hot day?
What can you do on a cold day?

 On a hot day I …

 …

WB p. 10
1, 2

p. 9
1, 2

In the break

CD 1/10

Look and listen. What are the boys talking about?

CD 1/10

Listen and read along.

Jonty: Oh, no! Cheese sandwiches again! I hate cheese sandwiches! And an apple, ugh!

Luke: I like apples! Look, you can give me your apple and I can give you my banana. What do you think?

Jonty: Yeah, sure. That's a great idea. I like bananas. And can I swap my sandwich for your pizza?

Luke: Sorry, no. I love pizza! But you can have a little bit of it.

Jonty: Oh, thank you.

WB p. 11
1–4

p. 10
1, 2

Act out the dialogue.

CD
1/12 5
1/13 6

Listen to the chant and say it.

Make your own chant.

 Food chant

I like **pizza**, I like **pizza** a lot!
I like **pizza**, I like **pizza** a lot!
I like **pizza**, I like **pizza** a lot!
I love it!

Karla

Read about Karla. What do you understand?

Hello everybody! My name is Karla.

I'm eleven. I've got a little brother. His name is Josh. He is five. He likes football.

I like playing wheelchair basketball. I'm very good at it. I go to computer club at my school.

I love music. I've got lots of songs on my mobile.

I love dinosaurs, too. I've got four dinosaur posters in my room. Dinosaurs are so cool!

My favourite animals are pigs and rabbits. They are so cute! I have got a rabbit. His name is Hoppity. He eats carrots for breakfast. I like cornflakes and a glass of orange juice.

My best friends are Gillian and Rajiv. Goodbye!

 WB p.12
1,2

 p.11
1

The Notting Hill Gate song – Part 1

Listen to the song. Then sing along.

 CD
1/15 7
1/16 8

♫ Come to London City,
it's time to meet
a lot of nice children
walking down the street.

Some live in Notting Hill,
a perfect place to stay!
Some live in Hendon,
that's not so far away!

So let's meet the friends
and all their pets, too.
I really want to meet them!
What about YOU?

People and places

In diesem *Theme* ...

- lernst du, andere zu begrüßen und dich und deine Freunde vorzustellen.

- Zielaufgabe *(target task)*: Du gestaltest ein Poster über dich selbst.

- erfährst du etwas über Notting Hill und lernst, von deiner Wohngegend zu erzählen.

- Zielaufgabe *(target task)*: Du entwickelst zusammen mit deiner Klasse Ideen für eine Traumstadt und präsentierst sie.

name: Leonie
town: Berlin
age: 12
favourite colour: red
hobby: Football ⚽
pet: no pet 🐈
best friends: Semra and Alexander

A1 Welcome to Notting Hill

Primary pick-up

a) **What can you see?**

b) **Listen. What can you hear?**

 CD
1/17 9

c) **Work with a partner.**

 WB p. 13
A1–A3

Show me the bus.

...

 p. 12
A1, A2

A2 New friends

CD
1/18 10

a) Look at the comic and listen.

1

Look, there's my cousin Gillian and her friends. Hi Gillian!

2

Hi David. These are my friends, Karla and Rajiv.

Hello! And this is Vanessa and that's Charlie.

Hi!

Hello!

3

Sorry, what's your name again?

I'm Rajiv.

Yes, I am.

Are you from Notting Hill?

4

Come on, let's go to the park.

Is it far?

No, it isn't.

It's around the corner.

WB p. 14
A4

b) Read what the children say.

p. 14
A3

c) Work in groups. Draw the scene in the park. Act it out.

A3 What's your name?

p. 14
A4

LiF p. 162
1a, d

Walk, stop and talk. Talk to your classmates like this:

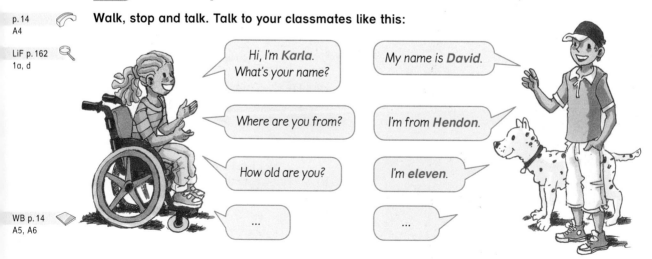

Hi, I'm *Karla*. What's your name?

My name is *David*.

Where are you from?

I'm from *Hendon*.

How old are you?

I'm *eleven*.

...

...

WB p. 14
A5, A6

A4 Charlie

 Work with a partner. Look at the picture. Collect words about Charlie.

p. 15
A5

a) Listen to Charlie and read along. What does he talk about?

CD
1/19 13

> Hi everybody! My name is Charlie. I'm from Hendon. That's in London.

> I've got three goldfish. There's a goldfish poster in my room. I've got a red bike. I like riding my bike, but my favourite hobby is football. I'm a big football fan. I think Arsenal is the best football team.

> My parents are from Barbados. I've got two sisters. Their names are Josephine and Sharon.

> My best friends are David and Vanessa. They live in Hendon, just like me.

> I love burgers and chips with ketchup. But I hate tomatoes!

how to p. 138
listen

b) Write about Charlie. Complete the sentences.

☆ Charlie is from …
Charlie has got two …
Charlie has got three …
Charlie has got a red …

☾ Charlie is from …
He has got two …
He loves …
But he hates …
He has got a red …
His best friends are …

☼ Charlie is from … in …
He has got two … and three …
He loves … , but he hates …
He has got a … in his room and a …
He likes …
His … is football.
He thinks Arsenal … team.
His … friends … David and Vanessa.

c) Match the questions and answers.

1. Is Charlie from Hendon?
2. Are his parents from Barbados?
3. Is Charlie a big basketball fan?
4. Are his best friends Josephine and Sharon?

a) No, they aren't.
b) No, he isn't.
c) Yes, he is.
d) Yes, they are.

LiF p. 163
1c

WB p. 16
A7, A8

A5 Meet the children

Work with a partner. Look at the pictures and point.

Show me the cat.

Show me the red cap.

Show me Gillian.

...

LiF p. 164
2a, b

a) Look at the pictures. What have the children got?

Vanessa has got a football.

Gillian has got ...

CD
1/20 16

b) Listen to the children and read along.

Hello! My name is Gillian. I'm from Notting Hill. I'm twelve years old. I've got a cat. Her name is Butterfly. My favourite colour is red. My best friends are Karla, Rajiv and my cousin David.

1

2 Hi, my name is Vanessa. I live in Hendon with my parents. I'm in a football team. We are really good. I also like music and dancing. I haven't got a pet.

model text

Hey! My name is David. I live in Hendon. I'm eleven. I've got a dog. His name is Kenny Hoover. I love football. I always wear my red cap.

3

Hi, I'm Rajiv. I'm twelve. My parents are from India. At home we speak English and Hindi. We **4** live in Notting Hill. I'm a good cook. I play the guitar. I love my parrot Ruby. My best friends are Gillian and Karla.

Hello! My name is Karla. I've got a little brother. My hobby is wheelchair basketball and I also go to computer club at school. I've got a rabbit. His name is Hoppity.

5

LiF p. 165
2d

c) Work with a partner. Who has got what?

p. 16
A6, A7

WB p. 17
A9, A10

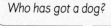
Who has got a dog?

David.

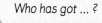
Who has got ... ?

...

A6 The Notting Hill Gate song – Part 2

Listen to the song and sing along.

Charlie's three goldfish
swim all day.
Karla's rabbit, Hoppity,
really loves to play.

Gillian's cat, Butterfly,
loves to chase mice.
Rajiv's parrot, Ruby,
is really, really nice.

David's dog, Kenny Hoover,
likes to play all day.
We like to learn English –
let's start right away!

CD
1/21 18
1/16 8
1/22 19
1/23 20

p. 18
A8

WB p. 18
A11

A7 That's me! ▶

Watch the video clip. What has Kai got?

Watch the video clip. What can you say about Kai?
Tell your partner in German.

DVD
10

WB p. 18
A12

A8 Choose

1. Draw a picture of your best friend and present him or her.

   This is ...   ... has got ...

2. Write about your best friend.

3. Make a recording about the friends from Notting Hill.

4. Make a character and present him or her.

WB p. 19
A13

A9 Target task: A class puzzle

a) Make a puzzle piece about yourself.

name: Leonie
town: Berlin
age: 12
favourite colour: red
hobby: Football ⚽
pet: no pet 🐹
best friends: Semra and Alexander

My name is Cem.
I'm from Hamburg.
Hamburg is in Germany.
I'm 11 years old.
I speak German, Turkish and English.
My favourite colours are 🟠 and 🔵.
I play basketball.
My favourite animals are zebras.
I've got two brothers and one sister.
I've got a dog.
My best friends are Cihan and Luka.

model text

p. 19
A9, A10

WB p. 19
A14

b) Put the pieces together and make a class puzzle.

P1 Explain

Explain what you have to do.

1. Work in groups.
2. Work with a partner.
3. Complete the sentences.
4. Listen to Charlie and read along.
5. Look at the comic and listen.

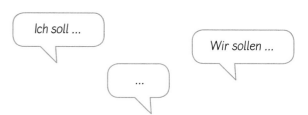

Ich soll ...

Wir sollen ...

...

P2 Who's this?

Talk about the friends.

Who's this?

This is Gillian. She's from Notting Hill.

P3 Long and short

a) Find the matching forms. Write them down in your exercise book.

there is	I am	what is	what's	that's	who's
that is	I have got	who is	I'm	there's	I've got

there is = there's

b) Be a language detective: look at A3 and A4 again. Find sentences with these forms. Read them out to a partner. Take turns.

P4 I'm – I am

Read the short forms. Write the long forms in your exercise book.

I'm Gillian.

You're my friend.

We're from London.

What's your name?

She's from Notting Hill.

They're from Hendon.

LiF p. 162
1a

🔍 I am Gillian.

☼ **Be a language detective: look at the long forms in your exercise book. When do you use "am", when do you use "are" and when do you use "is"?**

Practice matters

P5 Friends from Notting Hill

Write about the friends. You can look at A5 for help.

LiF p. 162
1a

| Gillian's best friends
David
Rajiv
Vanessa
Karla's hobby
… | is
are | wheelchair basketball.
eleven.
a good cook.
Karla, Rajiv and David.
in a football team.
… |

Gillian's best friends are Karla, Rajiv and David.

P6 Yes or no?

a) Match the questions and answers.

1. Is Vanessa in a football team?   No, he isn't.
2. Is Rajiv eleven?   Yes, it is.
3. Are Gillian and David cousins?   No, they aren't.
4. Is David from Notting Hill?   Yes, they are.
5. Are Rajiv's best friends David and Charlie?   Yes, she is.
6. Is red Gillian's favourite colour?   No, he isn't.

LiF p. 163
1c

b) Listen to the CD and check your questions and answers.

CD
23

P7 Six friends

a) Read the text. Say the words for the pictures.

1. Vanessa's 👩🧑👧🧑👨 are from London.   2. David and Vanessa like ⚽.

3. Rajiv and Vanessa like 🎵🎵🎵.   4. Karla loves her 🐰.

5. David has got a 🐆, Gillian has got a 🐈 and Charlie has got three 🐟.

b) Listen to the CD and check your words.

CD
24

P8 What have they got?

a) What have the children got?

1. Tom: a sister
2. Sara and Lynn: lots of comics
3. Diego: a new football
4. Sophie and Pete: a cat
5. Ben: a blue bike

Tom has got a sister.

LiF p. 164
2a

b) Listen to the CD and check your sentences.

CD
25

B1 In and around Notting Hill

a) Talk about the photos.

b) **What have you got where you live? What haven't you got?**

I can see ...

...

We've got ...

We haven't got ...

WB p. 20
B1

LAND & LEUTE 1

Notting Hill

Notting Hill ist ein Stadtteil der riesigen, weltberühmten Stadt London. Eine bekannte Straße und eine U-Bahnstation dort heißen Notting Hill Gate – wie dieses Buch. Die Holland Park School ist eine Gesamtschule. Sie liegt gleich neben dem Holland Park, einem großen Freizeit- und Erholungsgelände mit Spielplatz, Blumenbeeten, einem Café und einem japanischen Garten mit Fischteich.

Jeden August findet in Notting Hill der *Carnival* statt. Drei Tage lang wird auf den Straßen getanzt und gefeiert.
In der Portobello Road ist jeden Tag Markt. Samstags bauen dort auch die Antiquitätenhändler und Secondhand-Geschäfte ihre Stände auf und locken viele Touristen an.

**Schau dir den Videoclip an und finde mehr über Notting Hill heraus.
Was gibt es in deinem Ort Besonderes?**

DVD
11

B2 Butterfly's blog

a) Who is Butterfly? What do you think the blog is about?

b) Read the blog.

http://butterflythecat.wordpress.com/

how to p. 139
read

Monday 3 March – **A new home!**
Yay, I've got a new home! Now I live with Gillian, her mum and her mum's girlfriend. We have got a lovely blue house in Notting Hill! Gillian saw me at the animal shelter and I saw her and … here I am. I love this place! Miaow! Gillian is very happy and I'm very happy. Gillian knows what a cat likes! :)

Tuesday 11 March – **A little update from my new home!**
Our house isn't big but it has got a nice garden. There are lots of mice – yummy! We've got friendly neighbours. They sometimes give me cat food! And they've got a cat, too: Purry.

> Comment by Furry Friend in March:
> I hope the cat is friendly. Be careful, Butterfly!

Friday 21 March – **My new neighbourhood!**
Gillian wants to buy a basket for me. There is a big market with lots of shops on Portobello Road. I like markets but Gillian says markets aren't a good place for cats. I am so sad I can't go with her. Tell me where you live.

Miaow! Butterfly

Work with a partner. What does Butterfly say?

I've got a new home.   I live …   I love …

p. 21
B1

c) Write about Butterfly and her new home.

LiF p. 162
1a, b

Butterfly		friendly.
The house	is	sad.
Gillian	are	good for cats.
Butterfly and Gillian	isn't	big.
The neighbours	aren't	Gillian's cat.
Markets		happy.
…		…

Butterfly is Gillian's cat.

p. 22
B2

WB p. 21
B2–B4

d) Be a language detective: Find the sentences with "there is" and "there are" in the blog. When do you use "there is" and when do you use "there are"?

B3 Your area

a) Listen to the CD. What does the girl talk about?

 What is in your area? Collect words. supermarket, ...

CD 1/24

b) Walk, stop and talk. Ask your partner about his or her area.

> Is there a ... ?

> Yes, there is.

> No, there isn't.

> Are there ... ?

> Yes, there are.

> No, there aren't.

park • market •
zoo • shop •
shopping centre •
museum • café •
playground •
supermarket •
swimming pool •
cinema • school

LiF p. 163
1c
how to p. 136
work with
words

c) Talk about your house or street. Bring a picture and present it.

DVD 12

> This is my street.
> It's quiet.

> This is my house.
> It's nice.

> We've got a
> small garden.

> This is my ...

> We've got ...

> There is ...

> There are ...

> ...

p. 22
B3–B5

WB p. 22
B5

Write about your house or street.

B4 Charlie's dream street

a) Listen and read about Charlie's dream street.

There is a big park in my dream street. In the park there is a big pond with lots of goldfish and a lemonade fountain. There are no cars. You can play football in the street and you can ride your bike. There is a cool café. I can meet my friends there. We all get free burgers and chips. It's great fun. Everybody is friendly.

CD 1/25 27

model text

p. 24
B6

WB p. 22
B6–B9

b) What is special about Charlie's dream street?

You can play football in the street.

B5 Target task: Our dream town

a) Choose:

1. Draw a picture of your dream street and label it.
2. Make a collage about your dream street.
3. Write about your dream street.

b) Put your dream streets together to make a dream town.

p. 25
B7

P9 Explain

Explain what you have to do.

1. Write about your house or street.
2. Draw a picture.
3. Talk about the photos.
4. Walk, stop and talk.
5. Bring a picture and present it.

> *Ich soll ...*

> *...*

> *Wir sollen ...*

P10 In town

> shops • café • playground •
> swimming pool • shopping centre •
> market • cars • bikes

a) Look at the words. Complete the sentences.

There is a

There are

There are

There is a

There is a

There is a

There are

There is a

CD 30

b) Listen to the CD and check your sentences.

P11 Butterfly's new area

LiF p. 162
1a

a) Complete the sentences.

> is • are

Butterfly ??? Gillian's new cat. She ??? happy in her new home. Gillian ??? happy, too.

There ??? a cat in the neighbourhood and there ??? lots of mice. The mice ??? not happy

about the cats. There ??? a big market in Notting Hill and there ??? lots of shops.

Butterfly is Gillian's new cat.

CD 31

b) Listen to the CD and check your sentences.

Practice matters

P12 One and one is one

a) Put the words together and write them down.

swimming	shopping	football	animal	cat	computer

centre	team	pool	club	shelter	food

swimming pool, ...

b) Listen to the CD and check your words.

CD 32

P13 What have they got?

a) Complete the sentences.

> have got • has got

LiF p. 164 2a

1. I ??? a little sister. She ??? a rabbit.

2. I ??? three brothers. They ??? lots of mice.

3. My friend ??? a brother and a sister. They ??? two cats.

4. Our neighbours ??? five children – four boys and a girl.

5. The boys ??? seven hamsters and the girl ??? a dog.

6. My teacher ??? a parrot.

1. I have got a little sister. She has got a rabbit.

b) Listen to the CD and check your sentences.

CD 33

P14 Rhyming pairs

a) Listen to the CD and repeat.

CD 34

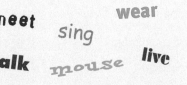

small   walk   there

stop   eat   house

fun   bring   give

meet   sing   wear

talk   mouse   live

sun   shop   all

b) Find the rhyming pairs and write them in your exercise book.

small - all, walk - ...

c) Listen to the CD and check your rhyming pairs.

CD 35

O Children in England

1 Hi, I'm Roshan. My friends call me "Rosh". I'm eleven years old and I live in Newcastle. I've got two sisters. They are nine and twelve years old.

My parents are from India. My sisters and I were born in England. My parents speak Punjabi with us but we speak English. I've got brown eyes and I'm quite small.

My dad works in a newsagent's. My mum hasn't got a job.

In my free time I play Indian drums called tabla.

2 Hi, my name's Alice. I'm nine years old and I live in Norwich.

My parents have got a veterinary practice, and so I see a lot of animals.

We've got two horses and a dog. We live next to the practice. Every morning I feed the horses apples and carrots. Our dog Skipper sleeps under my bed.

3 Hi, I'm TJ and I'm ten years old. I move to a new place every week because my parents work for a circus. So I go to a new school every week. I've got lots of friends, which is really cool.

We live in a caravan. I love juggling and I want to be an acrobat.

I love circus life – it's like a big family!

What do you find interesting?

It's interesting that …

I find it interesting that …

…

A fresh start 2

In diesem *Theme* ...

- erfährst du etwas über englisches Frühstück und sammelst Informationen über die Frühstücksgewohnheiten in deiner Klasse.

- **Zielaufgabe** *(target task)*: Du planst ein gemeinsames Frühstück in der Klasse.

- sprichst du über Dinge im Klassenzimmer, übst die Uhrzeiten und das Alphabet.

- **Zielaufgabe** *(target task)*: Du überlegst gemeinsam mit deiner Klasse, wie ihr euren Klassenraum verschönern könnt.

A1 Coconut soap rap

a) Look at the picture. What can you see? Collect words.

b) Listen to the song and act it out.

1 wash
  my hands

wash my arms

wash my
  elbows

Coconut soap

5 wash my feet

wash my knees

wash my legs

2 wash my face

wash my neck

wash my
  shoulders

3
  wash my
  hair with shampoo

brush my teeth
with toothpaste

4 wash my back

wash my tummy

wash my chest

A2 Hurry up, David!

 Work with a partner. Look at the comic. Point at body parts and say the words.

a) Look at the comic. Where is David?

b) Listen and read along. Why does David have to hurry up?

CD
1/27 42

It's eight o'clock.

David, brush your hair!

OK, Mum.

And wash your ears. They are always so dirty.

Hmm ... Tarzan has got cool hair ...

And don't forget your face!

Yes, Mum. And my eyes, my nose, my mouth, my feet ...

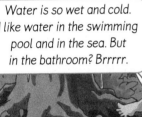

Water is so wet and cold. I like water in the swimming pool and in the sea. But in the bathroom? Brrrrr.

It's quarter past eight.

Hurry up, David, you're late!

OK, Mum. Just my hands.

c) Talk about David's morning.

d) Act out the scene.

e) Tell your partner what to do.

It's	are always dirty.
David	eight o'clock.
David's ears	and David is still in the bathroom.
The water	is in the bathroom.
It's quarter past eight	is cold.

| wash | face | teeth | neck | feet |
| brush | hair | hands | ears | ... |

Wash your hands!

p. 26
A1–A3

LiF p. 166
3

WB p. 31
A2–A5

A3 In the mirror

> Work with a partner. Look at the pictures. What does David see in the mirror?

CD
1/28 45

a) Listen and read along.

What's that? Big ears, red eyes, long nose? Hmm. No, I'm not green and scary. I haven't got three arms. I'm not a monster.

Wow, what a good-looking guy! Blond hair, white teeth, blue eyes. He's tall and strong. Hey, that's Tarzan.

Oh! A slim body, short brown hair, dark eyes and a small nose: that's me! Good morning, Mr Cool!

b) Which words describe the monster, Tarzan and David?

monster	Tarzan	David
big ears	good-looking	...
...	...	

LiF p. 162/4
1a, b, 2a, b

c) ☆ **Draw a picture of a fantasy character. Label the body parts.**

wordbank
me and my
body p. 150

☽ **Draw a picture of a fantasy character. Write a speech bubble.**

p. 28
A4

☼ **Work with a partner. Write a text about Rajiv or Karla.**

WB p. 33
A6

Hi, my name is Clive. I'm from Mars. I'm small and green. I've got five arms. I've got one eye, one nose and two ears. I like books. They are yummy!

Rajiv has got ... and ...
His ... He is ... ...

Karla has got ... and ...
Her ... She is ... ...

A4 Grandpa Phil tells a story: Bath in the bedroom ▶

Watch the video clip.
What does Tabby the cat do in the story?
What happens to her?

DVD
13

CD
1/29

A5 Who is it?

Listen to the CD. Who is who? Look at
page 18 for help.

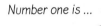
Number one is ...

...

CD
1/30

A6 Choose

1. Describe yourself like this:

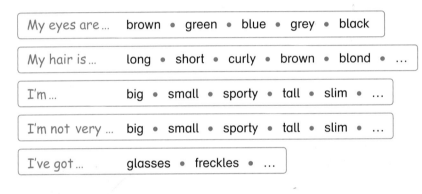

My eyes are ...   brown • green • blue • grey • black

My hair is ...   long • short • curly • brown • blond • ...

I'm ...   big • small • sporty • tall • slim • ...

I'm not very ...   big • small • sporty • tall • slim • ...

I've got ...   glasses • freckles • ...

🔍 LiF p. 162/4
1a, b, 2a, b

💡 how to p. 136
work with
words

🧰 wordbank
me and my
body p. 150

2. Write a poem about yourself.

Black hair
Brown eyes
White teeth
I smile

I
I am
I am so
I am so tall

Me
Not so tall
Not so slim
Average
That's me
And I like me

✏️ model text

3. Write about a famous person. Read your text but do not say the name of the person.
Your classmates guess who it is.

He has got ...
His eyes are ...
He is ...
...

She has got ...
Her eyes are ...
She is ...
...

I think it's ...

🔍 LiF p. 162/4
1a, b, 2a, b

📞 p. 28
A5–A6

A7 At the breakfast table

> Work with a partner. Look at the comic. Collect breakfast words.

CD
1/31 46

DVD
14

a) Listen and read along. What does David have for breakfast today?

It's half past eight. David sits down for breakfast in the kitchen.

Come on, David! You've only got five minutes! The cornflakes and milk are on the table.

Cornflakes again! I don't like cornflakes every day... I wish it was Sunday!

Mmh ... cooked Sunday breakfast! Dad makes the best Sunday breakfast. Orange juice, toast with lots of butter, baked beans and fried eggs. Yummy! But my favourite food of all ... sausages! Dad always gives me an extra sausage.

David! Stop dreaming! Hurry up, please! You're late!

Don't forget to brush your teeth!

David puts his bowl and spoon into the dishwasher.

Then he hurries to the bathroom.

I want more Sundays!

b) Talk about David.

| David
He | sits down
has only got
doesn't like
dreams
likes
puts
hurries
wants | cornflakes every day.
his bowl and spoon into the dishwasher.
for breakfast.
to the bathroom.
more Sundays.
of a cooked breakfast.
sausages.
five minutes. |

LiF p. 166
4a, b

☼ **Be a language detective: what do you notice about the verbs? When do you use "want" and "don't"? When do you use "wants" and "doesn't"?**

p. 29
A7

WB p. 34
A7

A8 Sunday breakfast

a) Listen to David's dad. What do David's mum and dad drink in the morning?

CD
1/32 48

> *Let me think – what do we need? Oh yes, it's Sunday! So it's eggs and sausages for David. He really loves sausages! Now where are the baked beans? Oh, here they are!*

> *So that's eggs, sausages, beans, what else? Oh yes, toast for David's mum. She likes toast and jam with a cup of tea. So tea for us – and David drinks orange juice.*

> *Now, is that everything? Oh, I know – bacon for me! David doesn't like bacon, but I love it! Oh, I love our Sunday breakfasts ... Wait, where's the milk? And, oh yes: plates, knives and forks ...*

b) Find the correct answers.

1. Does David make breakfast on Sunday?
2. Does David's mum like tea?
3. Does David's mum hate toast and jam?
4. Does David like bacon?
5. Does David's dad like bacon?

Yes, he does.   No, he doesn't.
Yes, she does.   No, she doesn't.

LiF p. 168
4c

c) ☆ **What does David have for breakfast on school days and on Sundays? Write two lists.**

school days	Sundays

☾ **Look at A7 again. Write about David's morning.**

It is half past eight. David ...

☼ **Write wrong sentences. Your partner corrects them.**

You: *David likes bacon.*
Your partner: *No, he doesn't like bacon. He likes ...*

p. 30
A8

WB p. 34
A8

A9 The Sunday breakfast table

 Work with a partner. Say the words in the box and point at the things in the picture. What is not on the table?

cup •
orange juice •
toast • glass •
milk • butter •
jam • plate •
cornflakes •
sausage • tea •
bowl • fried egg •
knife • fork •
bacon • spoon •
baked beans

wordbank
food and
drink p. 155

WB p. 35
A9

a) **Talk about the breakfast table.**

b) **Write about the breakfast table.**

There are three …

There is …   There are …   There is no …   There are no …

LAND & LEUTE 2

Englisches Frühstück

Ein traditionelles englisches Frühstück ist schon etwas Besonderes! Ein typischer Teil ist ein warmes Gericht, zum Beispiel gebratener Schinkenspeck *(bacon)* mit Ei, kleine Bratwürstchen, Bohnen in Tomatensauce *(baked beans)* und Grilltomaten.

Außerdem gibt es oft Toast mit Butter und Orangenmarmelade. Auf Englisch heißt Orangenmarmelade *marmalade*, Marmelade aus anderen Früchten heißt *jam*. Zum Frühstück trinkt man schwarzen Tee mit Milch, Kaffee oder Orangensaft.

Für so ein ausgiebiges Frühstück ist meist nur am Wochenende Zeit. Während der Woche isst man oft nur Müsli, Cornflakes, Haferbrei *(porridge)* oder Toast.

Kennst du ein typisches Frühstück aus einem anderen Land?

DVD
15

A10 A healthy morning

Listen to the radio ad. What is it about? Tell your partner in German.

☀ Work with a partner. Write and record your own radio ad. Present it to the class.

CD
1/33

A11 Karla's breakfast

a) Read Karla's blog entry. What does she think about Mega Muesli?

> Mega Muesli, Mega Muesli! I listen to the radio and all I hear is "Mega Muesli". I know that it's healthy, but I don't like it. I like cornflakes or toast with butter and honey. And when there's time I have a cooked breakfast – with hot, sweet tea. Muesli is more for my little brother and my mum. They love it.

b) Who likes what for breakfast? Talk to your partner.

WB p. 35
A10, A11

A12 Breakfast time ▶

a) Watch the video clip. What do you find interesting? Help out your classmates in German.

DVD
16

b) Talk about breakfast with your classmates.

What do you eat before school?

What do you have for breakfast at the weekend?

What do you eat at school?

Before school I eat ...

At the weekend I have ...

An apple.

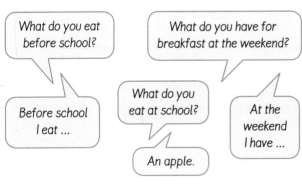

LiF p. 169
4d

c) Do a class survey on a poster. Hang it up in your classroom.

d) Write about your breakfast. What do you like? What don't you like? What do you have on school days and at the weekend?

wordbank
food and
drink p. 155

WB p. 36
A12, A13

A13 Target task: Breakfast in class

Plan a breakfast in your class.
Write a menu.
Make a shopping list.
Decide who brings what.
Make a breakfast phrase book.

It's breakfast time!
Have breakfast in class. Label everything on the table. Take photos. Later you can make a picture dictionary or think of your own product. During breakfast, use your breakfast phrase book.

how to p. 144
work together

p. 31
A9

P1 Explain

Explain what you have to do.

1. Act out the scene.
2. Describe yourself.
3. Point at body parts and say the words.
4. Read Karla's blog entry.
5. Do a class survey.

Ich soll …

…

Wir sollen …

P2 Rhyming pairs

CD 52

a) Listen to the words and repeat them. Which words rhyme? Write them down in pairs.

eight – late, …

> eight • cold • hair • small • old •
> feet • tall • blue • late •
> shampoo • sweet • pool • please •
> where • knees • school

CD 53

b) Listen to the CD and check your pairs.

c) Think of more pairs.

P3 One and one is one

a) Put the words together and write them down.

break	sun	bath	corn	tooth	week
paste	flakes	end	room	day	fast

breakfast, …

CD 54

b) Listen to the CD and check your words.

P4 Mime it!

LiF p. 166 3

a) Unscramble the commands. Tell your partner what to do. Your partner mimes it.

b) Think of more commands to mime.

1. arms – wash – your – !
2. tea – drink – your – !
3. cornflakes – your – eat – !
4. your – read – comic – !

P5 My morning

LiF p. 166 4a

Write about your morning.

First I …
Then I …
For breakfast I …
At the weekend I …
…

> wash • brush •
> have • eat •
> drink • …

Practice matters

P6 This is …

Write about a friend or
a family member.
Look at A6 for help.

This is Jan.
His eyes are …
…

This is my sister Paula.
Her eyes are …
…

🔍 LiF p. 162/4
1a, b, 2a, b

📦 wordbank
me and my
body p. 150

P7 Rajiv's Sunday

a) What does Rajiv do on Sundays? What doesn't he do?

🔍 LiF p. 166
4a, b

play the guitar •
read books • go to
school • play
football • work
on the computer •
listen to music

1. Rajiv plays the guitar on Sundays.

b) Listen to the CD and check your sentences.

💿 CD
55

P8 Do you like …?

**Work with a partner.
Ask and answer
questions.**

Do you like …?

Yes, I do.

No, I don't.

bacon • baked beans •
butter • cheese •
cornflakes • eggs •
jam • muesli •
orange juice • sausages •
tomatoes • …

🔍 LiF p. 168
4c

P9 Scrambled questions

a) Unscramble the questions.

1. for – like – breakfast – do – you – What – ?
2. have – Where – you – do – breakfast – ?
3. school – before – What – eat – you – do – ?
4. have – do – breakfast – When – you – ?
5. David – have – What – for – breakfast – does – ?
6. like – What – for – Karla – does – breakfast – ?

🔍 LiF p. 169
4d

b) Listen to the CD and check your questions.

💿 CD
56

c) Write answers to the questions.

B1 At Hendon School

DVD
17

Ruhe bitte!

Oh no, Lisa. It's so cold!

Can I open the window, please?

Oh, what is it?

It's "I love you so" by the Magic Boys.

What's "rubber" in German?

Radiergummi.

Can you spell it?

Oh dear ...

What a funny pen, Liz!

I'm so hungry!

Oh, great. Thanks.

I've got an apple. Would you like it?

It isn't a pen. It's my new USB stick.

Sorry I'm late, Mr Bennett.

What time is it?

Oh, David! You're always late.

It's five past nine.

Oh no, I haven't got my homework!

Here is my book. My homework is in it.

Yes, look at the poster.

School party?

a) **Look at the picture. What can you see?**

b) **Listen to the CD. Point at the things in the picture.**

 CD
1/34

p. 32
B1

blackboard •
computer •
whiteboard •
calendar •
window • chair •
pinboard • desk •
bin • map •
poster • cupboard •
sponge • chalk •
wall • clock •
school uniform

B2 In the classroom

a) **Listen to the dialogues and point to the pupils.**

 CD
1/35 57

b) **Listen to the dialogues again. Then act them out.**

☼ **Work with a partner. Write more dialogues and act them out.**

p. 32
B2

 WB p. 37
B1

B3 What does he say?

Listen to the German teacher. What does he say? Tell your partner in English.

CD
1/36

B4 Things in the classroom

CD
1/37 59

**a) Here is a list of things you can find in a classroom.
Listen to the CD and say the words.**

how to p. 136
work with
words

a pencil • a ruler • a pencil case •
a bookshelf • an English book • a pen •
a desk • a schoolbag • a window •
a door • a book • a bin •
an exercise book • a rubber •
an overhead projector • a wall • a map •
a cupboard • a lunchbox • a CD player

 Write words from the box on cards and label your classroom.

p. 33
B3, B4

**b) Work in groups. Look at the box in a)
again. Make two lists.**

LiF p. 170
5a

 **Be a language detective: when do you
use "a" and when do you use "an"?**

a	an
a pencil	an English book

LiF p. 170
5b

c) Work in groups. Write down the plural forms of the words.
pencil – pencils, ...

B5 Your classroom

 Put the words from B4 in alphabetical order.

a bin
a book
a bookshelf

 Make a list of the things in your classroom. **Write about your classroom.**

WB p. 37
B2–B5

a blue door
orange chairs

There is a brown ...
There are 27 blue ...

B6 Penny

CD
1/38 65

a) Listen to Penny. Who is she? **Why does Penny say "ouch"?**

b) Match the sentence parts and write down the sentences.

1. I've got ...
2. I'm very ...
3. I'm David's ...
4. I like the ...
5. Sometimes blue ink ...
6. I like it when David ...

a. green pencils best.
b. pencil case.
c. pencils and pens inside me.
d. important!
e. puts me on his desk.
f. comes out of David's pen.

CD
66

c) Listen to the CD and check your sentences.

B7 Good morning!

a) Look at the clock. How do you say the phrases in German?

b) Work with a partner. Ask the time.

> What's the time, please?

> It's ... o'clock.

c) Work with a partner. Ask the time.

You can answer: It's ten thirty. or: It's half past ten.

> What's the time, please?

> It's half past ten.

Tipp
Zahlenwörter findest du auf S. 263.

d) Work with a partner. Ask and answer questions.

You can say: It's ten twenty-five. or: It's twenty-five past ten.

You can say: It's eight forty. or: It's twenty to nine.

> Is it ten twenty?

> Yes, it is.

> No, it isn't. It's ten twenty-five.

p. 34
B5

e) Now answer these questions. Then ask your partner.

1. When do you get up in the morning?
2. When do you have breakfast?
3. When do you leave home for school?
4. When does school start?

I get up at ...

DVD
18

LiF p. 166
4a, d

WB p. 39
B6, B7

B8 Welcome to my day ▶

Watch the video clip.
What does Rhys do when?

> Rhys gets up at ...

DVD
19

WB p. 40
B8

B9 Rock around the alphabet

CD
1/39

a) Listen to the song. Then sing it and clap to it.

♫ Come on children sing it out
Come on children sing it loud
Come on children sing with me
This is the song of the ABC.

A B C D
E F and a G
H I J K
Oh, so far it is OK.
L M N O P
Q R S and T
U V W
X Y Z
That's the alphabet.

Hey, everybody, sing once more
Sing it as we've done before.
Come on, everybody, don't forget
This rock song of the alphabet.

A B C D …

Write a letter on your partner's back with your finger.

What is it?   It's an A.

b) Spell your name.

p. 35
B6

My name is Charlie, that's C-H-A-R-L-I-E. What about you?

c) Work with a partner. Think of a word. Write the letters on your partner's back with your finger.

P-E-N

Spell the word pen.

d) Work with a partner. Play a spelling game.

WB p. 40
B9

That's right.

B10 School things

Talk to your partner.

Have you got a pencil?

What's the English word for "Patrone"?   Cartridge.

Can I have your dictionary, please?   Yes, here you are.

Thanks!

p. 35
B7

WB p. 41
B10

Yes, here you are.

B11 Choose

1. Do you speak a language other than English or German? Say the alphabet in this language. Compare the alphabets.

The English alphabet has 26 letters, the ... alphabet ...

s _ h _ o _ b _ g
b _ o _
c _ a _ s _ o _ m
p _ n _ o _ r _

2. Work with a partner. Choose a letter. Write down all the words you know that start with this letter. You have five minutes.

3. Make a quiz about school things (for example words with missing letters, scrambled words or matching words and pictures).

eksd
amp
reptos
rynatiocid

4. Compare your classroom to David's classroom in B1.

In our classroom there is a poster about ..., but in David's ...
We've got ... in our classroom, but in David's classroom they have ...
We haven't got ..., but ...

B12 Perfect classroom poem

a) Listen and read along.
   What is special about this classroom?
   What is the only problem?

b) ☆ Draw the open-air classroom. Label it.

   ☾ Get into groups of four. Choose one of the verses. Each pupil learns one line by heart. Present your verse.

   ☼ Make a list of what the open-air classroom hasn't got. What has it got instead? Use your imagination and describe the classroom in more detail.

My perfect classroom has no walls,
No windows, doors or stairs
Because, you see, it's open-air
Just grass and trees and flowers.

My perfect classroom has no desks
No whiteboard, blackboard, chairs,
Because, you see, it's open-air
Just blue blue sky above us.

My perfect classroom's really cool
And there's really just one problem
I'm still not sure what we can do
When perfect rain falls on us!

 CD 1/40 69

WB p. 41
B11

B13 Target task: Improve your classroom

a) Work in groups. Look around your classroom. What do you like? What don't you like? Write two lists.

b) Talk about how to improve your classroom. What changes would you like to make? Make notes. You can use your dictionary.

c) Now talk in class. What changes can you really make? Make a plan.

 p. 36
B8

how to p. 144
work together

P10 Explain

Explain what you have to do.

1. Write words from the box on cards.
2. Label it.
3. Ask and answer questions.
4. Sing the song and clap to it.
5. Play a spelling game.

Ich soll ...

...

Wir sollen ...

P11 At school

a) Find the words and write them down.

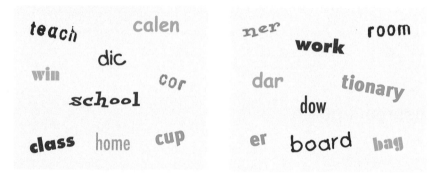

teach   calen   ner   room

dic   work

win   cor   dar   tionary

school   dow

class   home   cup   er   board   bag

teacher, ...

CD
71

b) Listen to the CD and check your words.

P12 Classroom words

a) Complete these words with the missing letters.

pncl	mbl phn	pstr
pn	crtrdg	rbbr
cmptr	rlr	lnch bx

b) Look at the picture and the words in a). Sort the words into the lists.

in the pencil case	not in the pencil case
pencil	...
...	

c) What have you got in your pencil case? Make a list.

Practice matters

P13 School things

What can you see in the picture? Write it down.

There is a ... and an ...
There are two ...
...

LiF p. 170
5

P14 When ...?

a) What do Rajiv and Vanessa do when?

LiF p. 166
4a

have breakfast • brush his/her
teeth • go to school

1. Rajiv has breakfast at ...

**b) Listen to the CD and check your
sentences.**

CD
72

P15 Spell the name!

a) Listen to the CD and write down the names.

b) Listen and check your names.

CD
73

CD
74

P16 Classroom questions

a) Unscramble the questions.

1. your – Can – pencil – please – have – I – ?
2. a – got – you – Have – ruler – ?
3. is – dictionary – Where – the – ?
4. it – time – What – is – ?
5. in – English – "Buchstabe" – What – is – ?
6. window – Can – please – I – open – the – ?

1. Can I have your pencil, please?

b) Listen to the CD and check your questions.

CD
75

c) Ask and answer the questions with a partner.

O1 All about eggs: experiments

Is the egg fresh?

There is an easy way to tell if an egg is fresh or not: put the egg into cold water with a spoon. If the egg stays at the bottom, it is fresh.
If it floats, it isn't fresh and you should not use it.

Can a fresh egg float?

Yes, it can. Put salt into the water before you put the egg in.

yolk   egg-white

shell

DVD
20

Do you know another experiment? Show it to the class.

O2 Eggs for breakfast? Yummy!

Boiled eggs

Put eggs in boiling water with a spoon. Wait for four minutes for a soft-boiled egg and for seven minutes for a hard-boiled egg. After that you can put the eggs under cold water.

Scrambled eggs

Put two or more eggs in a bowl. Add some milk or fizzy water. Beat the eggs with a fork. Put some butter in a pan. Add the eggs and keep stirring. When the eggs are ready, you can put them on a piece of toast and add salt and pepper.

Sunny side up or egg over easy?

Put some butter or oil in a frying pan. Wait until the butter or oil is hot. Put an egg in the frying pan. Fry for two minutes.

For **sunny side up** don't turn the egg over.

For an **egg over easy** turn the egg over and cook a little longer.

How do you like your eggs for breakfast? Have you got a special recipe?

Free time

Team table tennis

What... you need:
- 3 or more players
- everyone needs a table tennis bat
- 1 table tennis ball

Where... to play:
- at a table tennis table

How... to play:
- start like a normal game of table tennis.
- P1 starts the game. P3 waits behind P1. The players hit the ball and run around the table. Remember to take turns!
- If you miss the ball you're out!

P = player

Who... wins:
- the winner is the last person left.

Tip: run very fast!

In diesem *Theme* ...

- beschäftigst du dich mit den Themen *school clubs* und Sport.

- Zielaufgabe *(target task)*: Du erstellst eine Präsentation zu einer Sportart.

- sprichst du über Hobbys und lernst britische Kinder, ihre Hobbys und Haustiere kennen.

- Zielaufgabe *(target task)*: Du präsentierst deiner Klasse dein Hobby.

A1 What's on at Holland Park School?

a) Look at the posters. What clubs are there at Holland Park School?

Tipp
Club kann auch Schul-AG bedeuten.

b) Listen to the CD and point. Which posters are the children talking about?

c) Which club would you like to join?

d) What clubs and activities have you got at your school?

> At my school we've got ...

> There is ...

> I go to ... club.

CD · 1/41
DVD · 21
p. 37 · A1
WB p. 49 · A1, A2

Tipp
am: morgens, vormittags
pm: nachmittags, abends

A2 Drama club

Look at the poster for drama club.

1. Who is the teacher?
2. When is drama club?
3. Where is it?
4. What is "The Lion King"?
5. Who is welcome?

A3 Best school clubs

Watch the video clips.

- Where are the children?
- What are they talking about?
- Which is the best: cooking club or basketball club?

I think … is the best.

 DVD
22, 23

 p. 38
A2

 WB p. 50
A3–A6

A4 Holland Park School for the cup!

>
> **Look at the poster and answer the questions.**
>
> 1. Is the cup final for boys or girls?
> 2. Which schools are in the final?
> 3. When is the final?
> 4. Where is the final?

CD 1/42 81

p.38 A3

a) Listen to the children and read along.

1. What is Li's idea?
2. What is Gillian's idea?

how to p.145
mediate

b) Help Max to understand the poster. Explain it in German.

c) What do you think? Is it true that girls can't play football?

CD 1/43

d) Gillian and Li talk to their sports teacher Mrs Harnett. Listen to the CD. Can Mrs Harnett help the girls?

A5 Two teams

a) Listen and read along.

CD
1/44 82

how to p. 138
listen

Gillian: Hello?
Vanessa: Hi, Gillian, it's Vanessa.
Gillian: Oh hi, Vanessa. What's up?
Vanessa: Good news! We have now got eleven girls for our football team. We've got a great goalkeeper! We can have the match. What about your team?
Gillian: Well, there's a problem. Laura can't play. She's got a cold.
Vanessa: Oh dear! Well, what about Susan?
Gillian: Susan? Can she play?
Vanessa: Well, she doesn't like football but she can run fast.
Gillian: OK, why not? I can ask her.
Vanessa: Good. I hope she can come. I can't wait till Saturday. Come on, you Reds!
Gillian: Come on, you Blues! Bye, Ness!
Vanessa: See you soon!

b) What do you know about the two teams?

LiF p. 172
6a

p. 39
A4

| The girls
Laura
Susan
Gillian
Vanessa
… | can
can't | play.
have the match.
ask Susan.
wait till Saturday.
run fast.
… |

c) ☆ **Complete the sentences.**

1. The goalkeeper is …
2. Laura can't …
3. Laura has got …
4. Susan doesn't …
5. Susan can …
6. Vanessa can't …

☾ **Correct the sentences.**

1. Vanessa's football team has now got eight girls for the team.
2. Laura can't play because she doesn't like football.
3. Susan likes football and she can run fast.
4. Gillian can ask Laura.
5. Vanessa can't wait till Sunday.

☼ **Gillian calls Susan. Collect ideas and write a dialogue.**

WB p. 51
A7

A6 Two matches

CD
1/45

a) Listen to the radio report.

- Who is the winner of the boys' match?
- What is the score?

p. 39
A5

Tipp
1 – 0 heißt
one – nil

Fantastic match for Holland Park girls!

Holland Park girls beat Hendon girls 1–0 in a friendly match. Gillian Collins scored for Holland Park. What a fantastic match! Well done, girls!

b) Read the article.

- What is the final score in the girls' match?
- Who scored the goal?

WB p. 51
A8

DVD
24

LAND & LEUTE 3

Fußball

Das Fußballspiel wurde in England erfunden. Selbst in kleineren Vereinen gibt es gut organisierte *fan clubs*, deren Mitglieder mit großer Begeisterung zu den Spielen ihrer *clubs* mitziehen. Meistens kleiden sich die Fans in den Farben ihres Vereins. Die Spieler werden durch Sprechchöre oder Lieder angefeuert, ganz wie bei uns. Übrigens: Wenn Briten von *football* sprechen, meinen sie dasselbe wie wir mit

Fußball. Wenn Amerikaner *football* sagen, meinen sie damit *American Football*. Unser Fußballspiel heißt in den USA *soccer*.

Welche englischen Fußballwörter kennst du?

A7 In the stadium

Football fans love to sing and chant at matches.

CD
1/46 85

a) Listen and sing along.

b) What football songs or chants do you know?

c) What team do you like best? Talk to your partner.

My favourite team is ...

I haven't got a favourite team.

 Blue is the colour

Blue is the colour,
football is the game.
We're all together
and winning is our aim!

So cheer us on
through the sun and rain,
'cause Chelsea,
Chelsea is our name!

A8 Sports you can do

Play a guessing game. Mime and guess sports.

swim

ski

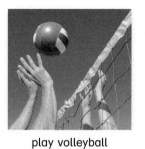

play volleyball

do gymnastics

play basketball

play hockey

skate

ride a horse

do karate

play football

ride a bike

?

...

wordbank
hobbies
and free time
p. 153

a) **Look at the pictures. Ask your partner. Take turns.**

b) **Write about what you can and can't do.**

I can ski, but I can't swim.

Can you play
football?

Yes, I can.

No, I can't.

LiF p. 172
6a,b

p. 40
A6

WB p. 52
A9, A10

A9 **Where?**

a) Where can you do the sports? Ask your partner. Take turns.

LiF p. 172
6

> play table tennis •
> play football • go swimming •
> play tennis • go skating •
> do gymnastics •
> play basketball • …

> on a playing field • at a sports centre •
> in a swimming pool • in a park • in the snow •
> on a tennis court • at home • in the street •
> in a gym • in a sports hall • in a playground •
> in the mountains • …

wordbank
hobbies
and free time
p. 153

> *Where can you do gymnastics?*

> *You can do gymnastics in a sports hall.*

> *Where can you go swimming?*

> *You can …*

p. 41
A7

b) Write down wrong sentences. Your partner must correct them.

You can go swimming on a tennis court.

> *No, you can't. You can go swimming in a swimming pool.*

A10 **Football for penguins**

Look at the cartoon. Why is it funny?

> *My cousin says that in England they play football with white balls. Imagine that!*

A11 **What's their sport?** ▶

a) Look at the photos. What sports do the children do? What do you think?

DVD
25, 26

b) Now watch the video clips and find out.

☼ **What do you need for your sport? Use a dictionary and tell your partner about it.**

A12 My favourite sport

What is your favourite sport? Make a word web.

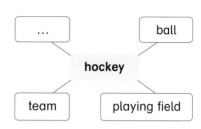

a) Read what Dennis and Inka write about their sport.

> I love football.
> Football is my favourite sport.
> I play for a club.
> Our shirts are blue.
> I've got new red football boots!
>
> Dennis

> Basketball is my favourite sport.
> I love it.
> At school I play in a basketball team.
> I am the captain of our team.
> I am very good at basketball.
> I've got my own basketball and my own
> basket in my garden so I can practise
> every day.
> Inka

model text

p. 41
A8, A9

how to p. 141
write

wordbank
hobbies
and free time
p. 153

b) Now write about your sport.

WB p. 53
A11

A13 Target task: Present a sport

Work in groups. Choose a sport.
Prepare a presentation. You can ...

- make a poster.
- collect pictures.
- explain the rules.
- mime the actions.
- make a chant and teach it to the class.
- ...

You can present your sport to another class.

Team table tennis

What ... you need:
- 3 or more players
- everyone needs a table tennis bat
- 1 table tennis ball

Where ... to play:
- at a table tennis table

How ... to play:
- start like a normal game of table tennis.
- P1 starts the game. P3 waits behind P1.
  The players hit the ball and run around
  the table. Remember to take turns!
- If you miss the ball you're out.

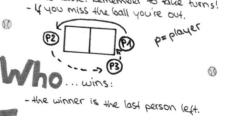

P2   P1   p=player
   → P3

Who ... wins:
- the winner is the last person left.

Tip: run very fast!

p. 43
A10

wordbank
hobbies
and free time
p. 153

model text

P1 Explain

Explain what you have to do.

1. Correct the sentences.
2. Read the article.
3. Listen to the radio report.
4. Listen and sing along.
5. Take turns.

Ich soll ...

Wir sollen ...

...

P2 Who?

a) Look at A5 again. Write questions and answer them.

Who
What

has got a problem with the team?
has Laura got?
doesn't Susan like?
can run fast?
can Gillian ask?
does Vanessa hope?
can't wait till Saturday?

Who has got a problem with the team? – Gillian.

CD 87

b) Listen to the CD and check your questions and answers.

P3 I can't wait

a) Match the sentences.

CD 88

b) Listen to the CD and check your answers.

1. Well, there's a problem.	a. Ach, du meine Güte!
2. Oh dear!	b. Ich kann es kaum abwarten.
3. Why not?	c. Bis bald.
4. I can't wait.	d. Nun, da gibt es ein Problem.
5. See you soon.	e. Warum nicht?

P4 Odd one out

Find the "odd one out".

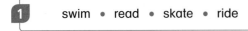
1 swim • read • skate • ride

3 tennis • football • karate • basketball

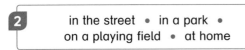
2 in the street • in a park • on a playing field • at home

4 captain • football • goalkeeper • sports teacher

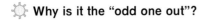
Why is it the "odd one out"?

Practice matters

P5 Can they or can't they?

a) What can the children do? What can't they do?

LiF p. 172
6b

1

Can the boy swim?

2

Can the girl ride a horse?

3

Can the boy play football?

4

Can the girl play hockey?

5

Can the boy ski?

6

Can the girls play basketball?

1. Can the boy swim? No, he can't.

b) Listen to the CD and check your answers.

CD
89

P6 Play, do or ride?

a) Find the pairs and write them in your exercise book.

			football	a horse	hockey	table tennis	
play	do	ride					
			tennis	a bike	gymnastics	karate	basketball

play football, play …

CD
90

P7 Who can?

Answer the questions. Look at pages 56–63 for help.

LiF p. 172
6b, c

1. When can you sign up for computer club?
2. Where can you go for a kickabout?
3. Can Max understand the poster for the Boys' Cup Final?
4. Who can't play in the girls' match?
5. Can you sing a football song?
6. What can the girl on page 62 do?
7. Who can play basketball? Dennis or Inka?

1. You can sign up now.

B1 At the market

a) Look at the market scene. What can you see?

CD

1/47 91
1/48 92
1/49 93

DVD

27

p. 44
B1, B2

WB p. 54
B1

b) You've got 15 pounds. Look at the picture. What can you buy?

c) Listen to the CD. There are three scenes. What do the people buy?

LAND & LEUTE 4

Britisches Geld

In Großbritannien wird in *pounds* und *pence* bezahlt. Für das *pound* gibt es dieses Zeichen: £. Das ist eigentlich ein „L". Es steht für *libra*, das lateinische Wort für Pfund. Ein Pfund hat hundert *pence*. Auf allen Münzen und Geldscheinen ist die britische Königin, Queen Elizabeth II, abgebildet.

So werden Preise angegeben: £2.30, aber du sagst: *two pound(s) thirty*. Bei *75p* kannst du *seventy-five pence* oder *seventy-five p* sagen.

Wie viel Euro muss man für ein Pfund bezahlen?

DVD
28

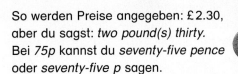

B2 One after the other

a) **Write the numbers in your exercise book. Start with one.**

3 three **15** fifteen **34** thirty-four **17** seventeen **1** one **56** fifty-six **20** twenty **22** twenty-two **16** sixteen **79** seventy-nine

100 one hundred **14** fourteen **47** forty-seven **8** eight **19** nineteen **68** sixty-eight **81** eighty-one **90** ninety **13** thirteen

Tipp
+ *plus*
− *minus*
x *times*
÷ *divided by*
= *equals*

b) **Listen to the sums and read along.**

 CD
1/50

17 + 4 = 21	5 x 6 = 30	8 + 19 = 27	3 x 9 = 27
30 − 2 = 28	60 ÷ 12 = 5	90 − 21 = 69	100 ÷ 5 = 20

p. 45
B3, B4

 Now listen to more sums and write them down.

  CD
1/51 94

B3 Choose

1. Add up all the green, all the blue, all the ... numbers in B2.

2. Make up sums for your partner.

3. Play "skip" in your group.

4. Play "number bingo" in your group.

WB p. 54
B2, B3

One. *Two.* *Skip.* *Four.*

B4 Buying and selling

p.46
B5, B6

a) Read the dialogue with a partner.

how to p.140
talk

Seller: Hi, can I help you?
Customer: Yes, hello. My son collects computer games. Have you got any new ones?
Seller: How about these? They are all new, you know.

Customer: Oh, this one looks interesting. How much is it?
Seller: It's 12 pounds.
Customer: 12 pounds?! That's too much.
Seller: All right, let's call it ten pounds then.
Customer: Ten pounds? OK then! I'll take it.

WB p.55
B4

b) Practise the dialogue and present it.

wordbank
shopping
p.156

☼ **Work with a partner. Write your own shopping dialogue. Practise and present it.**

B5 Collections

CD
1/52 98

Listen and point at the things.

DVD
29

comics • mugs • DVDs • stickers • posters • toy cars • marbles • cuddly toys • football cards • stones • postcards • elves and dragons • seashells • computer games

a) What things can you collect?

You can collect ...

LiF p.173
7R

b) Interview your classmates. Take notes.

p.47
B7, B8

What do you collect?

I collect model trains.

How many have you got?

I've got ...

DVD
30

c) Write about your classmates.

Mehmet collects ...

WB p.56
B5, B6

Do you collect ... ?

Yes, I do.

No, I don't. I collect ...

B6 At Gillian's

a) Listen and read along. What is *Teentalk?* Who are the guests? What do they talk about?

Gillian: Let's listen to *Teentalk.* It's my favourite radio show at the moment.

Vanessa: OK, turn the radio on then.

Nick Nelson: And now, *Teentalk.* Hello! My name is Nick Nelson. Today *Teentalk* starts with a quiz about collections. The winner can ask for his or her favourite song. Here's our number: 03800 100 100. My guests today are Justin, Carol and Sarah. Hi, guys!

Justin, Sarah and Carol: Hey! Hi!

Nick Nelson: So, tell us about yourselves.

Justin: Hi, my name is Justin. I'm 13. I'm from Hastings.

Carol: Hello, I'm Carol. I'm also 13. I live in London.

Sarah: Hi, my name is Sarah. I'm 12 and I'm from Liverpool.

Nick Nelson: OK. Now, describe what you collect. But don't say what it is. Sarah, let's start with you.

Sarah: I collect something that you can buy at a corner shop. It has got pictures in it. There are stories in it.

Nick Nelson: Hmm … that's not easy. Justin, what about your collection?

Justin: I collect things you can find on the beach. Some are white and some are grey.

Some are big and some are small. They are not stones.

Gillian: Oh, come on! That's easy.

Vanessa: Well, I don't know.

Nick Nelson: Carol, over to you!

Carol: I've got a collection of very special cuddly toys. They have got four legs, two small eyes and a short tail. They are pink!

Nick Nelson: OK! Thanks to all of you. So, listeners, here's our number again: 03800 100 100. Good luck.

Gillian: I know the answers. Let's call …

b) What do you think? What are the answers?

c) Listen to Gillian and find out.

CD
1/53 100

how to p. 138
listen

CD
1/54

p. 48
B9

WB p. 57
B7

B7 All about Teentalk

☆ **Complete the questions and answer them.**

Who • What • Where • Why

1. ??? does Carol live?
2. ??? collects cuddly toys?
3. ??? does Sarah collect?
4. ??? is the telephone number of *Teentalk?*
5. ??? does Gillian turn the radio on?

☾ **Match the sentence parts.**

1. What do
2. Who are
3. What does
4. Where does
5. Who knows
6. Why does

a. Nick's guests?
b. Sarah collect?
c. Gillian turn the radio on?
d. the answers?
e. Gillian and Vanessa listen to?
f. Justin come from?

LiF p. 174
7Rb

p. 48
B10

☀ **Work with a partner. Ask and answer questions. Use who, what, where and why.**

WB p. 57
B8–B10

B8 After school

a) Read the *Teentalk* forum. What do the children like doing after school?

Nick Nelson
Hey everyone! For the next show we want to know about what you like doing after school.

Amy
After school I like chilling with my friends. We sometimes play computer games or listen to music. My favourite kind of music is rap.

Eleanor
I like playing the piano. I love learning new songs. But my favourite hobby is teaching my dog, Bertie, new tricks.

Ishaan
Sometimes I play football with my brother in the garden – but I also really like reading. My favourite book is Billionaire Boy.

b) What do you like doing after school?

p. 49
B11

DVD
31

I like ...

My hobby is ...

playing computer games • reading •
teaching my dog tricks • watching TV •
listening to music • riding my bike •
meeting friends • playing an instrument •
chilling with friends • swimming • ...

B9 Meet our pets

DVD
32–34

Watch the video clips.

WB p. 58
B11, B12

1. What pets has Rhys got?

2. Which dog trick do you like best?

3. Where do the guinea pigs go on Saturdays and Sundays?

B10 Two pets

a) Read about the two pets.

Popeye, my guinea pig
My pet is a guinea pig. His name is Popeye. He's brown, black and white. He has got a pink nose. His favourite food is spinach. He lives in my room.   *Bill*

My dog Rainbow
My pet is a red dog with blue and yellow spots. His name is Rainbow. He's a cyberpet. He has got one orange eye and one brown eye. His ears are very long. They look funny. He has got a short green tail. I often feed him dog food and big bones. I play with him online.   *Eve*

  model text

  wordbank
animals p. 147

b) ☆ **Make a fact file for Popeye.**

☾ **Make a fact file for Rainbow.**

☼ **Make a fact file for your pet or dream pet.**

  WB p. 59
B13–B15

B11 Target task: Hobbies in your class

What is your favourite hobby? Present it to your class.

a) Collect words for your hobby and make a word web.

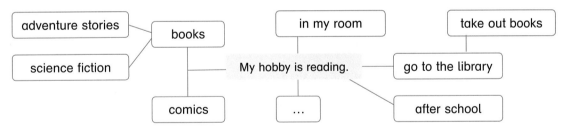

  wordbank
hobbies
and free time
p. 153

b) Write about your hobby.

What is your hobby?
When do you do it?
Where do you do it?
…

**c) Now put your products together and make a class exhibition.
Are you looking for a new hobby?
Get ideas from your classmates.**

  model text

⌒ p. 49
B12, B13

P8 Explain

Explain what you have to do.

1. Write the numbers in your exercise book.
2. Read the dialogue with a partner.
3. Collect words for your hobby and make a word web.
4. Watch the video clips.
5. Get ideas from your classmates.

Ich soll …

…

Wir sollen …

P9 Collection words

a) Put these words together and write them in your exercise book.

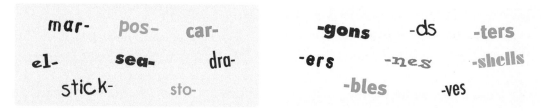

mar-   pos-   car-   -gons   -ds   -ters

el-   sea-   dra-   -ers   -nes   -shells

stick-   sto-   -bles   -ves

marbles, …

CD 107 **b) Listen to the CD and check your words.**

P10 Sound check: how to say the letter 'i'

CD 108 **Listen to the words and repeat them.**

idea   like   final   winner   article   girl

little   write   thirteen   fifteen   pictures

☼ **What do you notice about the 'i' sounds?**

P11 Lots of questions

a) Match the questions and answers.

LiF p. 173
7Ra

1. Does Charlie's sister like posters?
2. Has the seller got any new computer games?
3. Do your classmates collect football cards?
4. Is 72 divided by six twelve?
5. Are Popeye and Rainbow pink pigs?
6. Is Ishaan's hobby riding his horse?
7. Does Justin collect stones?

No, it isn't.
Yes, they do.
Yes, he has.
Yes, she does.
No, he doesn't.
Yes, it is.
No, they aren't.

CD 109 **b) Listen to the CD and check your answers.**

Practice matters

P12 Scrambled questions

a) Unscramble the questions. Write them down.

1 when • your friends • meet • you • do • ?

2 stickers • you • swap • do • ?

3 radio • listen • you • to • do • the • ?

4 like • do • spinach • guinea pigs • ?

5 got • cuddly • you • have • toys • any • ?

6 Charlie's pets • do • tricks • can • ?

LiF p. 173
7R

b) Listen to the CD and check your questions.

CD
110

c) Answer the questions.

P13 Opposites

a) Match the opposites. Write them in your exercise book.

love - hate, can - ...

love   can   come   funny
long   ask   listen   big

short   boring   small   can't
speak   answer   hate   go

b) Listen to the CD and check your pairs.

CD
111

Find more opposites and ask your partner.

What's the opposite of ...?

P14 Question words

a) Write the correct questions for the answers.

When?

Where?

What?

Who?

... does Gillian meet her friends?   – In the afternoon.
... do they meet?   – In the park.
... collects seashells?   – Justin.
... do you collect?   – Elves and dragons.
... are Gillian and Vanessa?   – In Gillian's room.
... is the winner of the radio quiz?   – Gillian.
... does Charlie buy at the market?   – A poster for his sister.
... colour is Popeye?   – Brown, black and white.

LiF p. 173
7Rb

When does Gillian meet her friends? – In the afternoon.

b) Listen to the CD and check your questions and answers.

CD
112

Optional

Ⓞ Unusual hobbies

Teenzone chat: Your comments

Last updated: Tuesday 25 November   11:25 GMT

What unusual hobbies do you have?

Do you love doing something that is a bit different?
Does nobody understand why you like it?
Perhaps you collect something funny?
Email us your stories.
Let the fun begin!

Your comments:

"I collect photos of insects. They are so interesting!
The walls in my room are full of photos."
John, 12, Liverpool

"I love juggling! I even juggle at school. You can juggle with anything –
pencil cases, sharpeners or rubbers."
Amir, 13, Enfield

"My friends think I'm crazy, but I collect the tags from the clothes I buy."
Susan, 13, Tenby

"I collect hair from different people. I've even got hair from Justin
Timberlake!"
Rebecca, 11, Norwich

"I know it's strange, but I collect pencil cases. I have got 35 of them. I
just love pencil cases."
Jem, 12, London

"I like sitting in my room all day. That's my
favourite hobby."
Rob, 13, Ramsgate

"When I'm in the woods I pick up sticks and peel
them."
Caroline, 11, York

"I love finding shapes in clouds. I often just stare
at the sky. Sometimes I take photos of the clouds."
Richard, 14, Leeds

Find out about one more unusual hobby. Tell the class about it.

At home

In diesem *Theme* ...

- sprichst und schreibst du über Aufgaben, die in einer Familie erledigt werden müssen.

- Zielaufgabe *(target task)*: Du präsentierst deiner Klasse, was du jede Woche regelmäßig machst.

- beschäftigst du dich mit der Planung eines Wochenendbesuchs und übst Einkaufsdialoge.

- Zielaufgabe *(target task)*: Du sammelst in Gruppen Ideen für einen schönen Abend mit Freunden oder der Familie und stellst gemeinsam mit der Klasse ein Ideenbuch her.

A1 Two rooms

DVD
36

a) Look at the two pictures. Say what you see.

wordbank
at home p. 154

b) Talk about Rajiv's room.

There's a red desk.

There are books.

There's a ...

There are ...

Rajiv has got ...

I like the ...

I don't like the ...

wardrobe   duvet

lamp   pillow

cage   shelves

desk

chair   bed

DVD
37

WB p. 67
A1, A2

p. 51
A1

c) Talk about Vanessa's room.

A2 Rooms, rooms, rooms

a) **Compare the two rooms.**

b) **Talk about your room.**

> There's a ... in Vanessa's room.

> There isn't a ... in Rajiv's room.

> ... is tidy.

> ... is untidy.

> Rajiv has got ... but Vanessa hasn't.

LiF p. 175 8a

p. 52 A2

A3 Things in the children's rooms

a) **Where are the things in Rajiv's room? Look at the picture and listen to the CD.**

CD 2/1

> **Partner A:** Where are the things in Rajiv's room? Listen to partner B and point.
> **Partner B:** Where are the things in Rajiv's room? Tell partner A.

p. 52 A3

b) **Where are the things in Vanessa's room? Write sentences.**

The books		on	the wall.
The computer	is	above	the floor.
The football	is not	in	the shelves.
The rucksack	are	under	the desk.
The shelves	are not	next to	the wardrobe.
...		behind	...

WB p. 68 A3–A5

A4 Dream rooms

a) **Read about one of the dream rooms and find the missing words. Write down the text.**

model text

My dream room has got a basketball basket. There are ??? of dinosaurs on the green wall. My computer is on my ??? . There are DVDs and computer games on the ??? . My ??? looks like a big red car.

> posters • shelves • bed • desk

My dream room is very big. I sleep on a comfortable blue ??? . On the blue wall there are green crocodiles and yellow fish. There's a terrarium on my ??? . That's where my three spiders live. I've got a very big TV. Next to the TV there is a ??? . In the middle of my room there is a ??? . I can watch TV or read books there. It's my favourite place in my room.

b) ☆ **Draw and label your dream room.**

☾ **Draw, label and describe your dream room.**

☼ **Write about your dream room. Leave out some words and let your partner find them.**

> sofa • popcorn machine • bed • desk

how to p. 141 write

WB p. 69 A6, A7

p. 53 A4

A5 Choose

1. Your partner asks you ten questions about Rajiv or Vanessa's room. How much can you remember? Take turns.

2. Write about your room.

3. Make a collage about your dream room.

4. Interview your partner about his or her dream room.

5. Bring a photo of your room into class. Present it.

> Where is the wardrobe?
>
> It's next to the bed.
>
> What's on the desk?

A6 Busy Saturdays

CD
2/2 121

a) Listen to the CD and read along. Why does Vanessa help her dad with the shopping?

At Vanessa's house everyone is very busy on Saturdays. Vanessa's dad is a great cook – he is always in the kitchen! He often does the cooking. Sometimes Vanessa helps him. On Saturday mornings he makes a nice breakfast for the family. After breakfast Vanessa's dad cleans the kitchen. But he never does the washing up. That's Vanessa's job. Then Vanessa goes to her room. She always tidies her room on Saturdays. Then she helps her mum to clean the bathroom. Vanessa's mum always tidies the living room on Saturdays. She vacuums the floors, too. Vanessa's dad does the shopping on Saturdays. Vanessa usually helps him – then she can choose her favourite food!

 Play a guessing game. Mime and guess jobs at home.

LiF p. 174/5
7Rb, 8a

b) Who does what on Saturdays? Write down questions and answers.

do the cooking • vacuum the floors • clean the bathroom • tidy ... • do ... • help ...	Vanessa • Vanessa's mum • Vanessa's dad

WB p. 70
A8, A9

p. 54
A5

Who does the cooking? – Vanessa's dad.

A7 Boys have an easy life

CD
2/3

how to p. 138
listen

a) Listen to the CD. What are Vanessa and Charlie talking about? How do you think they feel?

b) What do you think? Do boys really have an easy life?

A8 Jobs at home

LiF p. 169
4e

a) Unscramble the sentences.

1. the cooking • often • Vanessa's dad • does

2. cleans • Charlie • his bike • always

3. Vanessa's mum • the living room • tidies • always

4. the washing up • never • does • Vanessa's dad

5. her dad • helps • Vanessa • sometimes

6. her bed • usually • makes • Vanessa

1. Vanessa's dad often does the cooking.

b) Complete the sentences with a word from the box.

> his • her

LiF p. 175
8b

1. Vanessa usually tidies ??? room.
2. Charlie always feeds ??? fish.
3. David helps ??? parents in the shop.
4. Vanessa helps ??? mum to clean the bathroom.

p. 55
A6

A9 My jobs at home

a) Write about your jobs.

I usually make my bed.
I never tidy my room.

wordbank
at home p. 154

b) Work with a partner.
Ask and answer questions.

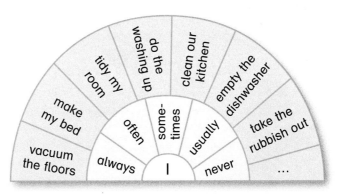

Do you do the washing up?

Well, sometimes.

No, never.

Yes, always.

...

WB p. 71
A10, A11

p. 55
A7

A10 The chores chant

Listen to the chant and say it. Act out the chores.

CD
2/4 125
2/5 126

DVD
38

 I tidy my room and make my bed,
I tidy so much it hurts my head.
What a life, what a life,
what a hard, hard life!

I empty the dishwasher, clean my bike,
but it's riding my bike that I really like!
What a life, what a life,
what a hard, hard life!

I tidy the living room, vacuum the floors,
every day it's just chores, chores, chores!
What a life, what a life,
what a hard, hard life!

I take out the rubbish, make Mum a cup of tea,
I work really hard, can't you see?
What a life, what a life,
what a hard, hard life!

A11 Charlie's week

CD
2/6 127

DVD
39

a) Listen to the CD and read about Charlie's week.

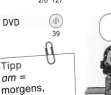

Tipp
am =
morgens,
vormittags

pm =
nachmittags,
abends

Monday 4.15 pm

Oh, Charlie!

On Monday afternoons Charlie takes his sister to ballet school with his mum. They wait for her. Sometimes Charlie gets a good idea and dances, too. The girls think that Charlie can't dance.

Hey, look at Charlie.

Tuesday 6.30 pm

Charlie goes to football training on Tuesday evenings. After training, he talks to his friends and drinks lemonade. He often shows them some dance steps. It's good fun.

Wednesday 7 pm

Charlie is president of the Hendon Goldfish Club. There are four members. On Wednesday evenings Charlie writes articles for the club magazine *Our Goldfish*. This week Charlie wants to write something on: "Do goldfish dream?"

Charlie doesn't like Thursday mornings. He has science at school. He thinks it's boring.

Thursday 9.30 am

I hate Thursdays!

It's a good thing I'm here to look after you!

Friday 7.30 pm

Charlie often looks after Sharon on Friday evenings. He makes beans on toast. Sometimes he forgets about the beans. But Sharon helps him.

On Saturday mornings Charlie plays football. He is very good at it. In the afternoons he sometimes goes to an Arsenal match with his dad.

Saturday 10 am

Sunday 8.30 am

On Sunday mornings Charlie sometimes makes his mum a cup of tea. Then she gets up and makes breakfast. Charlie goes back to bed.

 Look at the pictures. Write about Charlie's week.

Charlie takes Sharon to ballet school on …
Charlie goes to football training on …
Charlie writes articles …

Charlie has science …
Charlie looks after Sharon …
Charlie plays football …

Charlie takes Sharon to ballet school on Monday afternoons.

b) ☆ **Write about Charlie's week. Match the sentence parts.**

1. Charlie takes Sharon
2. He writes articles
3. He makes beans on toast
4. He goes to football training
5. On Thursday mornings

a) he has science at school.
b) on Tuesday evenings.
c) to ballet school on Monday afternoons.
d) on Friday evenings.
e) on Wednesday evenings.

🔍 LiF p. 166
4a

☾ **Write about Charlie's week. Complete the sentences.**

On Monday afternoons …
On Tuesday evenings …
On Wednesday evenings …

On Friday evenings …
On Saturday afternoons …
On Sunday mornings …

☼ **Write about Charlie's week. What do you think his favourite days are? Why?**

I think Charlie likes … because … He also likes …

 WB p. 72
A12

p. 56
A8

A12 Target task: Your week

a) **What do you do on Mondays, on Tuesdays, …? Think about jobs at home and activities. You can make a collage, draw pictures, write a text, make a recording, …**

b) **Present your product to the class.**

p. 57
A9

 how to p. 142
present

P1 Explain

Explain what you have to do.

1. Listen to the chant and say it.
2. Draw and label your dream room.
3. Interview your partner about his or her dream room.
4. Bring a photo of your room into class.
5. Compare the two rooms.

Ich soll ...

Wir sollen ...

...

P2 The things in your room

Where are the things in your room? Tell your partner. Take turns.

My computer is on my desk.

| computer • shelves • books • DVDs • posters • desk • ... | next to • under • in • on • behind • above |

P3 In my room

Write about your room.

There is a ...   There are ...   I have got ...
Next to the desk there is ...   The computer is ...

P4 Vanessa and Charlie

LiF p. 175
8b

a) Unscramble the two texts about Vanessa and Charlie. Write them down.

Vanessa has got a small room. Charlie has got three goldfish. She sometimes helps with the cooking. He often rides his bike. He goes to football training on Tuesdays. He always feeds his goldfish. She usually makes her bed. She always tidies her room on Saturdays. She likes her room. He sometimes makes his mum a cup of tea.

CD
129

b) Listen to the CD and check your two texts.

P5 Sundays

LiF p. 166
4a, b

a) What does Vanessa do (+) on Sundays? What doesn't she do (−) ?
   Write sentences.

listen to music   read comics

help her dad with   play football in
the cooking   the park

+

play tennis   do homework

tidy her room   clean the bathroom

−

On Sundays Vanessa listens to music. She doesn't play tennis.

b) What about you? What do you do on Sundays? What don't you do? Talk to your partner.

Practice matters

P6 Jobs

a) Look at A6 again and complete the sentences with the words in the box.

usually • often • always • always • sometimes • never

LiF p. 169
4e

1. Vanessa's dad ??? does the cooking.
2. He ??? does the washing up.
3. Vanessa ??? helps with the cooking.

4. Vanessa's mum ??? tidies the living room.
5. Vanessa ??? tidies her room on Saturdays.
6. Vanessa ??? helps with the shopping.

b) Listen to the CD and check your sentences.

CD
130

sein ihr

P7 His or her?

a) Complete the sentences.

LiF p. 175
8b

1. Rajiv has got a guitar in ??? room.
2. Vanessa has got books in ??? room.
3. Charlie takes ??? sister to ballet school.

4. Sharon helps ??? brother with the beans.
5. Charlie sometimes goes to a football match with ??? dad.
6. Vanessa helps ??? dad with the shopping.

1. Rajiv has got a guitar in his room.

b) Listen to the CD and check your sentences.

CD
131

machen, tun

P8 Makes or does?

a) Complete the sentences.

1. Charlie ??? his mum a cup of tea.
2. Vanessa's dad ??? the cooking.
3. He also ??? the shopping.

4. Vanessa usually ??? her bed.
5. Vanessa usually ??? the washing up.
6. Vanessa ??? lots of jobs at home.

LiF p. 166
4a

1. Charlies makes his mum a cup of tea.

b) Listen to the CD and check your sentences.

CD
132

P9 Things

a) Write down who the things or animals belong to.

LiF p. 175
8a

1. Sally

2. John

3. Peter

4. Emma

5. Mr Miller

6. Mrs Smith

1. It's Sally's computer.

b) Listen to the CD and check your sentences.

CD
133

B1 A weekend visit

CD 2/7 134

a) Listen to the CD and read along.

Vanessa: Hi, Gillian. Do you want to come to my house on Saturday for a sleepover? I've got a second bed in my room now.

Gillian: Good idea, but I have to ask my mum first. Hang on a minute. – Mum says yes.

Vanessa: Great!

Gillian: Have you got a big room?

Vanessa: No, not really, but it's OK. We can read some ghost stories!

Gillian: Good idea!

Vanessa: We can turn out the light and make it spooky!

Gillian: Wow, cool!

Vanessa: And we can listen to music. I can't wait to play you my favourite new song.

Gillian: And I can bring some chocolate.

Vanessa: OK. See you on Saturday then. I can pick you up at the station at 4.30. I have to go now. It's my turn to help make dinner.

Gillian: OK, that sounds good. See you on Saturday.

b) ☆ **Are the sentences true or false?**

Vanessa and Gillian talk about …
1. … Vanessa's room.
2. … Vanessa's visit on Sunday.
3. … ghost stories.
4. … Vanessa's collection of cuddly toys.

☽ **Correct the sentences.**

1. Vanessa and Gillian can sleep in Gillian's room.
2. They want to read comics.
3. They can watch a DVD.
4. Gillian can bring some apples.

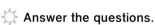 **Answer the questions.**

1. Where can Gillian sleep?
2. What can Vanessa and Gillian do?
3. What can Gillian bring?
4. When is Gillian's visit?

p. 58
B1, B2

B2 Choose

1. **Act out the dialogue in B1 with your partner.**

wordbank
English in action p. 157

2. **Make your own dialogue about a weekend visit with your partner. Act it out.**

3. **Make a list of things you can do at the weekend with a friend.**

B3 On the way

a) Listen and read along.

CD
2/8 135

It is Saturday afternoon and Gillian is on the way to Vanessa's house. It's a long way from Notting Hill to Hendon, so Gillian takes the Tube. She knows the way because she often visits her cousin David in Hendon. On the Tube she usually reads a comic.

First she walks to Westbourne Park station. Then she takes the Hammersmith & City Line to King's Cross. There she changes to the Northern Line and gets out at Hendon Central.

b) Write about Gillian's trip.

p. 59
B3

Gillian lives	at Hendon Central.
She's on the way	the Hammersmith & City Line.
First she walks	to Vanessa's house.
Then she takes	in Notting Hill.
She changes	to Westbourne Park station.
She gets out	to the Northern Line.

c) Listen to the children. What are they talking about?

CD
2/9

WB p. 73
B1–B3

LAND & LEUTE 5

Die Londoner U-Bahn

London hat die älteste U-Bahn der Welt. 1863 wurde die erste Strecke eröffnet. Damals zogen Dampfloks die unterirdischen Züge. Viele der alten Bahnhöfe sind gut erhalten und sehenswert. Der erste Netzplan einer U-Bahn wurde 1933 veröffentlicht. Er war das Modell für U-Bahnpläne auf der ganzen Welt. Die Londoner haben ihrer U-Bahn einen lustigen Namen gegeben: „the Tube", das heißt „die Röhre".

Schau dir die Karte an und finde den Weg, den Gillian zu Vanessa gefahren ist.

Hammersmith & City Line

Northern Line

DVD
40

WB p. 74
B4

www.tfl.gov.uk/tube

B4 Food

Say what you see.

WB p. 75
B5

p. 60
B4

B5 Find the food

Work with a partner. Find the things in the picture.

tomatoes   cakes   crisps   apples   ...

Show me the ...

wordbank
food and
drink p. 155

Look at the picture. Ask and answer questions.

| Where | is
are | the | milk,
apples,
vegetables,
chocolate,
biscuits,
fruit,
... | please? | next to
under
between
in front of
behind
above |

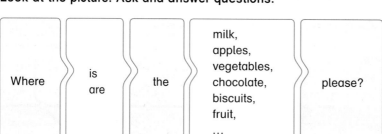

Where is the milk, please?

Where are the apples, please?

...

The milk is next to the ...

The apples are between the ...

WB p. 75
B6, B7

p. 60
B5

B6 At the corner shop

 Listen to the CD and point at the food and drink.

CD
2/10 141

a) Listen to the CD and read along.

Shopkeeper: Hello, girls, can I help you?

Vanessa: Yes, please! We can't find the cheddar cheese. Have you got any?

Shopkeeper: Yes, it's over there, next to the milk.

Vanessa: Ah, thank you!

Shopkeeper: Is there anything else I can help you with?

Gillian: Yes, how much are those cakes, please?

Shopkeeper: They are 75 pence each.

Gillian: Could we have two of them, please?

Shopkeeper: Of course! Here you go. Anything else?

Gillian: That's everything, thanks.

Shopkeeper: OK, what have we got? Lemonade, chocolate, crisps, cheddar cheese, cakes … that's 9 pound 30 altogether, please.

Vanessa: Here you are.

Shopkeeper: Thanks. Here's your change.

Vanessa and Gillian: Thanks. Bye.

Shopkeeper: Bye!

b) Read the dialogue in groups of three. Use props and gestures.

c) Write your own shopping dialogue in your group and act it out.

 WB p. 76
B8

p. 61
B6, B7

 wordbank
shopping,
English in action
p. 156/7

B7 Let's go shopping!

Watch the video clip.

What is on the shopping list?
What else do they buy?
Tell your partner in German.

 DVD
41

 how to p. 145
mediate

 WB p. 77
B9, B10

B8 Tongue twister

CD
2/11 144

a) Listen to the tongue twister. Now you say it.

> Chips or crisps? Crisps or chips?
> Chips with fish and crisps with dips!

WB p. 77
B11

b) Explain in German the difference between chips and crisps.

B9 Meeting Dan and Janet

CD
2/13 146

a) Listen to the CD and read along.

Vanessa: Come and meet my dad. Dan, this is Gillian.

Dan Ross: Hi, Gillian. Nice to meet you.

Gillian: Hello, Mr Ross. How are you?

Dan Ross: I'm fine, thanks. But don't call me mister. Dan is fine.

Janet Ross: Hello, Gillian. I'm Janet. Vanessa always calls us Dan and Janet.

Dan Ross: You can call us Dan and Janet, too. OK?

Gillian: OK, Mr Ross, I mean, Dan.

Janet Ross: Anyway, it's nice to meet you, Gillian. It's so cold today, isn't it? Would you like a hot chocolate?

Vanessa: Great idea, Janet!

Gillian: Yes, please!

Janet Ross: And I hope you're hungry, Gillian. It's Dan's spaghetti special on the menu tonight.

Gillian: Mmm! That sounds good.

Janet Ross: Vanessa, why don't you show Gillian your room?

how to p. 140
talk

Vanessa: OK. Come on, Gillian! I'll show you my room. I have this …

b) Work in groups of four. Two of you play the parents. Two of you play the friends. Introduce your friend to your parents.

> Mum, this is …

> Dad, this is …

> How are you?

> Nice to meet you.

> I'm fine, thanks.

> …

wordbank
English in
action p. 157

p. 63
B8

B10 A great evening

a) **What do you remember about Gillian and Vanessa's plans for the evening? Make notes.**

b) **Listen to Gillian, Vanessa and her parents. Compare with your notes.**

 CD 2/14

c) ☆ **What is right? Listen again and take notes.**

1. Gillian loves Dan's spaghetti special / pizza special.
2. Dan and Janet can do the shopping / washing up.
3. Vanessa and Gillian want to read ghost stories / comics.
4. They have tea / chocolate first.

☾ **Listen again and take notes. Correct the sentences.**

1. Gillian thanks Dan for the breakfast.
2. Vanessa and Gillian can switch on the lights and read funny stories.
3. Vanessa shows Gillian a big torch and her collection of comics.
4. The girls want to have some ice cream before they read the stories.

☼ **Listen again and take notes. Then answer the questions.**

1. Who can do the washing up?
2. Where do Vanessa and Gillian go after dinner?
3. What do they want to do?
4. What kind of stories does Vanessa collect?
5. What is good for their nerves?

p. 64 B9

B11 Voices in the dark

 Record spooky words and sounds.

a) **Listen to Gillian and Vanessa. What is the story about?**

 CD 2/15

b) **What do you like about the story?**

☼ **Write an ending to the story.**

 WB p. 77 B12

B12 Target task: Ideas for a fun evening

a) **Work in groups. Plan a fun evening with your family or friends.**
Present your ideas on a piece of paper.
Think about:

* What can you do? Sleepover? Games evening? Dinner? …
* What do you need? Shopping list? Games? …

 p. 65 B10

b) **Collect your ideas to make a book for the class.**

P10 Explain

Explain what you have to do.

1. Tell your partner in German.
2. Compare with your notes.
3. Make your own dialogue with your partner.
4. Listen again and take notes.
5. Record spooky words and sounds.

Ich soll ...

...

Wir sollen ...

P11 Lots of questions

You plan a sleepover with a friend.

LiF p. 172
6c

a) Write down questions.

What	can I	come • sleep •
When	can we	bring • eat • do •
Where	can you	pick me up • meet •
		drink • read

?

What can I bring?

b) Work with a partner. Ask and answer questions. Take turns.

P12 Food and drink

Write down the words in alphabetical order.

chocolate • milk • tomatoes • apples •
vegetables • crisps • cakes • biscuits •
sandwiches • cheese • lemonade

P13 Where is Ruby?

a) Write down where Ruby is.

next to
on
in
in front of
behind
under

1. Ruby is under the box.

CD 148

b) Listen to the CD and check your sentences.

Practice matters

P14 Let's go shopping

a) Sort the two dialogues and write them down in your exercise book.

Dialogue 1

Oh yes. How much is it?
It's one pound twenty.
Yes, please. I can't find the milk.
OK, thank you.
Hello, can I help you?
It's over there.

Dialogue 2

Of course. That's one pound fifty, please.
Hello, how can I help you?
Goodbye!
Here you are – five pounds.
Can I have one of those cakes, please?
Thank you. Here's your change. Bye!

b) Listen to the CD and check your dialogues.

 CD
149

P15 Prices

Work with a partner. Ask and answer questions.

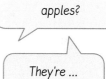

> How much is the milk?

> It's ...

> How much are the apples?

> They're ...

P16 Meeting people

a) Match the sentence parts and write them down.

Come and   my friend.
This is   fine, thanks.
Hello. Nice to are you?
How   meet you.
I'm   meet my parents.

b) Listen to the CD and check your sentences.

 CD
150

P17 Sound check: how to say the letter 'a'

 CD
151

Listen to the CD and repeat the words.

Janet • have • Dan • thanks •
at • apple • plan • can • and

[O] The London Underground

1. Did you know that …

… the London Underground is called 'the tube' because of the shape of the tunnels?

… the tube is quicker than a bus or a taxi?

… about 2.5 million passengers use the tube every day?

… about half a million mice live in the Underground?

… there are 12 lines, 287 tube stations and 409 escalators?

… it was the world's first underground network? The first line opened in 1863.

What do you find most interesting? Why?

2. Stories about ghosts on the London Underground

- On the Bakerloo Line, people look in the window and see someone next to them – but there is no one there!
- At Ickenham station there is a ghost who wears a red scarf. She waves at people and then disappears!
- On the Victoria Line there is a ghost who is more than 2 metres tall.

Find out more about ghosts on the London Underground and tell the class about them.

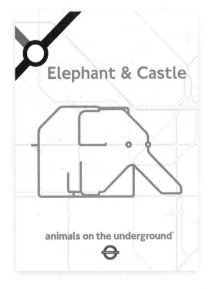

3. Animals on the London Underground

You can find animal shapes on the London Underground map. Look at these examples from an art project called 'animals on the underground'.

Have a look at the map on page 85. Put a thin piece of paper over it and draw another animal.

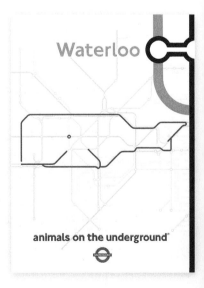

Day by day

In diesem *Theme* ...

- erfährst du etwas über den britischen Schulalltag.

- **Zielaufgabe** *(target task)*: Du präsentierst deinen Traumschultag.

- sprichst du über Geburtstage und Familie.

- **Zielaufgabe** *(target task)*: Du sammelst mit deiner Klasse Ideen, wie ihr eure Geburtstage im Englischunterricht feiern könnt.

A1 Our school ▶

a) Look at the pictures. What can you see?

DVD
43, 44

b) Now watch the video clips. What do the children talk about?

A2 Friday at last!

> **Work with a partner.**
> **Look at Gillian and David.**
> **Talk about the school uniforms.**
>
> *David has got a red and blue tie, …*
>
> *Gillian has got …*

CD
2/17 157

a) Listen to the CD and read along.
   Where do Gillian and David want to go?

Gillian: Hi, David! The weekend at last! History on a Friday afternoon is so boring. It's my last lesson before the weekend. I hate it.

David: Really? I love it. History is my favourite subject. But my last lesson on Friday is maths! That's terrible!

Gillian: I have maths on Friday, too – before lunch. But Friday mornings are great. My first lesson is music – that's really cool. And then I have art with Mr King …

David: Oh, he's your favourite, isn't he?

Gillian: Well, yes, his lessons are really good. But, I mean, I just really like art … And some other lessons are so boring, like science or maths …

David: Oh, you can say that again. By the way, nice new school uniform! You're lucky! I like the blue shirts.

Gillian: Well yes, the shirts are OK – but the boys' ties: blue and black …

David: You're right about that. Our ties look better.

Gillian: I'd rather wear no school uniform at all – but who asks me?

David: I know. Anyway, I'm so hungry. I missed lunch in the canteen today.

Gillian: I never eat in our canteen. I always take sandwiches for lunch. But I'm hungry, too. Let's go to Burger Queen.

David: OK! Let's go. You know what? The best thing about Fridays is that …

b) **What is the best thing about Fridays? Tell your class what you like about Fridays.**

c) **Now listen to David. What does he like about Fridays?**

CD 2/18

d) **Copy Gillian's timetable for Friday and fill in the subjects. Gillian also has English on Fridays. When is it?**

	1	2		3	4		5
Friday	???	???	break	???	???	lunch	???
	music	art		(maths)	maths		history

p. 66 A1, A2

e) ☆ **Answer the questions.**

1. Does Gillian like history?
2. Does she like music?
3. Who is her favourite teacher?
4. Does she like school uniforms?
5. What does Gillian have for lunch?
6. Does she eat in the canteen?

☾ **What does Gillian like? What doesn't she like?**

☼ **Collect information about Gillian and David. Think about subjects, favourite teacher, school uniform, ... Then write about Gillian and David.**

WB p. 85 A1, A2

LAND & LEUTE 6

Schulalltag in Großbritannien

Ein Schultag in Großbritannien dauert etwa von 9 bis 16 Uhr. Viele Kinder kommen mit dem Schulbus zur Schule. Häufig beginnt der Tag mit der Überprüfung der Anwesenheit *(registration)*. Oft gibt es auch noch eine Schulversammlung *(assembly),* in der Ankündigungen gemacht werden, zum Beispiel für Projektwochen, Sportveranstaltungen und Theateraufführungen.

Die Lehrerinnen und Lehrer haben eigene Unterrichtsräume für die verschiedenen Fächer. Die Schülerinnen und Schüler gehen also für jedes Fach in einen anderen Raum. Die Jacken und Bücher können in einem eigenen Spind *(locker)* untergebracht werden. In der Mittagspause kann man in der Mensa *(canteen)* eine warme Mahlzeit essen. Danach geht der Unterricht weiter.

Nach dem Unterricht nehmen viele Schulkinder an Arbeitsgemeinschaften *(clubs)* teil. Hier können sie Sport treiben, musizieren und vieles mehr. Wenn sie am Nachmittag zu Hause sind, machen sie ihre Hausaufgaben.
An den meisten britischen Schulen trägt man eine Schuluniform.

Kennst du andere Länder, in denen es Schuluniformen gibt? Was weißt du noch über den Schulalltag in anderen Ländern?

DVD 45

www.hendonschool.co.uk; www.hollandparkschool.co.uk; wwww.mrc-academy.org

A3 David's timetable

> **Work with a partner. Point at these subjects in David's timetable:**
>
> Englisch   Mathe   Musik   Deutsch   …

YEAR 7		1	2		3	4		5	
time	8.40– 9.00	9.00– 10.00	10.00– 11.00	11.00– 11.20	11.20– 12.20	12.20– 1.20	1.20– 2.15	2.15– 3.15	3.15– 3.20
Monday		German	English		maths	science		drama	
Tuesday	registration/ assembly	ICT	history	break	RE	maths	lunch	science	afternoon registration
Wednesday		English	maths		art	geography		music	
Thursday		science	German		PE	PE		English	
Friday		history	ICT		geography	English		maths	

p. 68
A3, A4

LiF p. 166
4a, b

a) Talk about David's timetable.

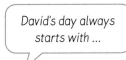
David's day always starts with …

On Mondays David has …

David has … lessons a week.

There are … subjects.

There are … breaks.

…

b) Talk to your partner.

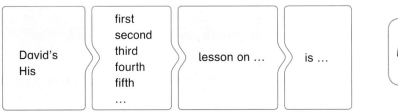

| David's His | first second third fourth fifth … | lesson on … | is … |

David's first lesson on Mondays is German.

c) Write your timetable in English. Do you speak a language other than English or German? Write down the subjects in that language, too.

d) ☆ **Make a word web of school words. Think about subjects, things in the classroom, …**

   ☾ **Write about David's school day.**

wordbank
at school
p. 152

   David's school day starts at 8.40. His day starts with … It ends …

   ☼ **Compare your timetable with David's timetable. Think about registration, assembly, breaks, lessons, subjects, when the school day ends, …**

WB p. 85
A3–A5

   David's school day starts at 8.40 in the morning, but my school day starts at …
   His day starts with …

A4 Before and after school

a) **Look at the pictures. When do the things happen – before or after school?**

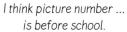

I think picture number ... is before school.

I think picture number ... is after school.

p. 70
A5, A6

how to p. 138
listen

b) **Listen and put the pictures in the correct order.** 3, 2 6 5, 1, 4

CD
2/20 161

c) **Listen again and answer the questions.**

1. Who gets up at 7.30 am? *David*
2. Who gets up at 7 am? *Gillian*
3. Who has breakfast at 7.30 am? *Gillian*
4. Who walks to school? *David*
5. Who goes to school by bus? *Gillian*

6. Who walks the dog at 4.15 pm? *David*
7. Who often plays with friends at 4.30 pm? *Gillian*
8. Who has dinner at 6.30 pm? *Gillian*
9. Who starts their homework at 6.30 pm? *David*
10. Who goes to bed at 9.30 pm? *David*

LiF p. 166
4a

1. David gets up at ...

d) **Listen to Gillian on her way to school. When is the next bus?** 8.28 am
What does she decide? *goes back & gets her bike*

CD
2/21

Bus 390 Notting Hill Gate		
7 to 8 am	8 to 9 am	9 am to 10 pm
7 12	8 13	about every
7 27	8 28	*11–13*
7 42	8 43	minutes
7 57	8 58	

Tipp
Bei Zeiten wie 8.13 sagt man *eight thirteen* oder *thirteen minutes past eight.*

WB p. 87
A6–A9

A5 When, what, where, why?

CD
2/22 166
2/23 167

a) Listen to the song. What is it about?

♫ **Song of the day**

When do you get up every morning?
I get up at half past six.

When do you … What do you … Where do you … Why?
When do you have breakfast and leave your house for school?

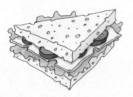

What do you have for lunch on a school day?
I have a sandwich, an apple and juice.

When do you … What do you … Where do you … Why?
What do you do or play in the break?

Where do you do your homework in the afternoon?
I do my homework at my desk.

When do you … What do you … Where do you … Why?
Where do you have dinner with your family?

Why do you go to bed at half past seven?
I ask my mum that every night!

When do you … What do you … Where do you … Why?
Why are we still singing? It's time to end this song.

b) Sing the song and act it out.

 Work with a partner. Act out your day. Mime and guess.

LiF p.169
4d

 c) Write down all the questions in the song. Then write answers about your day.

d) Ask your partner about his or her day.

WB p.88
A10

☼ **Write more verses.**

A6 Choose

1. **Make a fact file about a subject from your timetable. What do you do in the lessons? What do you need? Who is your teacher? …**

2. **Make notes about your dream subject and give a short talk on it.**

3. **Write your dream timetable and present it to your classmates. You can think of new subjects if you want to.**

A7 Karlotta's email

Gillian's class takes part in the eTwinning project "School days around the world".

a) Read the email they get from Karlotta. What are Karlotta's favourites?

p. 72 A7

Hi everyone!

I'm Karlotta Nissen. My friends call me Lotta. I go to school in Aalborg in Denmark.
I usually go to school by bike but sometimes I go by bus.
Our school year is from August to June. My school starts at 8 am every day and finishes at 3 pm. We have a 30-minute break for lunch.
There are 20 pupils in my class. My favourite teacher is my class teacher Arne Jensen and my favourite subjects are geography and maths.
The school library is my favourite place at school. I often go there after lessons and work on a computer. On Wednesdays I go to a photography course at the Youth Club next to my school. What about your school day?
Bye for now!

Karlotta

model text

b) What does Karlotta write about in her email? Talk about it in German.

how to p. 141 write

c) Write an email to Karlotta about your school day.

WB p. 89 A11–A13

A8 Target task: Your dream school day

a) What is your dream school day like? You can draw pictures, make a poster or make a recording. These questions can help you:

- When do you get up?
- How do you get to school?
- What subjects do you have?
- What does your dream school look like?
- What do you do all day?

wordbank at school p. 152

b) Present your dream school day. Here is an example. You can make notes like this:

how to p. 142 present

model text

My dream school day
- get up at 10 o'clock
- fly to school by helicopter
- first lesson: breakfast - cake
- lots of flowers in the classroom
- class party every day

p. 73 A8

You can listen to an example of a presentation on the CD.

CD 170

P1 Explain

Explain what you have to do.

1. Copy Gillian's timetable.
2. Fill in the subjects.
3. Ask your partner about his or her day.
4. Write an email about your school day.
5. Write down all the questions in the song.

Ich soll ...

...

Wir sollen ...

P2 Sound check: how to say the letter 'u'

CD 171

Listen to the words and repeat them.

lunch • bus • pupil • put • Ruby • club • June • subject • uniform • much

What do you notice?

P3 School words

a) Find the words and write them down.

lu-	regist-	les-	sci-	-ject	-son	-nch
geogr-	assem-	can-	-tory	-ration	-form
br-	tea-	sub-	uni-	-bly	-eak -aphy -table -cher
his-	time-	Eng-	-ence	-teen	-lish

lunch, registration, ...

CD 172

b) Listen to the CD and check your words.

Choose at least five words and use them to write sentences.

P4 Odd one out

Find the odd one out.

1. cornflakes – egg – pizza – toast
2. teacher – orange – pupil – classroom
3. weekend – Monday – Tuesday – Wednesday
4. shirt – tie – cap – canteen
5. music – English – burger – geography
6. walk – read – run – go

Practice matters

P5 Headwords

a) What are these things? Find the headwords.

1. PE – maths – art – history
2. pizza – sandwich – spaghetti – chips
3. Monday – Saturday – Sunday – Friday
4. cornflakes – egg – toast – milk

days

breakfast

subjects

lunch

b) Write down more word groups. Your partner has to find the headwords.

P6 Find a classmate who ...

a) Draw this table in your exercise book. Write down the questions and add more subjects. Now ask your classmates.

Find a classmate who	question	name
... likes geography.	Do you like ... ?	
... likes history.	Do you ... ?	
... likes RE.		
... likes PE.		
... likes music.		
... hates music.		
... hates PE.		
...		

Do you like ... ?

Yes, I do.

No, I don't.

🔍 LiF p. 168
4c

b) Report to your partner.

P7 Gillian's afternoon

a) Complete the text with the correct forms of the verbs in the box.

> ride • come • listen • dance • have • meet • help • play • make

Gillian usually 🔲🔲🔲 home from school at half past three.
Then she often 🔲🔲🔲 to music in her room and 🔲🔲🔲 to it.
Sometimes she 🔲🔲🔲 her friends in the afternoon. They 🔲🔲🔲
lots of games together and sometimes they 🔲🔲🔲 their
bikes. Gillian often 🔲🔲🔲 her mum in the kitchen and 🔲🔲🔲 a
salad for dinner. They usually 🔲🔲🔲 dinner at half past six.

Gillian usually comes home ...

🔍 LiF p. 166
4a

b) Listen to the CD and check your text.

 CD
173

B1 The calendar song

CD
2/24

WB p.91
B1

Listen to the song and sing along. Stand up when you hear your birthday month.

January February March April May June
July August September October November December

B2 Birthday plans

CD
2/25

p.74
B1

WB p.91
B2, B3

David is planning his birthday party. He wants to invite some friends.

a) **Listen to David and his mum. What is David's idea?**

b) **What does David check on the Internet?**

c) **What do David and his mum decide to do?**

15

April

David's
birthday

B3 David's birthday party

Look at the pictures. Where is the party? Who is at the party? What can you see?

CD
2/26 176

DVD
47

a) **Listen and read along.**

It's three o'clock on Sunday afternoon. David's family are in the living room. His mum is putting food on the table and his dad is helping her. Aunt Fay and Uncle Morgan aren't helping. Aunt Fay is sitting at the table and reading. And what is Uncle Morgan doing? Uncle Morgan is doing magic tricks. But nobody is watching. Then David's friends arrive.

Gillian: Hi, David, happy birthday.
David: Hey, Gillian, thanks! Come in.
Rajiv: Here's your present. Hope you like it.
David: Hi, Rajiv, thanks. Hello, Vanessa, hi, Karla.
Vanessa and Karla: Hi, David, happy birthday.
Mrs Williams: Hello, children. Nice to see you all. Is anybody hungry?
Charlie: Oh, yeah. I'm hungry.

Gillian: You're always hungry, Charlie.

Mrs Williams: Well, come on, then. The food's in the living room. David, can you get your friends something to drink, please?

David: Sorry, Mum, but I can't. I'm just opening my presents. – Wow, fantastic poster!

The music is great. Gillian, Karla and Charlie are dancing. Uncle Morgan is doing another magic trick.

Then the phone rings. Mrs Williams answers it.

Mrs Williams: David, it's for you.

b) Look at the pictures. Say what the people are doing.

David Karla Uncle Morgan Gillian David's mum Aunt Fay The friends …	is are	dancing. opening presents. putting food on the table. coming in. saying hello. looking at … …

> In picture number three David is opening presents.

p. 75
B2

> In the last picture the friends are dancing.

LiF p. 176
9a

c) Make an ABC of birthday party words.

A – apple juice
B – balloon
…

☾ **Right or wrong?**
Correct the wrong sentences.

1. David's party starts at three o'clock.
2. Aunt Fay is putting food on the table and Uncle Morgan is helping her.
3. Uncle Morgan is watching TV.
4. Charlie is always hungry.
5. David gets a poster from his friends.
6. Gillian, Karla and Charlie are singing.
7. Mr Williams answers the phone.

☼ **Write the end of the story. Think about:**

- Who is on the phone for David?
- What do they talk about?
- What happens after the phone call?
- …

 WB p. 92
B4–B6

B4 On the phone

CD 2/27

Listen and answer the questions.

1. How many people are on the phone? Who are they?
2. What are the birthday presents?
3. Does David like his presents?

B5 Party pictures

LiF p. 176
9

a) Work with a partner. Look at the pictures. What is everyone doing? Ask and answer questions.

Gillian	sleep under the table
Aunt Fay	eat cake
David's mum	dance to the music
David's dad	make pizza
Uncle Morgan	drink tea
Kenny	pour the drinks
...	...

What is Gillian doing?

Gillian is eating cake.

p. 76
B3

WB p. 93
B7, B8

b) Now write down what the people are doing.

Gillian is eating cake.

B6 Let's talk about birthdays

DVD
48

a) Watch the video clip. What do the children like about birthdays?

b) What do you like about birthdays?

B7 Family tree

> **Work with a partner. Point at these people in the family tree.**
>
> David's mother   Gillian's grandparents   ...
>
> Morgan's brother   Gillian's father

a) Talk about David and Gillian's family.

1. Thomas is Alice's ...
2. Morgan is Thomas's ...
3. Ivor is Gillian's ...
4. Gwen is David's ...
5. David is Gillian's ...
6. Gillian is Janet's ...
7. Morgan is David's ...
8. Janet is ...

girls and women:	boys and men:
daughter	son
grandmother	grandfather
mother	father
sister	brother
aunt	uncle
granddaughter	grandson
wife	husband
cousin	cousin
niece	nephew

LiF p. 175
8

Can you say it the other way round, too?

1. Alice is Thomas's wife.
2. Thomas is ...
...

Ivor Williams
13 Sep

Janet Williams
17 Dec

Gwen Collins
21 Apr

divorced

Paul Collins
31 May

Fay Williams
14 Nov

Morgan Williams
20 Aug

Thomas Williams
31 Dec

Alice Williams
18 Oct

Gillian Collins
15 Jan

David Williams
15 Apr

b) ☆ **Work with a partner. Write about the family.**

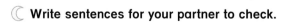

Gillian is David's cousin. Gillian's birthday is on 15 January. ...

p. 77
B4, B5

☾ **Write sentences for your partner to check.**

You:
David is Gillian's brother.
Gillian's birthday is in January. ...

Your partner:
No, that's wrong. He is her cousin.
Yes, that's right. ...

Make a quiz for your class about the family.

Who is David's uncle? – It's Morgan Williams.
Whose first name starts with an F? – Aunt Fay's.
How many brothers has Gwen got? – ...

WB p. 94
B9, B10

B8 Choose

1. Do you speak a language other than English or German? Then present the words for family members in that language.

> In Turkish mother is "anne" and father is "baba".

2. Choose photos of your family and present them to your classmates.

> In this photo you can see ...

wordbank people p. 151

3. Draw your own family tree and write about it.

B9 Birthdays

wordbank time p. 148

a) Work with a partner. Ask and answer questions.

> When is Daniel's birthday?

> It's on the first of April.

1 April — Daniel

19 September — Tim

26 March — Robert

12 January — Sarah

22 July — Emily

30 June — Lucy

5 November — Ben

23 May — Becky

6 February — Oliver

15 August — Katie

3 October — Anna

31 December — Karim

Tipp
Man schreibt:
1st April oder
1 April,
man sagt: *the first of April.*

1st	first	11th	eleventh	21st	twenty-first
2nd	second	12th	twelfth	22nd	twenty-second
3rd	third	13th	thirteenth	23rd	twenty-third
4th	fourth	14th	fourteenth	24th	twenty-fourth
5th	fifth	15th	fifteenth	25th	twenty-fifth
6th	sixth	16th	sixteenth	26th	twenty-sixth
7th	seventh	17th	seventeenth	27th	twenty-seventh
8th	eighth	18th	eighteenth	28th	twenty-eighth
9th	ninth	19th	nineteenth	29th	twenty-ninth
10th	tenth	20th	twentieth	30th	thirtieth
				31st	thirty-first

WB p. 95
B11–B13

b) Ask each other:

> When is your birthday?

> It's on the second of March.

> When is your mum's birthday?

> It's in June.

p. 77
B6

c) Make a birthday calendar for your class.

B10 Grandma says

a) **Listen to the poem and read along. What is the poem about?**

b) **What problem is the person in the poem talking about? Explain it in German.**

c) **What should the person do if Grandma asks? Lie? Tell the truth?**

Grandma says

Grandma says I shouldn't lie,
The truth is always better.
I just hope she doesn't ask
If I like my birthday sweater.

Judy Lalli

CD
2/28 182

B11 Choose

Make a word web about your birthday. Now choose:

1. **Tell your class about your birthday. Make notes first.**

2. **Draw a picture of your birthday and label it. Show it to a classmate.**

3. **Write about your birthday. You can write a text or a poem. Read it to a classmate.**

My birthday is in winter. It is on 4th January. I go to the cinema with my friends. We always have crisps and lemonade. It is a cool day!

 how to p. 141 write

 model text

 wordbank birthdays p. 154

My birthday is on 27th August. It's in summer and I usually go to the park with my friends. We play games and have a picnic. We always have pizza, doughnuts and crisps and a big chocolate birthday cake. When I blow out the candles my friends sing "Happy birthday to you". It's always such a fun day.

 p. 78 B7

B12 Target task: Birthday parties in your class

How can you celebrate your birthdays in your class?
Collect ideas for birthday parties in your English lessons.
Think about:

- songs
- games
- decoration
- recipes
- things you need
- a poster with "Happy birthday" in many languages
- ...

Present your ideas in class.

 Can we ... ?

 Let's ...

What about ... ?

I like the song ... best of all.

 p. 79 B8

 how to p. 144 work together

wordbank birthdays p. 154

Practice matters

P8 Explain

Explain what you have to do.

1. Say what the people are doing.
2. Write sentences for your partner to check.
3. Make a quiz for your class about the family.
4. Make a word web about your birthday.
5. Ask each other.

Ich soll …

…

Wir sollen …

P9 One and one is one

a) Find the words and write them in your exercise book.

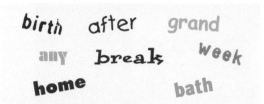

birth   after   grand
any   break   week
home   bath

work   body   day
fast   room   end   mother   noon

birthday, afternoon, …

CD 🔘 183   **b) Listen to the CD and check your words.**

P10 Party day

a) Unscramble the sentences.

LiF p. 176
9a

1. David's father – for the party – pizza – making – is – .
2. drinking – Vanessa and Gillian – are – lemonade – .
3. giving – his present – They – David – are – .
4. to the music – Charlie – dancing – is – .
5. eating – cake – are – Aunt Fay and Uncle Morgan – .
6. playing – David's friends – are – with him – .

1. David's father is making pizza for the party.

CD 🔘 184   **b) Listen to the CD and check your sentences.**

P11 Activities

a) Look at the pictures. Write about the old man and the cat. What are they doing?

LiF p. 176
9a

1. The old man is cleaning. The cat is …

CD 🔘 185   **b) Listen to the CD and check your sentences.**

P12 Everybody is busy

a) Write down the text and complete it.

It is quarter past two on Saturday afternoon. Charlie and his family are busy. Mrs Batson is in the living room. She ??? a birthday card for her mother. Josephine is in her room. She ??? to music. Sharon ??? at the kitchen table and ??? a birthday picture for her grandmother. Mr Batson ??? a cup of tea. And Charlie? Charlie is in the park with his friends. They ??? football. What a busy family!

| make • draw • |
| listen • play • |
| sit • write |

LiF p. 176
9a

b) Listen to the CD and check your text.

CD
186

P13 Sorry, I can't

a) Work with a partner. Look at the pictures. Ask and answer questions.

LiF p. 176
9a

Can you help me?

Sorry, I can't. I'm doing my homework.

Are you ready?

Wait! I'm ...

do homework • brush teeth •
watch TV • tidy room •
play table tennis

b) Make up more dialogues with your partner.

DVD
49–51

P14 A family quiz

a) Read the sentences. Who is it?

1. He is my mother's son.
2. She is my son's sister.
3. He is my father's father.
4. He is my son's son.
5. She is my mother's daughter.
6. He is my father's brother.
7. She is my sister's daughter.
8. She is my father's wife.

LiF p. 175
8

1. He is my mother's son. He is my brother.

b) Listen to the CD and check your sentences.

CD
187

c) Write more sentences for your partner.

Optional

O1 Party drinks

Cherry cheer
1 litre cherry juice
1 litre pineapple juice
1 litre bitter lemon/
    lemonade
fruit: lemon,
        pineapple,
        cherries
sugar, lemon juice
cocktail sticks

Fruit fun
1 litre apple juice
1/2 litre ginger ale
1/2 litre pineapple juice
1/2 litre orange juice
fruit: orange, apple,
        pineapple,
        grapes
sugar, lemon juice
cocktail sticks

Dip the glasses in the lemon juice and then in the sugar. Mix the drinks. Cut pieces of fruit. Put the fruit on the cocktail sticks. Add a cocktail stick and a straw to each glass.

Collect recipes for more party drinks.

O2 Party games

Chocolate bean game

Play it in a group of three or four.
Put chocolate beans on a big plate. Give everyone a straw and a small plate. Suck hard – put the chocolate beans on your own plate! The person who has the most chocolate beans on their plate wins.

The egg box game

Take an old egg box and write numbers on it like this:

Put the box at the end of the table. Everyone has six chocolate beans and throws them into the box. How many points can you get?

Find out about more party games and tell your class about them.

O3 A magic trick

DVD 52

Watch the video clip. Then try the trick yourself.

Out and about

In diesem *Theme* ...

- sprichst du über die Ferien und erfährst, was die Kinder aus Notting Hill im Sommer machen.

- **Zielaufgabe** *(target task)*: Du sammelst mit deiner Klasse Ideen, was man am eigenen Wohnort in den Ferien machen kann.

- liest und hörst du Geschichten und erfährst, was britische Kinder gerne lesen.

- **Zielaufgabe** *(target task)*: Du schreibst gemeinsam mit anderen eine Geschichte.

A1 A trip to Kentish Town City Farm

It's the last week before the holidays. Gillian, Rajiv, Karla and their classmates go on a school trip to Kentish Town City Farm.

a) Look at the picture of the farm. What animals can you see?

CD — 2/29

b) Listen to the animals and point.

CD — 2/30 190

c) Listen to the people and point.

DVD — 53

p. 80
A1, A2

Primary pick-up

13 We've got 35 sheep, 13 lambs and 8 goats.

14 Do they get on well together?

16 Stop! What's going on?

15 Yes, they do.

17 That goat is eating your rucksack!

18 Ugh! Does it bite?

19 No, don't worry.

A2 A day at the farm

a) **Listen to the CD and find out what Rajiv tells his family about his day.**

b) **Now write about Rajiv's day.**

It was really …	We saw …
There was …	We rode …
There were …	It was …
They had …	I liked the … best of all.

ponies • ducks • pigs • horses •
cows • goats • a bull •
a lot of chickens • sheep •
an information stand • a field •
a café • a big tractor •
a hen house • a bridge • the water •
interesting • fun • great • …

 LiF p. 178
10a, b

 CD
2/31

 p. 81
A3

 wordbank
animals p. 147

 WB p. 103
A1–A4

☼ **What does the boy in the red sweatshirt tell his family?**

A3 School's out for summer

CD 2/32 192

DVD 54

a) Listen to the CD and read along.

Last Saturday was the first day of the summer holidays. Gillian and Vanessa had breakfast at Gillian's house. It was warm and sunny. Vanessa opened the window.

Vanessa: Oh, it's great to be on holiday at last.
Gillian: Yeah! And it's fun having you here. Why do you live so far away?
Vanessa: I know … but it's only until next month. I'm glad we're moving to Notting Hill, at last.
Gillian: Yeah, me too.

Suddenly a parrot landed on the table.

Vanessa: Hey, Ruby! What are you doing here?
Ruby: Rajiv is my best friend.
Gillian: We know, Ruby, we know. But where is Rajiv? He can't be far.

Ruby flew out of the window. Gillian jumped up and looked out. Rajiv and Karla were outside the house. Gillian waved to them.

Gillian: Hi, you two. Look up!
Rajiv: Oh no, Ruby, not again!
Gillian: I think she's flying to the park.
Rajiv: Can you come and help us find her?
Gillian: OK. Vanessa is here, too. Just a minute.

So off they went to the park. They searched for a while and finally they found Ruby in a tree.

Rajiv: Ruby, there you are! Come down now!
Ruby: Bananas, bananas!
Rajiv: Come down and you can have a banana!

Ruby flew onto Rajiv's shoulder.

Rajiv: There's a good parrot. Let's take Ruby home. She can have her banana and we can play together. What do you think, girls?
Karla: Great idea, Rajiv!
Gillian: OK!
Vanessa: Let's go!

b) ☆ **Write about the first day of the summer holidays.**

p. 82
A4

Vanessa and Gillian A parrot Rajiv and Karla Ruby The children …	had were flew went landed	to the park. outside the house. onto Rajiv's shoulder. on the table. out of the window. breakfast.

☾ **What does Vanessa tell her dad in the evening? Complete the sentences.**

LiF p. 178
10a, b

I had breakfast with …
Suddenly a parrot …
Rajiv and Karla were …
We all went to …

There we found …
Ruby flew onto …
Then we went to …
It was …

how to p. 141
write

☼ **What does Gillian write in her diary?** This morning I had breakfast with …

WB p. 105
A5, A6

A4 It's time for the holidays

a) Listen and sing along.

CD
2/33 195
2/34 196

♫ No teachers, no homework, no lessons, no school.
It's time for the holidays – cool!

It's the end of July and it's time for some fun –
time to play with my friends, be outside in the sun!

No teachers, no homework, no lessons, no school.
It's time for the holidays – cool!

In my town in the summer there's so much to do –
at the beach, at the park, at my house – yes, it's true!

No teachers, no homework, no lessons, no school.
It's time for the holidays – cool!

I've got a favourite place for ice cream, a favourite place to skate,
a favourite place to meet my friends, my town is really great!

No teachers, no homework, no lessons, no school.
It's time for the holidays – cool!

So who needs a plane or a holiday in the sun,
when you can stay at home and have so much fun?! Yeah!

No teachers, no homework, no lessons, no school.
It's time for the holidays – cool!

b) What do you like best about the song?

A5 A crush on Duncan

 Look at the pictures. What can you see?

CD
2/35 197

a) Listen to the story. Does Charlie like Duncan?

Vanessa, Gillian and Charlie are at the park.

Charlie: Hey, I've got a new pair of skates, let's go skating next weekend!

Vanessa: I went to the skatepark last Sunday with Susan and Duncan. Susan and I hired skates, but Duncan has got a brilliant pair of skates! He's a very good skater. He lives next door.

Charlie: Hmm. And did you have a good time?

Vanessa: Yes, we skated for an hour, and then they had the club championship.

Charlie: What about Duncan?

Vanessa: Well, he was the champion. Everyone cheered for him … he was great. The audience shouted: Two, four, six, eight! Who do we appreciate? Duncan! Duncan! Skate, man, skate!

Charlie: Hmm! I think you've got a crush on Duncan. Duncan. What a silly name.

Vanessa: You're silly. We're just … oh, look, there's Gillian with our ice creams.

Gillian: OK, you two. You can have vanilla, vanilla, or vanilla!

b) Work in groups of three. Read the dialogue.

c) Work with a partner. Ask and answer questions.

p. 83
A5

Who went to the skatepark?	**Who** cheered for Duncan?
Who skated for an hour?	**Who** thinks Vanessa has got a crush on Duncan?
Who was the champion?	**Who** has got ice creams for Charlie and Vanessa?

> Vanessa, Susan and Duncan.
> …

Match the sentence parts.

1. Vanessa, Susan and Duncan	a. for Duncan.
2. Susan and Vanessa	b. vanilla ice creams.
3. Duncan has got	c. Duncan is a silly name.
4. They had the club championship	d. a brilliant pair of skates.
5. Everyone cheered	e. went to the skatepark last Sunday.
6. Charlie thinks that	f. at the skatepark.
7. Gillian brings them	g. hired skates.

Duncan tells his best friend about his day at the skatepark.

LiF p. 178
10a, b

What does he tell him? Write it down. Here are some ideas to help you.

WB p. 106
A7, A8

I had a really great time on Sunday! I went skating with … We had …

A6 A skater's paradise

BaySixty6

THE ONLY INDOOR SKATEPARK IN LONDON!

56–66 Acklam Road

BaySixty6 – A SKATER'S PARADISE

- for beginners and professionals

- inline skaters, skateboarders and BMX bikers welcome

- We offer skateboard lessons!

Tube: Ladbroke Grove or Westbourne Park

Bus: 23, 28, 31, 228

 p. 84 A6

OPENING HOURS

MON:	12:00 – 21:00
TUE – THU:	12:00 – 22:00
FRI:	12:00 – 21:00
SAT – SUN:	10:00 – 21:00

Free membership
£6 per session per person

a) **Look at the leaflet. How can you get to the indoor skatepark and what can you do there? Tell a classmate in German.**

how to p. 145 mediate

b) **Is there a place like this in your town? Work in groups. Make a leaflet for English-speaking visitors.**

A7 Holiday fun

LiF p. 176
9a

a) Talk about the photos. Where are the children? What are they doing?

activities	places	people	other
going to a museum	museum	grandpa	no school

how to p. 136
work with words

b) Collect holiday words.

WB p. 107
A9, A10

c) Sort the words.

A8 Grandpa Phil tells a story: A trip to Blackpool ▶

CD
2/36

a) Listen to Grandpa Phil. What happens in Blackpool?

DVD
55

b) What about you? Have you got a funny family story?

A9 Holiday weather

a) **What are your favourite holiday activities?**

- What can you do in rainy weather?
- What can you do in sunny weather?

b) **Compare your answers with your partner's answers. What is the same? What is different?**

DVD
56

wordbank
weather p. 147

A10 Free time

Work with a partner. Do the role play.

Partner A:

Hello.

Let's go to the swimming pool.

What about inline skating?

Let's have a game of football then.

Let's go to the cinema!

Well, what do you want to do then?

OK, let's go.

Partner B:

Sag hallo.

Es ist dir zu kalt.

Du kannst nicht skaten.

Du magst keinen Fußball.

Du hast kein Geld.

Du möchtest …

wordbank
English in
action p. 157

WB p. 108
A11

☼ **Work with a partner. Make plans for a day out together. Write a dialogue and present it to the class.**

A11 Target task: Holidays at home

What can you do in your area?
Make a page for a class holiday booklet.
Think about:

- your favourite activities
- events
- your favourite places
- …

Now put your pages together to make a class holiday booklet.

p. 85
A7

BEST ICE CREAM IN TOWN

CAFÉ BOTTICELLI

DOUBLE CHOCOLATE CHIP

Best Flavours

STRAWBERRIES AND CREAM

11:00-22:00 Hochstraße 8, Gelsenkirchen

P1 Explain

Explain what you have to do.

1. Compare your answers with your partner's answers.
2. Write about the first day of the summer holidays.
3. Make plans for a day out together.
4. Make a page for a class holiday booklet.
5. Look at the leaflet.

Ich soll ...

Wir sollen ...

...

P2 Ice creams

a) How many words can you make out of "ice creams"?

am, me, ...

b) Compare with your partner.

P3 At Kentish Town City Farm

LiF p. 172
6b

**Rajiv's mum has got a lot of questions about the farm.
Do you know the answers?**

1. Can you feed the sheep?
2. Can you feed the pigs?
3. Can you feed the cows?
4. Can you feed the goats?
5. Can you feed the chickens?
6. Can you buy drinks at the farm?
7. Can you ride the ponies?
8. Can you play with the animals?
9. Can you ride on a tractor?

Can you ... ?

Yes, you can.

No, you can't.

P4 Rajiv's day at the farm

What does Rajiv tell his family? Write sentences.

	a café	pigs	toilets
There was	a black pony	a tractor	lots of sheep
There were	a bridge	a hungry goat	a picnic area
	a big bull	lots of children	ducks

at the farm.

There was a café at the farm.

Practice matters

P5 Sound check: how to say the letter 'r'

a) **Listen to the words and repeat them.**

CD
199

b) **Listen again and write them down.**

c) **Check your words with a partner and say them.**

☼ **What do you notice? You can talk in German.**

P6 Verbs

a) **Match the verb forms and write them in your exercise book.**

🔍 LiF p. 178
10b

have	do	saw	went	go	did
was	said	be	say	had	see

have – had, do – ...

b) **Listen to the CD and check your pairs.**

CD
200

P7 Who did it?

a) **Look at A3 again. Answer the questions.**

1. Who opened the window?
2. Who flew out of the window?
3. Who jumped up and looked out?

> Vanessa.

4. Who saw Rajiv and Karla?
5. Who went to the park?
6. Who flew onto Rajiv's shoulder?

b) **Listen to the CD and check your answers.**

CD
201

P8 Rhyming pairs

a) **Listen to the words and repeat them.**

CD
202

b) **Find the rhyming pairs for these words from A5.**

got   can   great   late   hair   fast

look   two   last   pair   game   rhyme   hot

name   time   skate   book   who   man   plate

c) **Listen to the CD and check your pairs.**

CD
203

d) **Find other words that rhyme with the words above.**

☼ **Start your own rhyming dictionary.**

B1 My favourite stories

a) Read about Gillian. What does she like to read?

model text

I read a lot of books and I go to the library every week. I like ghost stories and funny stories. My favourite stories are about old castles and houses. The coolest story I know is about the ghost of Catherine Howard. She walks through the rooms of Hampton Court near London. She carries her head under her arm. Ooooooaaaahh!!! I like funny stories after a ghost story – then I can laugh! I love comics, too. Yes, I love reading.

how to p. 141
write

p. 86
B1

WB p. 109
B1, B2

b) What about you? What do you like to read? Make notes.

c) Write about what you like to read.

B2 Survey time: What do you like to read? ▶

DVD

57

a) Watch the video clip. What do the children like to read?

b) What do children in Germany read?

c) Find out more about one of the books.

p. 87
B2

d) Now report to your class in German.

B3 Up high into the sky

a) **Listen to the CD and read along.**

CD
2/37 204

> Holidays, fun days, model plane days. I watch the model planes in the park. It's a lovely day. I close my eyes. A model plane lands next to me. I pick it up, and it takes off with me, up high, into the blue sky.

> Higher and higher the little plane flies. All of London is below me. The River Thames, Tower Bridge and there is London Zoo, my favourite place. I see the giraffes and the tigers. Suddenly there is no more wind. I go down, down, down and land ...

1 ... right in the middle of the penguins. They push me into the water. One penguin wants to give me a fish but ugh, I hate fish! I swim to the rock. I crawl out of the water. The keeper says: ...

2 ... right in the middle of the elephants. I'm scared! One of the elephants puts me on his back. Then the elephant walks to the keeper. The keeper says: ...

3 ... right in the middle of the guinea pigs. They are all over me!! I like a guinea pig or two but fifty guinea pigs! I get up and run. The keeper is there. He says: ...

4 ... right in the middle of the monkeys. They come closer and closer. They look at me and show me their big teeth. Help! I close my eyes. I hear the keeper say: ...

 Draw a picture for one of the stories. Label it.

b) ☆ **Which story do you like best? Read it to your partner.**

p. 88
B3

   ☾ **What does the keeper say? Complete one of the stories.**

   ☼ **Write another "... right in the middle of ..." story. You can record it.**

B4 An exciting day at Kentish Town City Farm

CD
2/38 205

Listen to the CD and read along.

It was a sunny day in spring. Joe and Milly, two volunteers at Kentish Town City Farm, were with the horses.

Suddenly the farmer shouted: "Come, quick, kids! Abby just had her foal!"

It's a boy. You can give him a name.

What a lovely foal!

The kids were very excited.

What about Toby?

OK, Toby it is.

Joe and Milly thought hard. Then Milly had an idea.

Good morning, Toby, how are you?

The next day the kids were at the farm very early. They wanted to say hello to the foal.

My baby brother is two months old, but he can't jump!

The children watched the foal. Milly was surprised.

WB p. 110
B3, B4

☼ **Tell the story in your own words.**

B5 An island story

 Look at the picture. What can you see?

Answer the questions. Use your imagination. Make notes.

Who are the children?	What is in the treasure box?
Where are they from?	What noises can they hear?
How do they feel? Why?	What do the children want to do?
Where are they?	Who is watching them in the jungle?
What do they see?	What do they not see?

how to p. 141
write

DVD
58

p. 90
B4

WB p. 112
B5, B6

☆☽ Tell your partner about the picture. Use your notes.

☼ Use your answers to write a story. Find a title. You can draw a picture, too.

B6 Target task: The story box

Work in groups. Make a story box.

Everyone gets three pieces of paper.
Write one word on each piece of paper.
Put the pieces of paper in the box. Mix them.

Then take three pieces of paper out of the box.
Look at the words and make up a story.
Record your story and present it to the class.

Optional

O Grandpa Phil's holiday photos

CD

2/39 208

It's a rainy afternoon. Grandpa Phil and his grandson, Ben, are at Grandpa Phil's house.
Ben wants to look at Grandpa Phil's holiday photos. Grandpa Phil tells him about the photos.

Look, Ben – this is me on holiday in Wales. Grandma
and I go there every summer and ride our bikes
and walk. Spot comes, too – she loves long walks!
Sometimes she swims in the sea, too!

This photo is from
last summer – look,
Spot and I are on a
really old train.
Grandma and I were
on holiday in Scotland.
It was a beautiful
train ride. Spot loved
it, too!

And look – this is me with you and Daniel at your house.
It was your birthday, and Grandma and I visited you
for a week, do you remember? We had lots of fun!

Look at Grandma, Spot, you and me
in this photo. That was in Germany
last year. The weather was really bad –
look at us in our coats!

And this is Spot and me in the garden at
home. Sometimes it's nice to have a holiday
at home. Then I work in the garden, go for
lots of walks and play with Spot a lot – I
think those are Spot's favourite holidays!

1. **What kind of holiday would you like to have? Write about it.**

2. **Send a holiday postcard in English to your class. After the holidays you can make a
   big holiday poster with all your postcards and photos and tell your class more about
   your holidays.**

BS1 Poems

CD
2/40 211
2/41 212
2/42 213

Wet weather

Wet weather
Windy weather
Very very windy weather
Very very wet weather
What will we wear?
Wellies!

Mice

I think mice are rather nice.

Their tails are long,
their faces small,
they haven't any chins at all.

Their ears are pink,
their teeth are white,
they run about the house at night.

They nibble things
they shouldn't touch
and no one seems
to like them much.

But I think mice are nice.

Rose Fyleman

Rain

There are holes in the sky
Where the rain gets in,
But they're ever so small
That's why rain is thin.

Spike Milligan

BS2 Word play

1 It can be black and white, it can be colourful. It can tell stories. What is it?

2 What is grey, has got four legs, a tail and a suitcase?

3 What has got four legs and says OOM?

4 It is round.
It is red, green and yellow.
You can eat it.
It is good for you.
It grows on a tree.

5 One night I see a man in white.
He is not old. He stands in the cold.
When he feels the sun, he starts to run.
Who could he be? Please answer me!

1: a book; 2: a mouse on holiday; 3: a cow walking backwards; 4: an apple; 5: a snowman

BS3 The snowmen's summer holiday

Imagine! Two snowmen have never seen the summer. They are very sad. The children say wonderful things about the summer. "What is summer like? Is it really so wonderful?" think the snowmen.

They go to see a man in the village. He has got a big freezer in his shop. "May we stay in your freezer until the summer?" they ask. "Of course," says the man. And there they stay until July, when the man tells them to come out. "It's summer!" he says.

What a wonderful world meets their eyes outside! The trees are green. The birds sing. The sky is blue. There are flowers and butterflies everywhere. Children play in the sun.

The two snowmen walk up to their usual place on the hill and look around. Tears roll down their cheeks. "I'm so happy!" says one. "It's wonderful to see this!" says the other. They smile at each other and then they very slowly turn to tears.

Soon nothing is left – only a puddle of water.

Melanie Beneke, Bremen

BS4 Spiders

Spiders live all over the world. Spiders live all around you. Spiders can live in a garden. They can live in your house. If you find a spider, it is better not to touch it. Some are poisonous. But most spiders are safe. So if you find a spider, stop and look at it. They are very interesting!

Spiders can be big, but most spiders are small.

Some are so small that they are difficult to see. Some spiders are brown and hairy. Some are yellow. Some are green. Spiders come in many colours!

There are lots of different kinds of spiders. Spiders have two parts to their bodies.

They have eight legs. Most spiders have eight eyes, too. But some have six eyes, or four eyes, or two eyes. Some spiders live in very dark places and don't have any eyes! All spiders make silk. They use silk in different ways. Many spiders use silk to build webs.

When a spider catches an insect in its web, it wraps the insect in silk threads. The spider eats the insect later. Spiders mostly eat flies but they eat other insects, too.

A mother spider carries her young on her back. When they are ready to leave her, she makes a long thread of silk. The silk carries the young spider up into the air. Some of the young spiders land far away. They all begin new lives alone.

BS5 Working dogs

Lots of people have got a dog as a pet. But many dogs aren't pets – they are working dogs. These dogs help people. There are different types of working dogs.

Guide dogs for the blind

Many blind people have got guide dogs. The dogs go to a special school for guide dogs. They learn to be guide dogs when they are six weeks old. The dogs go to school for a year or longer. Then they work as guide dogs for seven years. The dogs help blind people in traffic.

St Bernard's dogs

St Bernard's dogs are big brown and white rescue dogs. They come from Switzerland. They help to find people in the mountains. They have got good noses and are very strong. Their feet are big so they can walk on snow and ice. They can find people under a lot of snow. St Bernard's dogs save many people. They are very friendly and are good pets.

Sheepdogs

Sheepdogs look after sheep. They make sure that the sheep stay together. A sheepdog can also bring together cows, ducks or even people.

Police dogs

Some dogs work for the police. They help to find drugs and explosives. They also help to find criminals. You can see police dogs in railway stations, airports, football stadiums and many other places.

BS6 A knife in the back

CD
2/43 214

Scene: The library in an old house. A man sits at a desk, sleeping. Enter the butler.

Butler: Good afternoon, Dr Goldman, here's your tea!

He puts the tea on the desk and goes out. Enter old Mrs Thorn, the cook. She can't hear very well.

Mrs Thorn: Dr Goldman! I can't find my bike. I want to go to the shops but my bike isn't there. Where is my bike, Dr Goldman? Oh dear. He never knows a thing.

Exit Mrs Thorn. Enter Jack Goldman, Dr Goldman's son.

Jack: Hello, Dad. Can you give me some money, please? Five pounds? I want to go to the cinema. Dad? Ugh. Always sleeping! Oh, well!

Jack goes out, angry. Enter Jill Goldman, Dr Goldman's daughter.

Jill: Oh, Daddy! Wonderful news. I'm the winner of the school reading competition.

She runs to her father. He falls onto the desk. There is a knife in his back.

Jill: Aaargh!

Enter Detective Blake.

Detective Blake: Calm down, Jill. Let me see your father. Dr Goldman! Dr Goldman! Oh no, he's dead. We must call the police.

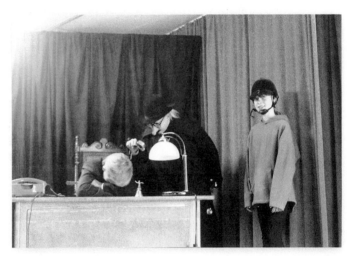

Jill: But you are a detective. Can't you find out who killed him?

Detective Blake: OK. First I must talk to all the people who were in the house. Can you get them all, please?

Jill goes out. Enter Mrs Thorn, Jack, the butler and Jill.

Detective Blake: Right. Sit down everyone. Now then … I must ask you all some questions …

CD
2/44

BS7 Summer holiday

We're all going on a summer holiday.
No more working for a week or two.
Fun and laughter on a summer holiday.
No more worries for me or you
For a week or two.

We're going where the sun shines brightly.
We're going where the sea is blue.
We've seen it in the movies
Now let's see if it's true.

Everybody has a summer holiday
Doing things they always wanted to.
So we're going on a summer holiday
To make our dreams come true
For me and you.

Music & lyrics: Brian Bennett and Bruce Welch

BS8 At the ghostel

2/45 215 CD

Two London ghosts, Mo and Joe, are on holiday in Scotland.

I'm Mo.

And I'm Joe.

The night is dark and they are tired.
"Oh look, this place looks good. Let's go in."

A grey ghost is in the hall:
"Welcome to the ghostel, I'm Mrs McHowl."
"Hello. Have you got a double room, please?"
"Yes, come with me."

"Nice room … but I can hear a child laughing."
"Maybe the room is haunted!"
"This was a child's room, before this place was a ghostel. But don't worry, they're friendly!" says Mrs McHowl.

"Eugh … I'm a b … b … bit scared of children!" says Joe.
"Me, too," says Mo.
"Don't be scared," says Mrs McHowl. "Come to the living room and meet the other guests."

"This is Scary Mary and Miss White." "Scary Mary hasn't got a head!" says Mo.
"She always loses her head after a glass of wine. It's in her bag!" says Miss White.

Mo and Joe sit down in front of the warm fire. Suddenly, the ghosts hear a 'bump!' from upstairs.
"It's the children!" screams Joe.
"Help!" shouts Mo.

"Don't worry," says Mrs McHowl. "The children are just playing. Sometimes they like to scare us." They hear footsteps on the stairs.
"I'm scared," says Mo. "What shall we do?!"

A voice comes from Scary Mary's bag.
"Let's cook marshmallows on the fire and tell each other spooky children stories!"

BS9 The pickpockets

Stella and Ben are at Camden Lock Market. Suddenly Stella shouts, "Look at those boys – they're pickpockets!"

"Let's follow them!" says Ben.

"Don't be silly," Stella answers. "They're going into the market hall. We can't find them in there. Look at all the people!"

"Quick, let's go upstairs to the gallery," says Ben. "You can see everything from there."

Up on the gallery the two friends look down on the people below.

"There they are!" Stella shouts and points to a stall. "At the stall with the CDs."

"Look!" Ben says. "Watch the woman in the purple jacket next to them. She's looking at that CD. One of the pickpockets is talking to her … and the other pickpocket is stealing her purse from her bag!"

"Come on, we have to stop them!" Stella says. "But how?"

"I've got an idea!" says Ben. "There must be a policeman on Camden High Street!" He runs down the stairs and out onto the street.

Five minutes later Ben sees a policeman. "Sir! Sir!" he shouts. "There are two pickpockets at the market."

"That's very interesting, Sherlock Holmes," the policeman laughs.

"No, really! You must come and stop them," Ben shouts. "My friend is watching them, but we must be quick!"

At the market Stella is nervous. Where is Ben? Stella watches the pickpockets from the gallery.

Finally, Ben and the policeman arrive. Ben looks around. He can't see the pickpockets. He looks up at Stella. Stella points to her mobile. Ben gets out his phone.

"OK," Stella says. "Turn right, then left and left again. They are at the stall with the T-shirts now." Ben and the policeman go to the stall – and there are the pickpockets!

"These children say you're pickpockets," says the policeman.

"What?" one of the boys laughs. "That's a joke. We're just looking at the stalls."

"Well?" the policeman looks at Ben.

Stella arrives from the gallery. "Look in their jackets!" she says. "They've got purses in their pockets!" Suddenly the boys start to run away. But the policeman stops them and the purses fall out of their jackets.

"What a surprise," the policeman says to the pickpockets. Then he looks at Ben. "Thanks, Sherlock Holmes!" he says. "Don't forget Dr Watson!" says Ben, looking at Stella and smiling. "We're a great team!"

BS10 The dare

Sophie listens to her classmates as they tell her about *the dare*. She is nervous. She does not want to do the dare. But every new pupil has to do it.

Every day on her way to school, Sophie passes the old house. It looks terrifying and everyone says it is haunted. No one is sure if people live there or not. People are too scared to find out. Most pupils never knock on the door. Only brave children finish the dare and knock.

Sophie's classmates tell her the old story again:

One afternoon a young boy is bored. He wants to go to the old house. His parents tell him not to go. They tell him it's dangerous. But the young boy doesn't listen …

When he gets to the house he knocks on the door and waits. Nothing. He knocks again. Finally, the door opens. But there is nobody there. The boy walks inside. The door shuts quickly behind him.

The house is dark and it smells disgusting. The boy hears a noise. A scratch. He walks along the hallway. The noise gets louder. Where is it coming from? Suddenly, he trips. His head hits the wooden floor with a BANG!

The boy lies on the floor, shocked. He hears the noise again. Scratch, scratch, SCRATCH, SCRATCH. It is coming from under the floor. The boy is too scared to move. He wants the scratching to stop. Finally, it does. The boy slowly stands up and looks around.

And there, in front of him, is a dark figure in a hood. The figure stares at him. It says nothing. Terrified, the boy runs to the door. It's locked. He is trapped. A cold, white hand grabs him. The boy screams.

Nobody ever sees the boy again. People say that sometimes you can still hear his screams. Some people say he is dead. Others are not so sure.

Sophie thinks about the story as she walks slowly along the icy path. She reaches the garden wall. THUMP, THUMP. THUMP, THUMP. Her heart beats quickly. She walks into the garden.

She shivers when she sees graves by the path. She tries not to look at them as she walks up to the house. For a second Sophie thinks she sees a dark figure at the window. She walks slowly to the door. She knocks and waits.

That's it, that's the dare. She can go now. But Sophie wants to be really brave, so she knocks again. She waits. After a while, the door opens. A little old lady looks at her.

"How lovely to see you," the little old lady says. "Most children knock but then they run away. I wonder why … anyway … you are the first to stay."

Then she asks Sophie to come in. THUMP, THUMP. THUMP, THUMP. Sophie's heart beats faster. She looks behind her, then walks inside …

So kannst du dir Wörter merken

In deinem Buch gibt es ab Seite 185 eine nach Kapiteln sortierte Wortliste, die auf Seite 182 erläutert wird.

- Die Wörter, die du lernen willst, kannst du dir mit einem Beispielsatz immer wieder laut vorlesen, bis du sie dir eingeprägt hast.
- Wenn du gut durch Zuhören lernst, kannst du die Wörter und Beispielsätze auch aufnehmen und sie dir immer wieder anhören.
- Englische Wörter von Gegenständen aus der Wohnung kannst du auf Klebezettel schreiben und diese Zettel an die Gegenstände heften. So hast du sie stets im Blick.
- Eine weitere gute Möglichkeit, sich Wörter einzuprägen ist, einen *chant* mit diesen Wörtern zu schreiben und zu sprechen (zum Beispiel nach einem bestimmten Silbenmuster wie 2 Silben – 3 Silben – 1 Silbe):

café – museum – zoo, café – museum – zoo
café – museum, café – museum
café – museum – zoo

- Wenn du gern mit dem Computer lernst, kannst du die Vokabeln auch mit der Lernsoftware lernen oder mit einer Handy-App.

So lernst du mit den *wordbanks*

- Wörter, Ausdrücke und Sätze zu bestimmten Themen stehen in den *wordbanks* ab Seite 146.
- Solche *wordbanks* kannst du auch selber machen: Zeichne oder schneide Bilder aus und schreibe Wörter oder Sätze neben die Bilder.

Einen Vokabelordner anlegen

- Mit eigenen *wordbank*-Seiten kannst du dir auch einen Vokabelordner anlegen. Er kann dir helfen, den Überblick über die Wörter zu behalten. Neue Wörter kannst du hinzufügen und farbig markieren.
- Bei einer *wordbank* ist wichtig, dass du Gruppen von Wörtern bildest, die zusammen gehören, weil du sie dir dann leichter merken kannst.

pets	family
dog	brother
rabbit	mother
...	...

- Du kannst in deinem Vokabelordner auch **Wortnetze** *(word webs)* zu einem Thema anlegen.

our house

a nice garden

neighbourhood

friendly neighbours

shops

...

- Außerdem kannst du dir **Listen** aufschreiben, zum Beispiel
  - von deinen persönlichen Lieblingswörtern: *cat, dog, rabbit, ...*
  - von Gegensatzpaaren: *right – wrong, big – small, ...*
  - von Reimwörtern: *small – all – tall ..., house – mouse ...*
  - von besonders schwierigen Wörtern: *religious education, science, ...* Versuche, dir Sätze mit besonders schwierigen Wörtern zu überlegen. Vielleicht fallen dir sogar lustige Sätze ein? Dann kannst du dir die Wörter bestimmt noch besser merken: *I talk to my goldfish about science.*

- Manche Teile eines Wortes sind besonders schwierig zu schreiben oder zu sprechen. Du kannst dir die Schreibweise und die Aussprache besser einprägen, wenn du die schwierigen Buchstaben farbig hervorhebst oder wenn du sie sortierst.

> fr**ie**nd, dr**ea**m, gr**ea**t, cent**re**, neig**h**bour

- Bei **Wortkombinationen** *(chunks)* lernt man nicht die einzelnen Wörter, sondern die ganze Wortkombination:

> **ea**: dr**ea**m, gr**ea**t, t**ea**m, w**ea**r, r**ea**d

> **ou**: of course, h**ou**se, c**ou**sin, c**o**l**ou**r, fav**ou**rite

What about *a friendly match?* / **I am very good at** *football.*
Schreibe in deinen Vokabelordner weitere Beispiele auf zu solchen *chunks*:

What about an ice cream?
I am very good at basketball.

So findest du die Bedeutung von Wörtern heraus

Manchmal musst du Wörter gar nicht nachgucken,
- weil du sie dir aus dem Zusammenhang eines Textes oder einer Situation erklären kannst.
- weil sie fast genau so aussehen wie im Deutschen und auch das Gleiche bedeuten. Viele dieser Wörter findest du auf Seite 184.

Wenn du aber ein Wort nachgucken musst, findest du es in der alphabetischen Liste im Buch ab Seite 239 oder in einem Wörterbuch. Dort sind die Wörter alphabetisch geordnet.
Du musst nicht nur auf den ersten Buchstaben achten, sondern auch auf den zweiten oder sogar dritten: Das Wort *back* steht zum Beispiel vor *banana.*

Ein Wort hat oft mehrere Bedeutungen. Suche dir die heraus, die für deinen Satz die passende ist.

The cup is on the breakfast table.
Hendon boys play for the cup.

> **cup** /kʌp/ Tasse 2/A9
> cup /kʌp/ Pokal, Cup 3/A4

Manche Wörter können zum Beispiel Adjektive und Verben sein:

Rajiv's room is tidy.
Vanessa always tidies her room on Saturdays.

> **tidy** /ˈtaɪdi/ ordentlich, aufgeräumt 4/A2; aufräumen 4/A6

Ohren auf: Worum geht es eigentlich?

Du musst nicht jedes einzelne Wort verstehen, wenn du Geschichten und Gespräche auf Englisch hörst. Hier sind einige Tipps, die dir helfen können:

1. Vor dem Hören

- Welche Hinweise geben dir die Überschrift und die Bilder zu einem Hörtext?
- Worum könnte es gehen? Stelle Vermutungen an.
- Was weißt du schon über das Thema?

2. Beim Hören

- Höre dir den Hörtext einmal ganz an.

- Mache dir Notizen zu diesen Fragen:

  Who?   Wer spricht? Um wen geht es? Wer ist beteiligt?
  Where? Wo findet das Gespräch oder die Geschichte statt?
  When?   Wann findet das Gespräch oder die Geschichte statt?
  What?   Was wird besprochen? Was passiert?

  Bei 1A4 „Charlie" auf Seite 23 kannst du dir zum Beispiel Folgendes notieren:

Who?	Charlie
Where?	in Charlie's room
When?	—
What?	family, food, hobbies, friends

- Auch die Stimmen der Personen und Geräusche können dir Hinweise darauf geben, was in dem Hörtext passiert.

- Gibt es eine Höraufgabe im Buch? Dann lies sie dir genau durch. Was sollst du herausfinden? Höre dir die Geschichte oder das Gespräch ein zweites Mal an. Wenn du die Höraufgabe noch nicht lösen kannst, dann höre ein weiteres Mal.

3. Zu guter Letzt

Vergleiche deine Ergebnisse mit denen einer Partnerin oder eines Partners. Was habt ihr herausgefunden? Haben sich eure Vermutungen bestätigt?

TIPP   Nutze jede Gelegenheit, um Englisch zu hören!

- Mit der CD zu *Notting Hill Gate* kannst du zu Hause dein Hörverstehen trainieren.
- Höre dir englische Musik an und achte auf den Text. Was kannst du schon verstehen?
- Sieh dir einen Film auf DVD an, den du schon kennst. Auf einer DVD kannst du fast immer den englischen Ton (mit oder ohne Untertitel) einschalten.

Lesen leicht gemacht!

Im Englischunterricht begegnen dir ganz viele Texte: Dialoge, Geschichten, Comics, Gedichte, Zeitungsartikel, … Was kannst du tun, damit dir das Verstehen der Texte leichter fällt? Hier sind einige Tipps:

1. Vor dem Lesen

- Überschriften und Bilder können dir wichtige Hinweise darauf geben, worum es gehen könnte. Sieh sie dir genau an. Was erwartest du?

2. Beim Lesen

- Überfliege den Text erst einmal. Dabei ist es nicht wichtig, jedes einzelne Wort zu verstehen. Wenn du eine Idee hast, worum es gehen könnte, mache dir Notizen zu folgenden Fragen:

Who?	**Where?**	**When?**	**What?**
Wer ist dabei?	Wo passiert es?	Wann passiert es?	Was passiert?

Schau dir zum Beispiel 1B2 „Butterfly's blog" auf Seite 30 an:

> Who?   Gillian's cat Butterfly
> Where?   at her new home
> When?   Monday 3 March
> What?   Butterfly about her new home

- Wenn es zu einem Text eine Aufgabe gibt, dann lies sie dir genau durch. Was sollst du herausfinden? Versuche, die Frage zu beantworten, indem du den Text noch einmal gründlich durchliest.

- Auf Kopien oder in deinen eigenen Büchern kannst du auch wichtige Textstellen markieren.

3. Zu guter Letzt

- Vergleiche deine Ergebnisse mit denen einer Partnerin oder eines Partners. Was habt ihr herausgefunden? Haben sich eure Erwartungen bestätigt?

 TIPP   Geh auf die Suche nach interessanten Texten und nimm dir Zeit zu lesen.

Welche Themen und Texte interessieren dich? Schau zum Beispiel einmal im Internet oder in einer Bücherei nach englischsprachigen Texten zu Themen, die du spannend findest. Du kannst auch deine Lehrkraft nach einer Auswahl schöner Bücher fragen. Vielleicht kann sich auch die ganze Klasse eine Bücherkiste anschaffen.

Du kannst reden!

Rollenspiele sind eine gute Methode, um dein Englisch zu trainieren.
Hier findest du einige Tipps, damit du deine Rolle überzeugend spielen kannst.

1. Vor dem Rollenspiel

- Versetze dich in die Person hinein, die du darstellen wirst. Überlege dir zum Beispiel, in welcher Stimmung die Person ist. Vielleicht kannst du auch einige Requisiten benutzen, die es dir erleichtern, in die Rolle zu schlüpfen (zum Beispiel Münzen in einem Verkaufsgespräch).
- Was möchtet ihr sagen? Schreibt euch Fragen und Antworten auf einzelne Kärtchen. Nummeriert sie und legt sie so hin, dass sie in der richtigen Reihenfolge liegen.
- Mit der Methode *read – look up – speak* (man liest seinen Satz still, sieht dann auf und spricht ihn) könnt ihr eure Rollen auswendig lernen.
- Wenn ihr auch mal die Rollen wechselt und mit anderen Partnern übt, lernt ihr, spontan zu reagieren.

> Seller: 1
> Hi, can I help you?
>
> Customer: 2
> Yes, hello. My son collects computer games. Have you got any new ones?

2. Während des Rollenspiels

- Benutze beim Sprechen Mimik (Gesichtsausdruck) und Gestik (Bewegungen).
- Halte den Augenkontakt zu deinem Gesprächspartner.
- Wenn dir mal ein Wort nicht einfällt, kannst du versuchen, es zu umschreiben. Du kannst aber auch „mit Händen und Füßen reden", um dich verständlich zu machen.
- Frage nach, wenn du etwas nicht verstanden hast: „Sorry, what was that again?" oder: "Sorry, can you say that again, please?"
- Versuche, langsam und deutlich zu sprechen.

TIPP   Sprich Englisch, so oft du kannst!

- Höre dir die CD zu *Notting Hill Gate* an und lies die Texte laut mit. Versuche, die Aussprache der Sprecherinnen und Sprecher nachzuahmen.
- Singe englische Lieder mit, die dir gefallen.
- Lies einen Text aus dem Buch laut vor oder sprich Englisch und nimm dich auf. Dann kannst du dich selbst anhören und überprüfen, wie dein Englisch klingt.
- Sprich Englisch mit jemandem, der ebenfalls Englisch sprechen kann.

So macht Schreiben Spaß!

Wenn du einen Text schreibst, gehst du am besten Schritt für Schritt vor.

1. Plane deinen Text

- Überlege: Was für einen Text willst du schreiben – eine E-Mail, ein Gedicht, eine Geschichte? Für wen soll der Text sein?
- Sammle Ideen und Wörter zum Thema deines Textes in einem *word web* oder einer Liste. Die *wordbanks* ab Seite 146 und das *German-English dictionary* ab Seite 257 können dir dabei helfen. Wenn du eine Geschichte schreiben willst, kannst du dich an den Fragewörtern *who*, *where*, *when* und *what* orientieren.
- Du kannst dir auch Texte im Buch ansehen, die sich mit dem Thema deines Textes beschäftigen und dieselbe Form haben. Du kannst sie als Muster für deine eigenen Texte benutzen, wie zum Beispiel bei 3A12 „My favourite sport" auf Seite 63.
- Überlege dir eine Reihenfolge. Was schreibst du zuerst, was folgt darauf, was kann am Ende stehen?

2. Schreibe den Text

- Schreibe erst einmal kurze, einfache Sätze auf.
- Nun überarbeite deine Sätze.
- Fange deine Sätze unterschiedlich an, damit dein Text abwechslungsreicher wird. Zum Beispiel:

Football is great. Football is my favourite sport. ☹
Football is great. It is my favourite sport. ☺

- Verbinde Sätze mit *and*, *or*, *but*, *so* oder *because*. Zum Beispiel:

My football boots are red. My shirt is blue. ☹
My football boots are red and my shirt is blue. ☺

- Überlege dir eine passende Überschrift zu deinem Text.
- Wie wär's mit einem kleinen Bild?

3. Überarbeite deinen Text

- Sieh dir deinen Text noch einmal genau an.
  - Überprüfe schwierige Wörter mit dem *dictionary*.
  - Bist du bei der Grammatik unsicher? Schau im LiF-Teil ab Seite 162 nach.
  - Tauscht eure Texte untereinander aus. Sprecht darüber, was euch an den Texten gefällt, was noch ergänzt und was verbessert werden könnte.
  - Ist der überarbeitete Text gut zu lesen oder solltest du ihn noch einmal sauber abschreiben?

4. Präsentiere deinen Text

- Du kannst deinen Text vortragen, aushängen oder in einem *class book* oder auf der Homepage deiner Schule veröffentlichen.
- Sammle deine besten Texte in deiner Portfolio-Mappe.

Etwas präsentieren

Du kannst verschiedene Dinge vor deiner Klasse präsentieren, zum Beispiel mit Hilfe eines Posters dein Hobby vorstellen, eine Geschichte vorlesen, ein Gedicht vortragen, ...

Hier findest du ein paar Ideen für eine Präsentation:

1. Bevor du etwas vorträgst

- Überlege: Was möchtest du zu deinem Thema sagen?
- Sammle deine Ideen und schreibe sie auf, zum Beispiel in einem *word web* oder in einer Liste.
- Lege die Reihenfolge fest, in der du deine Ideen vorstellen möchtest und überlege dir einen interessanten Einstieg. Vielleicht kannst du zum Beispiel zum Thema *„My week"* einen Gegenstand hochhalten, verbunden mit der Frage *„What do I do on Mondays? What do you think?"*
- Du kannst ein Poster oder eine Folie verwenden, um deinen Vortrag anschaulich zu machen. Auch eine Computer-Präsentation ist möglich.
- Übe deinen Vortrag vor dem Spiegel, vor Freunden oder deiner Familie. Du kannst ihn auch aufnehmen, zum Beispiel mit einem Handy oder einem Easi-Speak-Mikrofon.

> **TIPP** So sieht ein gelungenes Vortragsposter aus:
>
> - ansprechende Überschrift
> - interessante Informationen
> - verständliche Sätze, aber nicht zu viel Text
> - große Bilder und Schrift, damit sie für alle im Raum lesbar sind
> - saubere Schrift
> - Bilder mit Bildunterschriften

2. Bei deiner Präsentation

- Sprich langsam und deutlich.
- Sieh dein Publikum an, wenn du sprichst.
- Versuche, frei zu sprechen. Du kannst zur Unterstützung die wichtigsten Punkte auf Karteikarten schreiben und als Gedankenstütze benutzen.
- Dein Publikum kann dir besser folgen, wenn du auf einem Poster oder einer Folie zeigst, worüber du gerade sprichst.

3. Nützliche Redewendungen

Zu Beginn deines Vortrags:	*Hello everybody. My talk is about ... /I want to present ... / I want to talk about ...*
Im Hauptteil:	*On my poster you can see ... This picture shows ... / In the picture you can see ...*
Zum Schluss:	*Thank you. Are there any questions?*

Grammatikregeln auf der Spur

Grammatik kann spannend sein: Spiele Sprachendetektiv und versuche, Grammatikregeln selbst aufzuspüren. Das folgende Beispiel zu Einzahl und Mehrzahl zeigt dir, wie das gehen kann.

1. Sammeln

- Schau dir englische Texte an.
- Sammle Wörter, von denen du meinst, dass sie Einzahl oder Mehrzahl sind.

2. Sortieren

Schreibe die Beispiele untereinander.

one hand	–	two hands
a chair	–	five chairs
my friend Gillian	–	his friends David and Rajiv

3. Beschreiben

Sieh dir deine Beispiele gut an. Was kannst du erkennen? Beschreibe und notiere dann deine Regel.

> Wenn ein englisches Wort in der Mehrzahl steht, dann wird ein -s angehängt.

4. Überprüfen

Schaue nun im LiF-Teil auf Seite 170 nach, ob du richtig liegst. Ändere und ergänze deine Regel, falls nötig.

5. Achtung Ausnahmen!

Manchmal gibt es auch Ausnahmen, zum Beispiel bei den Wörtern *tooth* und *foot*.

| tooth | – | teeth |
| foot | – | feet |

Diese Beispiele musst du dir besonders gut einprägen.

TIPP   Spielt in der Klasse *grammar games.*

Zu vielen Grammatikthemen gibt es schöne Spielideen, zum Beispiel "I'm standing, I'm sitting". Fragt eure Lehrerin oder euren Lehrer nach einer Anleitung.

Zusammen seid ihr stark!

Es gibt viele verschiedene Methoden, die dir helfen, gut mit anderen zusammenzuarbeiten. Hier lernst du ein paar Arbeitsformen kennen:

1. Milling around

Mit der Methode *milling around* (auf Deutsch: umherlaufen) kannst du dich mit deinen Klassenkameraden zu einem Thema austauschen.

1. Gehe durch die Klasse, ohne dass du dabei sprichst.
2. Wenn dein Lehrer / deine Lehrerin ein Zeichen gibt oder „Stop!" sagt, sprich mit der Person, vor der du gerade stehst. Tauscht euch über die Aufgabe aus.
3. Notiere deine Ergebnisse und gehe weiter.

2. Think – pair – share

Um etwas zu einem Thema herauszufinden, kannst du in drei Schritten vorgehen:

1. *Think:* Sammle deine Gedanken und Ideen und mache dir Notizen.
2. *Pair:* Tausche dich mit einem Partner / einer Partnerin aus. Ergänze neue Ideen in deiner Liste.
3. *Share:* Teilt dann eure Gedanken und Ideen mit einem anderen Paar. Nun habt ihr schon Ideen und Meinungen von vier verschiedenen Leuten kennengelernt.

3. Double circle

Auch dies ist eine Arbeitsform, bei der du die Ideen und Gedanken von vielen verschiedenen Personen in deiner Klasse erfährst.

1. Bildet in der Klasse zwei Kreise: einen Innenkreis und einen Außenkreis.
2. Diejenigen von euch, die sich gegenüberstehen, unterhalten sich über ein vorher bestimmtes Thema (zum Beispiel *free time activities*).
3. Wenn dein Lehrer / deine Lehrerin ein Zeichen gibt, dreht ihr euch in den beiden Kreisen in entgegengesetzte Richtungen weiter. Nun tauscht ihr euch mit einem neuen Partner / einer neuen Partnerin über das Thema aus.

So kannst du jemandem sprachlich aushelfen

Du kannst anderen Menschen helfen, die sich in einer Fremdsprache nicht so gut auskennen wie du. Hier erfährst du, wie das funktioniert:

1. Gib den Sinn wieder

Stell dir vor, du bist mit einer englischen Austauschschülerin und einem deutschen Freund unterwegs. Sie spricht kaum Deutsch, er kaum Englisch. Du musst jetzt nicht Wort für Wort übersetzen. Wichtiger ist es, den Sinn wiederzugeben. Das kannst du auch in deinen eigenen Worten machen.

I just love ponies! They're so cute! Really, I just love them!

Sie ist verrückt nach Ponys.

Wollen wir Fußball spielen?

What about a game of football?

2. Benutze Redewendungen

Versuche, dich an Redewendungen aus dem Unterricht zu erinnern, zum Beispiel, dass man mit „*What about …*" etwas vorschlagen kann.

3. Bilde kurze Sätze

Bilde einfache, kurze Sätze, wenn du den Sinn wiedergibst.

Worum geht es hier?

Das Basketballteam sucht noch Spieler.

4. Umschreibe Wörter

Wenn dir ein wichtiges Wort nicht einfällt, kannst du es umschreiben. Du weißt zum Beispiel nicht, was „Geschenk" auf Englisch heißt. Du kannst dann sagen: *You give it to a friend. It's for a birthday.* Natürlich kannst du auch Hände und Füße benutzen, um deutlich zu machen, worum es geht.

Clothes

hat

helmet

for your head

cap

glasses

sunglasses

David has got a red cap.

socks

shoes

boots

wellies

for your feet

trainers

skates

football boots

coat

Have you got a black T-shirt in small?

sweatshirt

jacket

wear a shirt •
buy a new jumper

football shirt

shirt

T-shirt

jumper

dress

skirt

for your body

scarf

trousers

tie

shorts

gloves

jeans

Lily has got a lot of green clothes in her wardrobe.

I like to wear blue.

What's in your suitcase?

Gillian has got a new school uniform.

Colours

light blue • **dark blue**

purple • yellow • **blue** •
red • orange • **black** • white •
brown • green • **pink** • **grey**

I don't like green.

My favourite colour is purple.

Animals

Wild animals

 bird

bat • squirrel • fox • rat
insect • crocodile • elephant •
giraffe • tiger • penguin •
polar bear • fish • dolphin • dinosaur

Let's go to the zoo!

monkey

lion

fly • jump •
swim • run •
ride • feed

frog

hedgehog

Farm animals

bull • goat • lamb •
hen • duck • pony • foal

duck

Pets

dog • cat •
rabbit • goldfish •
parrot • hamster •
mouse

budgie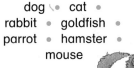

guinea pig

pig

cow

horse

sheep

aquarium •
terrarium •
animal shelter •
basket •
zoo • farm

Charlie's
goldfish live in
an aquarium.

chicken

Have you got
a pet?

spider

Weather

What can you do in rainy
weather?

sun • sunny

It is warm and
sunny today.

rain • rainy

cloud • cloudy

Weather can be …

hot
cold
warm
bad
wet

snow • snowy

wind • windy

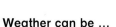

jump into puddles •
build a snowman • play in the snow •
fly my kite • sit in the sun

puddle • rainbow •
snowman • sky

What do you wear
on a cold day?

Time

clock

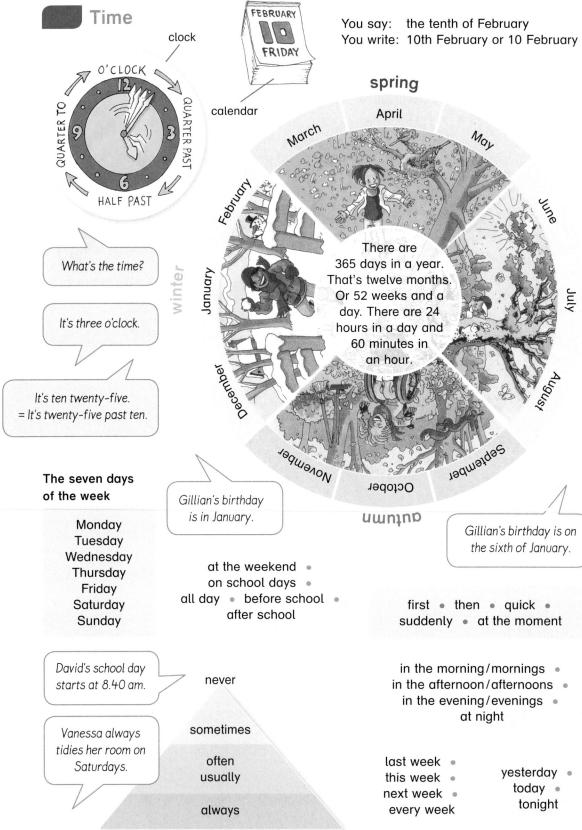

O'CLOCK

QUARTER TO

QUARTER PAST

HALF PAST

calendar

FEBRUARY
10
FRIDAY

You say: the tenth of February
You write: 10th February or 10 February

spring

March   April   May

February   June

January   July

There are 365 days in a year. That's twelve months. Or 52 weeks and a day. There are 24 hours in a day and 60 minutes in an hour.

winter   summer

December   August

November   September

October   autumn

What's the time?

It's three o'clock.

It's ten twenty-five.
= It's twenty-five past ten.

Gillian's birthday is in January.

Gillian's birthday is on the sixth of January.

The seven days of the week

Monday
Tuesday
Wednesday
Thursday
Friday
Saturday
Sunday

at the weekend •
on school days •
all day • before school •
after school

first • then • quick •
suddenly • at the moment

David's school day starts at 8.40 am.

never

Vanessa always tidies her room on Saturdays.

sometimes

often
usually

always

in the morning / mornings •
in the afternoon / afternoons •
in the evening / evenings •
at night

last week •
this week •
next week •
every week

yesterday •
today •
tonight

Places

farm • zoo • museum • castle • swimming pool •
circus • stadium • cinema • school • library • park •
vet's practice • youth club • indoor skatepark • market •
picnic area • café • playground • information stand

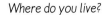
Where do you live?

home • house •
street • area •
neighbourhood

on

in front of

in

between • above •
through • below •
in the middle of

next to

under

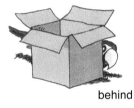
behind

flower

grass • stick • stone •
seashell • rock • hole

at the beach •
by the sea •
on the bus •
on the street •
at home •
outside

in the woods • in the mountains •
in the field • in the jungle •
in the pond • in the park •
in the city • in town

quiet ≠ loud

How can you get there?

By train.

read a map • know the
way • on the way •
a long way • far away

bridge •
(underground) station

*When is the next train
to Glasgow?*

plane

*The bus is leaving
at three.*

car • bike •
motorbike •
caravan • taxi •
bus • helicopter

take someone home •
pick someone up •
take the tube •
change trains •
get out • take off

train

bus stop

Me and my body

brush your hair

blond • black • brown •
long ≠ short •
curly • dark

open your eyes •
close your eyes

watch
read
look
see

speak
talk
eat
say
sing
ask
drink
answer
tell
shout
laugh

think

head

face

nose

hair

listen
hear

— ear

brush your teeth

— tooth

back

elbow →

sit
sit down

— bottom

stand up
jump
go
walk
come

— leg

foot

turn around
stop
stay

eyes

mouth

neck

shoulder

arm

chest

tummy

hand

finger

toe

play
help
work
draw
wave
make
pick sth up
push
give
throw

show
point at

tummy button

thumb

feet

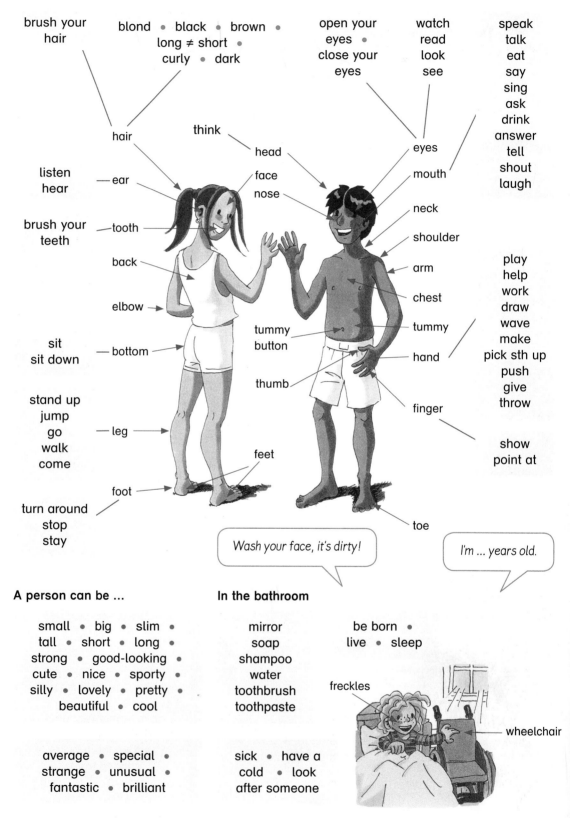

Wash your face, it's dirty!

I'm ... years old.

A person can be ...

small • big • slim •
tall • short • long •
strong • good-looking •
cute • nice • sporty •
silly • lovely • pretty •
beautiful • cool

average • special •
strange • unusual •
fantastic • brilliant

In the bathroom

mirror
soap
shampoo
water
toothbrush
toothpaste

be born •
live • sleep

freckles

wheelchair

sick • have a
cold • look
after someone

People

My parents are divorced.

child • children • everybody • someone • nobody • person • guy

Family members

Girls and women

(baby / little / big) sister •
mother • mum •
wife • partner •
girlfriend •
grandmother • grandma •
granddaughter •
aunt • niece •
cousin

Boys and men

(baby / little / big) brother •
father • dad •
husband • partner •
boyfriend •
grandfather • grandpa •
grandson •
uncle • nephew •
cousin

together ≠ alone

(best) friend • neighbour •
guest • member •
passenger • volunteer •
(inline) skater •
skateboarder • biker •
character • beginner •
professional • champion •
audience • listener •
ghost • monster

Jobs

detective
teacher
acrobat
cook
singer
shopkeeper
captain
president

introduce •
meet •
get on well together

Feelings

be happy • be excited • be lucky • be surprised

Eve is scared of dogs.

Gillian is sad.

cry • smile • laugh • love • hate •
like • want • hope • dream • imagine •
forget • lie • tell the truth •
have a crush on someone

great fun • funny • friendly • nice • crazy • spooky

Be careful!

How do you feel?

Ouch!

Oh dear!

Don't worry!

Hooray!

I can't wait!

You're the best!

Thanks my dear.

I love you.

At school

Great idea. Well done!

In the classroom

learn • understand •
spell • describe •
explain • finish •
learn something by heart •
remember

whiteboard • blackboard •
pinboard •
overhead projector •
sponge • chalk •
schoolbag •
dictionary • desk

do a (class) survey •
do an interview •
make a table •
plan a presentation •
make a collage •
give a talk •
make a leaflet

In my schoolbag

cartridge • ink •
(English) book •
exercise book •
workbook •
piece of paper

present • find help •
look for help • give an example •
put something in alphabetical order •
mime • act • take turns

question
answer
sentence
page
comment
dialogue
scene
speech bubble
box
story
poem
verse
alphabet

rubber

pencil case

pen

ruler

pencil

important •
easy ≠ difficult •
interesting ≠ boring •
true ≠ false •
right ≠ wrong

My last lesson on a Monday is art.

English is my favourite subject.

Subjects in my timetable

I've got so much homework!

science • geography • history • maths • music •
art • drama • RE (religious education) •
PE (physical education) •
ICT (information and communication technology)

go to school •
go to a school club •
join a club •
after school activity

break • lunch break • lunchtime •
assembly • registration • lesson

go on a school trip • School's out! •
(summer) holidays • be on holiday

I can speak ...

German • English • Polish •
Turkish • three languages

Make notes for a presentation.

Listen and take notes.

Places at school

classroom • school library •
sports hall • sports field •
playing field • playground •
canteen • music room

teacher

partners

pupil

classmates

Hobbies and free time

Sports

play: football • tennis • basketball • wheelchair basketball • volleyball • table tennis • hockey

do: gymnastics • karate

ride: a bike • a horse

swim • ski • skate

I'm good at volleyball – I play in the school team.

gym • ballet school • tennis court • basketball basket • swimming pool

At a football match

the winners   the score

Come on, you Reds!

cheer someone on

football fan

Music

play: an instrument • the guitar • the drums

dance • go to a party • listen to music • song • chant • recording • CD player • MP3 player

see a musical • play in the school band

You can read ...

an article • a book • a comic • a magazine • science fiction • adventure stories • ghost stories • funny stories

listen to a radio report • tell a story • take photos • go to the cinema • watch a DVD

Collections

stickers • toy cars • model planes • toys • cuddly toys • marbles • postcards • football cards

Games

chase • run fast • beat • (to score) a goal • win

take turns • quiz • guessing game • odd one out • tongue twister • play skip • number bingo • opposites

football club • (cup) final • event • team • championship • game • (friendly) match • versus • one-nil • membership • football chant

What do you do in your free time?

I like meeting friends at the weekend.

My hobby is juggling.

video clip • blog • website • USB stick • play a computer game • email someone • send someone an email • search the Internet • work on the computer

At home

room • bedroom •
bathroom •
kitchen •
living room •
garden

bin • clock • picture •
photo • stairs • door • sofa •
table • dishwasher • bath

*In the middle
of my room
there is a ...*

tidy ≠ untidy •
comfortable ≠
uncomfortable

get up • go to bed

live in a house •
move to a new place

*Do you want to come to
my place after school?*

lamp   cupboard   window   desk
poster
wall
shelf
pillow
duvet
bed
wardrobe
chair

stay at home •
leave home •
a weekend visit •
visit someone •
sleepover

watch TV •
turn the radio on •
switch / turn on / out the light •
answer the phone •
the phone rings

Jobs at home / chores

do: the cooking • the washing up • the shopping •

make: breakfast • dinner • (someone) a cup of tea • your bed

clean: the kitchen • the bathroom • your bike

tidy a room • help with something •
empty the dishwasher • take the rubbish out • feed your pet

vacuum the floor(s)

Birthdays

plan a birthday party •
celebrate •
open a present •
eat birthday cake •
dance to music •
sing a birthday song •
play party games •
blow out the candles

*Happy birthday,
Ruby!*

party drinks •
cocktail sticks •
magic tricks •
balloons

Food and drink

Fruit and vegetables

apple • banana •
carrot • tomato •
coconut • spinach •
lemon • bean •
pineapple • cherry

Please can I have a banana?

Sweet food and snacks

(vanilla) ice cream • chocolate •
cake • biscuit • pudding •
doughnuts • crisps • dip

My favourite food is ice cream! Yummy!

sandwiches

Breakfast

cornflakes • toast • butter •
jam • marmalade • honey •
porridge • muesli • baked beans •
sausages • bacon •

eggs: fried • boiled • scrambled •
sunny side up • over easy

Lunch or dinner

burger • chips •
pizza • fish • spaghetti •
(cheddar) cheese •
beans on toast • vegetables

I'm hungry! Is it time for dinner?

I love having picnics in the summer.

On the table

bowl • glass • cup

ketchup •
salt •
pepper •
sugar

knife

fork

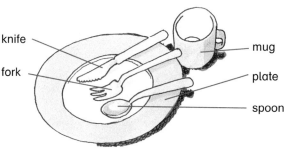

mug

plate

spoon

dishwasher •
do the washing up

Drinks

Cold drinks
lemonade • orange juice • apple juice •
milk • (mineral) water

Hot drinks
hot chocolate • tea • coffee

Jobs in the kitchen

peel vegetables • boil water •
stir beans • cook spaghetti •
fry bacon • beat eggs •
put food on the table • mix a drink

I have hot chocolate with my breakfast.

Please can I see the menu?

cut an apple

You can eat ...

at a café • at a restaurant •
at a table • at the breakfast table

Shopping

shop • clothes shop • shopping centre •
supermarket • newsagent's shop • corner shop

At the market

do the shopping

a market stall

sell ≠ buy

tag • product •
shopping list •
open • opening hours

cheap ≠
expensive

The seller says:

The customer says:

Can I help you?

How much is it?

Here you are.

Excuse me please,
where's the ...

one pound • six pound(s) fifty •
seventy-five p = seventy-five pence

 – =

That's one pound
fifty, please.

Have you got ... ?

Here's your
change.

I'm looking for ...

Numbers and quantities

number •
(mobile) phone number

a cup of tea •
a glass of water •
a bottle of milk

metre
litre

plus   +
minus   –
times   ×
divided by ÷
equals   =

full of •
anything •
something •
altogether

first
second
third
fourth
fifth

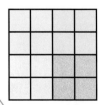

lots of •
a lot of •
a (little) bit of •
no more

sums •
set sums

Sixteen divided by
four equals four.

a piece of cake

English in action

So kannst du ...

... jemandem zustimmen.

That's a great idea.
Yes.
Yeah, sure.
OK.
That's right.
I like ..., too.
Good idea.
OK, that sounds good.
You can say that again!
You're right (about that).
Yeah, me too.
OK, why not?
That's true!

... dich verabschieden.

Goodbye!
Bye.
See you soon!
See you.

... jemanden begrüßen.

Hello everybody!
Hi.
Hello!
Hey.
Good morning!
Welcome!
It's nice to meet you.
How are you?
I'm fine, thanks.

... jemandem widersprechen.

Well, I don't think so.
Sorry, no.
That's not true.

... dich entschuldigen.

Sorry.
Sorry, no.
Sorry, I can't.
Sorry, I'm ...

... dich bedanken.

Thank you.
Thanks.
Thank you very much.
Thanks very much.

... jemanden vorstellen.

Come and meet ...
This is ...

... um etwas bitten.

Can I ..., please?
Can I have ..., please?
Can you ..., please?
Could we have ..., please?
I'd like ..., please.
Excuse me, where are
    the ..., please?

... etwas vorschlagen.

Let's ...
Come on, let's ...
Let's go!
What about ... ?
How about ... ?
Why don't you ... ?
Look, you can ...
We can ... .
What do you think?

Wenn man ankommt oder geht

Good morning.	Guten Morgen.
What's for homework?	Was haben wir als Hausaufgabe auf?
See you tomorrow.	Bis morgen.
Bye.	Tschüs.

Wenn es ein Problem gibt

Sorry, I'm late.	Tut mir leid, dass ich zu spät bin.
Sorry, I haven't got my exercise book with me.	Tut mir leid, ich habe mein Heft nicht dabei.
Sorry, I haven't got my homework with me.	Tut mir leid, ich habe meine Hausaufgaben nicht dabei.
What's the matter?	Was ist los?
I'm fine.	Mir geht's gut.
I feel sick.	Mir ist schlecht.
I've got a headache.	Ich habe Kopfschmerzen.
Can I open the window, please?	Kann ich bitte das Fenster öffnen?
Can I go to the toilet, please?	Kann ich bitte zur Toilette gehen?

Wenn man Hilfe braucht

Can you help me, please?	Können Sie/Kannst du mir bitte helfen?
I've got a question.	Ich habe eine Frage.
I don't understand this.	Ich verstehe das hier nicht.
How can I do this exercise?	Wie mache ich diese Aufgabe?
What's … in English/German?	Was heißt … auf Englisch/Deutsch?
What does … mean?	Was bedeutet …?
Is that correct?	Ist das richtig?
Can you write it on the board, please?	Können Sie das bitte an die Tafel schreiben?
Can you spell that, please?	Können Sie das bitte buchstabieren?
Can you say that again, please?	Können Sie/Kannst du das bitte noch einmal sagen?
Can we listen to the CD again?	Können wir die CD bitte noch einmal hören?
Sorry, I don't know.	Tut mir leid, das weiß ich nicht.
What page, please?	Auf welcher Seite bitte?

Wenn man zusammen arbeitet oder spielt

Whose turn is it?	Wer ist dran?
Do you want to work with me?	Möchtest du mit mir arbeiten?
Let's check …	Lass uns … überprüfen.
Let's compare …	Lass uns … vergleichen.

Classroom phrases

Wenn man mit dem Computer arbeitet

What's your email address?   Wie ist deine E-Mail-Adresse?
You can click on this link.   Du kannst auf diesen Link klicken.
Can I print that out?   Kann ich das ausdrucken?
Can I download it?   Kann ich es herunterladen?
I saved it.   Ich habe es gespeichert.
My computer has crashed.   Mein Computer ist abgestürzt.

Was die Lehrerin oder der Lehrer sagt

Open your books at page …   Öffnet eure Bücher auf Seite …
Turn to page …   Blättert zu Seite …
Look at line …   Seht euch Zeile … an.
Look at the next paragraph.   Seht euch den nächsten Absatz an.
Read the text on page …   Lies/Lest den Text auf Seite …

Work in pairs.   Arbeitet zu zweit.
Work in groups of four.   Arbeitet zu viert.
Sit in a circle.   Bildet einen Sitzkreis.

Listen to track number … on the CD.   Hör dir/Hört euch Nummer … auf der CD an.
Write about …   Schreibe/Schreibt über …
Talk about …   Sprich/Sprecht über …
Ask questions about …   Stelle/Stellt Fragen zu …
Answer the question, please.   Beantworte/Beantwortet bitte die Frage.
Match the sentences.   Ordne/Ordnet die Sätze zu.
Who wants to read the text?   Wer möchte den Text vorlesen?
Write down the answers.   Schreibt die Antworten auf.

Act out the dialogue.   Spiel/Spielt den Dialog vor.
Change roles.   Tauscht die Rollen.
Make your own dialogue.   Entwirf/Entwerft selbst ein Gespräch.
Take a card.   Nimm/Nehmt eine Karte.

Come to the board, please.   Komm/Kommt bitte zur Tafel.
Collect the exercise books, please.   Sammelt bitte die Hefte ein.
Do this exercise at home, please.   Macht diese Aufgabe bitte zu Hause.

Be quiet, please.   Sei/Seid bitte ruhig.
Sit down, please.   Setz dich bitte./Setzt euch bitte.
Please speak up.   Sprich bitte lauter.

You can do better.   Das kannst du besser.
Try again.   Versuch es noch einmal.
That's it.   Das ist es./Richtig!
Well done.   Gut gemacht.

Deutscher Begriff	Englischer Begriff mit Aussprache	Beispiele	LiF
Apostroph	apostrophe /əˈpɒstrəfi/	Gillian's cousin, David's dog	8a
Artikel (Begleiter)	article /ˈɑːtɪkl/		
bestimmt	definite /ˈdefnət/	the	5a
unbestimmt	indefinite /ɪnˈdefnət/	a, an	5a
Aussagesatz	statement /ˈsteɪtment/	I love pizza.	
bejaht	positive /ˈpɒzətɪv/	Charlie likes football.	4a, 6a, 9a
verneint	negative /ˈnegətɪv/	David doesn't like bacon.	4b, 6a, 9a
Befehlsform (Imperativ)	imperative /ɪmˈperətɪv/	Wash your hands. Don't forget to brush your teeth.	3
einfache Gegenwart (Präsens)	simple present /ˌsɪmpl ˈpreznt/	Vanessa lives in Hendon.	4
einfache Vergangenheit (Präteritum)	simple past /ˌsɪmpl ˈpɑːst/	It was warm and sunny.	10
Entscheidungsfrage (Ja/Nein-Frage)	yes/no-question /jesˈnəʊˌkwestʃən/	Are you from Notting Hill?	1c, 2c, 4c, 6b, 7Ra, 9b
Fragewort	question word /ˈkwestʃən wɜːd/	who, what, when, where, why	7Rb
Frage mit Fragewort	wh-question /ˌdʌbljuː ˈeɪtʃ ˌkwestʃn/	What's your name?	1d, 2d, 4d, 6c, 7Ra, 9b
Grundform des Verbs (Infinitiv)	infinitive /ɪnˈfɪnətɪv/	be, go, like	3, 4a, 6a
Häufigkeitsadverb	adverb of frequency /ˌædvɜːb ˌəv ˈfriːkwənsi/	always, sometimes	4e
Konsonant (Mitlaut)	consonant /ˈkɒnsənənt/		4a, 5b, 9a
stimmlos	voiceless /ˈvɔɪsləs/	k, p, t	
stimmhaft	voiced /vɔɪst/	g, b, d	
Kurzantwort	short answer /ˈʃɔːtˌɑːnsə/	Are you eleven? Yes, I am.	1c, 2c, 4c, 6b, 7Ra, 9b
Kurzform	short form /ˈʃɔːt fɔːm/	'm, 's, isn't, aren't	1a, 2a
Langform	long form /ˈlɒŋ fɔːm/	am, is, is not, are not	1a, 2a
Nomen (Substantiv, Hauptwort)	noun /naʊn/	school, book, cat	5
Plural (Mehrzahl)	plural /ˈplʊərəl/		
regelmäßig	regular /ˈregjʊlə/	schools, books	5b
unregelmäßig	irregular /ɪˈregjʊlə/	children, teeth	5b

Glossary

Deutscher Begriff	Englischer Begriff mit Aussprache	Beispiele	LiF
Possessivbegleiter (besitzanzeigender Begleiter, besitzanzeigendes Fürwort)	possessive determiner /pəˌzesɪv dɪˈtɜːmɪnə/	my, his, her	8b
s-Form (des Verbs)	s-form /ˈes fɔːm/	likes, goes, does	4a
s-Genitiv	s-genitive /ˈes ˌdʒenətɪv/	Gillian's cat, David's dog	8a
Singular (Einzahl)	singular /ˈsɪŋgjʊlə/	one cat, one apple	5b
Subjekt (Satzgegenstand)	subject /ˈsʌbdʒekt/	<u>Karla</u> likes rabbits.	7Rb
Verb (Tätigkeitswort) regelmäßig unregelmäßig	verb /vɜːb/ regular /ˈregjʊlə/ irregular /ɪˈregjʊlə/	play, like, watch, walk go, do, have	10a 10b
Vergangenheitsform	past form /ˈpɑːst fɔːm/	played, liked, went, did	10
Verlaufsform der Gegenwart	present progressive /ˌpreznt prəʊˈgresɪv/	We <u>are having</u> a party.	9
Verneinung verneint, negativ	negation /nɪˈgeɪʃn/ negative /ˈnegətɪv/	I <u>don't like</u> tomatoes.	1b, 2b, 4b, 6a, 9a
Vokal (Selbstlaut)	vowel /ˈvaʊəl/	a, e, i, o, u	5a

Theme 1

LiF1 Formen von *be* – *forms of be*

Be heißt auf Deutsch „sein". Du brauchst die Formen von *be* zum Beispiel dann, wenn du über dich selbst oder andere sprechen möchtest: *I am eleven years old. – He is from Notting Hill.*

a **Kurzformen und Langformen**

Zur Grundform *be* gehören die Formen *am, is* und *are.* Die Formen von *be* gibt es als Kurzformen und als Langformen. Die Kurzformen *(short forms)* verwendet man meistens beim Sprechen, in persönlichen Briefen, SMS, E-Mails oder Chats. Die Langformen *(long forms)* verwendet man eher beim offiziellen Schreiben.

I'm Rajiv. I'm from Notting Hill.

We're from Hendon.

*This is Rajiv.
He is from
Notting Hill.*

*They are
from Hendon.*

	Kurzform		Langform			
Singular	I'm	=	I am			Ich bin …
	You're	=	You are			Du bist/Sie sind …
	He's	=	He is			Er ist …
	She's	=	She is		eleven.	Sie ist …
	It's	=	It is			Es ist …
Plural	We're	=	We are			Wir sind …
	You're	=	You are			Ihr seid/Sie sind …
	They're	=	They are			Sie sind …

b **Verneinung von *be***

Die Formen von *be* kannst du verneinen, indem du *not* einfügst:
He is from Notting Hill. → *He is not from Notting Hill.* Oder: *He isn't from Notting Hill.*

	Kurzform	Langform		
Singular	I'm not	(= I am not)		Ich bin nicht …
	You aren't	(= You are not)		Du bist/Sie sind nicht …
	He isn't	(= He is not)		Er ist nicht …
	She isn't	(= She is not)	eleven.	Sie ist nicht …
	It isn't	(= It is not)		Es ist nicht …
Plural	We aren't	(= We are not)		Wir sind nicht …
	You aren't	(= You are not)		Ihr seid/Sie sind nicht …
	They aren't	(= They are not)		Sie sind nicht …

c Entscheidungsfragen und Kurzantworten mit *be*

Entscheidungsfragen sind Fragen, die man mit „Ja" oder „Nein" beantworten kann.
Wenn du eine Entscheidungsfrage mit *be* stellen möchtest, stellst du die Form von *be*
an den Satzanfang.

Gillian is from Notting Hill.   Gillian ist aus Notting Hill.

Is Gillian from Notting Hill?   Ist Gillian aus Notting Hill?

Auf Entscheidungsfragen antwortet man meist nicht mit einem ganzen Satz. Es klingt
aber oft unhöflich, nur „*Yes*" oder „*No*" zu sagen. Deshalb verwendet man häufig Kurzantworten:

Is this your book? – **Yes, it is./No, it isn't.**

	Entscheidungsfrage		Kurzantwort (positiv)		Kurzantwort (negativ)	
Singular	Am I			you are.		you aren't. (= you are not.)
	Are you			I am.		I'm not. (= I am not.)
	Is he			he is.		he isn't. (= he is not.)
	Is she	eleven?	Yes,	she is.	No,	she isn't. (= she is not.)
	Is it			it is.		it isn't. (= it is not.)
Plural	Are we			we are.		we aren't. (= we are not.)
	Are you			we are.		we aren't. (= we are not.)
	Are they			they are.		they aren't. (= they are not.)

d Fragen mit Fragewort und *be*

What, where und *who* sind Fragewörter. Wenn du eine Frage mit einem Fragewort stellen willst,
stellst du das Fragewort an den Satzanfang.

What is your name? – My name is Gillian.
Where are you from? – I am from Notting Hill.
Who is this? – This is Charlie.

Auch hier gilt, dass man die Kurzformen vor
allem in gesprochener Sprache (oder in
persönlichen Briefen, SMS, E-Mails oder
Chats) verwendet.

what's   (= what is)
where's   (= where is)
who's   (= who is)

LiF2 Formen von *have got* – *forms of have got*

Have got heißt auf Deutsch „haben". Man kann damit ausdrücken, dass jemand etwas besitzt oder etwas hat: *I have got a cat. – She has got a rabbit.*

a Kurzformen und Langformen

Wie bei *be* gibt es auch bei *have got* und *has got* Kurzformen und Langformen.

	Kurzform		Langform		
Singular	I've got	=	I have got		Ich habe …
	You've got	=	You have got		Du hast/Sie haben …
	He's got	=	He has got		Er hat …
	She's got	=	She has got	two sisters.	Sie hat …
	It's got	=	It has got		Es hat …
Plural	We've got	=	We've got		Wir haben …
	You've got	=	You've got		Ihr habt/Sie haben …
	They've got	=	They've got		Sie haben …

! *Has* und *is* haben dieselbe Kurzform:
She's got a new book. (*She has got a new book.*)
She's my sister. (*She is my sister.*)

b Verneinung mit *have got*

Wenn man sagen möchte, dass man etwas **nicht** hat, stellt man das Wort *not* zwischen *have* und *got* bzw. zwischen *has* und *got*. Meistens verwendet man die Kurzformen *haven't* und *hasn't*:

	Kurzform	Langform		
Singular	I haven't got	(= I have not got)		Ich habe nicht …
	You haven't got	(= You have not got)		Du hast/Sie haben nicht …
	He hasn't got	(= He has not got)		Er hat nicht …
	She hasn't got	(= She has not got)	two sisters.	Sie hat nicht …
	It hasn't got	(= It has not got)		Es hat nicht …
Plural	We haven't got	(= We have not got)		Wir haben nicht …
	You haven't got	(= You have not got)		Ihr habt/Sie haben nicht …
	They haven't got	(= They have not got)		Sie haben nicht …

c Entscheidungsfragen und Kurzantworten mit *have got*

c Entscheidungsfragen und Kurzantworten mit *have got*

Wenn du eine Entscheidungsfrage mit
have got stellen möchtest, stellst du
have oder *has* an den Satzanfang.

She has got a new book.

Has she got a new book?

Auf Entscheidungsfragen antwortet
man oft mit einer Kurzantwort.
Das ist höflicher als nur „*Yes*"
oder „*No*" zu sagen.

> Have you got
> a computer?

> Yes, I have.

	Entscheidungsfrage		Kurzantwort (positiv)		Kurzantwort (negativ)
Singular	Have I got Have you got Has he got Has she got Has it got	two sisters?	Yes,	you have. I have. he has. she has. it has.	No,	you haven't. I haven't. he hasn't. she hasn't. it hasn't.
Plural	Have we got Have you got Have they got			we have. we have. they have.		we haven't. we haven't. they haven't.

Bei den Kurzantworten lässt du *got* weg und wiederholst nur *have* oder *has* bzw.
haven't oder *hasn't*.

d Fragen mit Fragewort und *have got*

Wenn du eine Frage mit einem Fragewort stellen willst, stellst du das Fragewort
an den Satzanfang. An zweiter Stelle steht dann *have* oder *has:*

What have you got? — *I have got a dog.*
What have the children got? — *They have got pets.*
Who has got a cat? — *Gillian has got a cat.*

Auch hier verwendet man die Kurzformen
meistens beim Sprechen, in persönlichen
Briefen, SMS, E-Mails oder Chats.

> Who's got
> a cat?

> Gillian's got
> a cat.

Theme 2

LiF3 Die Befehlsform – *imperative*

Mit der Befehlsform (Imperativ) kannst du jemanden um etwas bitten oder eine Anweisung oder einen Befehl ausdrücken.

Im Englischen hat der Imperativ dieselbe Form wie die Grundform des Verbs (Infinitiv).

David, brush your hair!
Wash your ears.

Get out *your books, please.*

Wenn jemand etwas nicht tun soll, stellst du *don't* vor das Verb. *Don't* ist die Kurzform von *do not*.

Don't forget your face.

Der Imperativ hat nur eine Form. Es spielt also keine Rolle, ob du eine oder mehrere Personen ansprichst oder ob du die Person mit du oder Sie anredest:

Help me, please. – Bitte **hilf** mir. / Bitte **helft** mir. / Bitte **helfen Sie** mir.

!
■ Wenn du nur den Imperativ verwendest, kann das im Englischen sehr unhöflich klingen. Höflicher ist es, wenn du *please* hinzufügst.

LiF4 Die einfache Gegenwart – *simple present*

Das *simple present* verwendest du, …
- um über Gewohnheiten oder regelmäßige Handlungen zu sprechen:
  I brush my teeth every morning.

- um über aufeinander folgende Handlungen zu sprechen:
  David puts his bowl and spoon into the dishwasher. Then he hurries to the bathroom.

- um über Zustände zu sprechen, die längere Zeit andauern:
  David lives in Hendon.

a *Simple present* in Aussagesätzen

simple present: Aussagesätze

Singular				
	I	live		Ich lebe …
	You	live		Du lebst / Sie leben …
	He	live**s**		Er lebt …
	She	live**s**	in Notting Hill.	Sie lebt …
	It	live**s**		Es lebt …
Plural	We	live		Wir leben …
	You	live		Ihr lebt / Sie leben …
	They	live		Sie leben …

Bei *I, you, we* und *they* hat das *simple present* dieselbe Form wie die Grundform des Verbs (Infinitiv). In der 3. Person Singular (zum Beispiel bei *he, she* und *it*) hängst du ein *-s* an.

Aber Vorsicht: Es gibt bei der s-Form von Verben einige Besonderheiten bei der Rechtschreibung.

Endet das Verb mit -ss, -sh, -ch oder -x, hängst du in der 3. Person Singular ein *-es* an:

*David wash**es** his face in the morning.*
*David brush**es** his hair.*

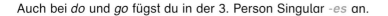

Auch bei *do* und *go* fügst du in der 3. Person Singular *-es* an.

*David do**es** his homework.*
*David go**es** to school.*

Bei Verben, die auf *y* enden (zum Beispiel *hurry*), gilt folgende Regel: Kommt ein Konsonant (zum Beispiel *r*) vor dem *y*, so wird das *y* in der 3. Person Singular zu *ies*:

*David hurr**ies** to the bathroom.*

Vorsicht auch bei der Aussprache von Verben in der 3. Person Singular:

Bei Verben, die auf einen Zischlaut, zum Beispiel /s/, /z/, /ʃ/, /tʃ/ oder /dʒ/, enden, wird das *-es* /ɪz/ ausgesprochen:

*I wash – he wash**es*** /wɒʃɪz/
*I brush – he brush**es*** /brʌʃɪz/

Bei *do* und *go* gibt es Folgendes bei der Aussprache zu beachten:

I do /duː/ *– he does* /dʌz/
I go /gəʊ/ *– he goes* /gəʊz/

Nach stimmlosen (harten) Konsonanten wird auch das *-s* zu einem stimmlosen /s/. Es klingt wie das Zischen einer Schlange.

/s/   SSSSS

*I put – she put**s*** /pʊts/

Nach stimmhaften (weichen) Konsonanten und nach Vokalen wird das *-s* /z/ ausgesprochen. Es klingt wie das Summen einer Biene.

/z/   ZZZZZ

I live /lɪv/ *– she live**s*** /lɪvz/
I see /siː/ *– she see**s*** /siːz/

b **Verneinung im _simple present_**

Sätze im _simple present_ verneinst du,
indem du _don't_ (= _do not_) vor das Verb
stellst. Bei der 3. Person Singular
verwendest du _doesn't_ (= _does not_).
Dabei verliert das Verb das _-s_ am Ende.

> I _don't_ like
> cornflakes every
> day.

David doesn't like cornflakes every day.

simple present: Verneinung

Singular				
	I	don't		Ich lebe nicht ...
	You	don't		Du lebst/Sie leben nicht ...
	He	do<u>es</u>n't		Er lebt nicht ...
	She	do<u>es</u>n't	live in Notting Hill.	Sie lebt nicht ...
	It	do<u>es</u>n't		Es lebt nicht ...
Plural	We	don't		Wir leben nicht ...
	You	don't		Ihr lebt/Sie leben nicht ...
	They	don't		Sie leben nicht ...

! Bei der Verneinung von Sätzen mit _be_, _have got_ oder _can_ brauchst du _don't_ oder _doesn't_ nicht:

He **isn't** from Hendon. (Er ist nicht aus Hendon.) (→ LiF 1b)
I **haven't got** a pet. (Ich habe kein Haustier.) (→ LiF 2b)
I **can't** play football. (Ich kann nicht Fußball spielen.) (→ LiF 6)

c **Entscheidungsfragen und Kurzantworten im _simple present_**

Wie man Entscheidungsfragen mit den
Verben _be_ und _have got_ bildet, hast du
schon bei LiF 1c und LiF 2c gesehen.

> _Do you like_ orange juice?

> Yes, I do.

Wenn du Entscheidungsfragen mit
anderen Verben im _simple present_
stellen möchtest, stellst du _do_ oder
does an den Satzanfang. Auch hier
verliert bei der 3. Person Singular das
Verb das _-s_ am Ende.

In den Kurzantworten wird _do_ oder
does aufgegriffen.

	Entscheidungsfrage			Kurzantwort (positiv)	Kurzantwort (negativ)
Singular	Do	I		you do.	you don't.
	Do	you		I do.	I don't.
	Do<u>es</u>	he		he do<u>es</u>.	he doesn't.
	Do<u>es</u>	she	live in Notting Hill?	she do<u>es</u>.	she doesn't.
	Do<u>es</u>	it	Yes,	it do<u>es</u>.	No, it doesn't.
Plural	Do	we		we do.	we don't.
	Do	you		we do.	we don't.
	Do	they		they do.	they don't.

d **Fragen mit Fragewort im *simple present***

Bei Fragen mit Fragewort rückt das Fragewort an den
Satzanfang. Es steht vor *do* oder *does*.

What do you have for breakfast? – *I have cornflakes.*
Where do you have breakfast? – *I have breakfast in
the kitchen.*
When do you have breakfast? – *I have breakfast
at 7.30.*

e **Aussagesätze mit Häufigkeitsadverbien**

Wenn man sagen will, wie oft man etwas macht, benutzt man Häufigkeitsadverbien.
Das sind Wörter wie *always* (= immer) oder *sometimes* (= manchmal).
Sie stehen meistens direkt vor dem Verb.

Dad always gives me an extra sausage.
The neighbours sometimes give Butterfly cat food.

Bei Sätzen mit *be* stehen dagegen
Häufigkeitsadverbien nach *am*, *are*
oder *is*:

You're always late.

Sorry I'm late.

Oh, David!
You're
always late.

LiF5 Nomen – *nouns*

a Nomen und ihre Artikel

„Der", „die" und „das" sind die drei bestimmten Artikel im Deutschen. Hast du eine andere Muttersprache als Deutsch? Wie viele Artikel gibt es in deiner Sprache? Im Englischen ist es eigentlich ganz einfach, denn es gibt nur eine Form des bestimmten Artikels: the.

the desk	*der Schreibtisch*
the school	*die Schule*
the book	*das Buch*
the chairs	*die Stühle*

! Achtung bei der Aussprache: Wenn das nach-folgende Wort mit einem Vokal beginnt, wird the nicht /ðə/ ausgesprochen, sondern /ði:/.

the /ðə/	**the** /ði:/
the book	the exercise book

„Ein" und „eine" sind die unbestimmten Artikel im Deutschen. Im Englischen heißt der unbestimmte Artikel a oder an. Ob du a oder an verwendest, hängt von der Aussprache des folgenden Wortes ab: Beginnt dieses mit einem Vokal, benutzt du an.

a /ə/	**an** /ən/
a book	an exercise book

! Vorsicht: Hier zählt nur die Aussprache. Das Wort *uniform* zum Beispiel wird /junifoːm/ ausgesprochen, deshalb heißt es hier *a uniform*.

a car

an apple

b Plural der Nomen

Die meisten englischen Nomen haben einen regelmäßigen Plural. Du bildest ihn, indem du ein -s an das Nomen anhängst.

Singular	Plural
book	books
pen	pens

Nomen auf -s, -ss, -sh, -ch und -x erhalten im Plural die Endung -es:

Singular	Plural
bus	buses
sandwich	sandwiches
box	boxes

Bei Nomen, die auf *y* enden, gilt folgende Regel: Kommt ein Konsonant vor dem *y*, so wird das *y* im Plural zu *ies*:

Singular	Plural
story	stories

Es gibt auch Nomen, die unregelmäßige Plural-formen haben. Am besten lernst du diese immer zusammen mit der Singularform. Sie stehen in der Wortliste ab Seite 185 in Klammern hinter dem Nomen: *child (pl children).*

Singular	Plural
bookshelf	bookshelves
child	children
foot	feet
goldfish	goldfish
knife	knives
man	men
mouse	mice
sheep	sheep
tomato	tomatoes
tooth	teeth
woman	women

Vorsicht bei der Aussprache:

Bei Nomen, die im Singular auf einen stimmlosen (harten) Konsonanten enden, wird auch das Plural-*s* zu einem stimmlosen / s /. Es klingt wie das Zischen einer Schlange.

a book – two books / bʊks /

/ s /   *sssss*

Bei Nomen, die im Singular auf einen stimmhaften (weichen) Konsonanten oder einen Vokal enden, wird das Plural-*s* / z / ausgesprochen. Es klingt wie das Summen einer Biene.

a pen – two pens / penz /
a window – two windows / wɪndəʊz /

/ z /   *zzzzz*

Bei Nomen, die im Singular auf einen Zischlaut, zum Beispiel / s /, / z /, / ʃ /, / tʃ / oder / dʒ /, enden, wird im Plural die Endung *-es* /ɪz / ausgesprochen:

a bus – two buses / bʌsɪz /
a sandwich – two sandwiches / sænwɪdʒɪz /

Theme 3

LiF 6 *Can*

Mit *can* kannst du sagen, ...

- was jemand **tun kann**: *He **can** play football.* – Er kann Fußball spielen.
- was jemand **tun darf**: *You **can** come on Saturday.* – Du darfst am Samstag kommen.

Mit *can* kannst du auch ...

- fragen, ob jemand etwas kann: ***Can** he play football?* – Kann er Fußball spielen?
- jemanden um etwas bitten: ***Can** you ask her, please?* – Kannst du sie bitte fragen?

Charlie can play football.

a *Can* in Aussagesätzen

Can steht mit der Grundform des Verbs (Infinitiv) und bleibt in allen Personen gleich. Wenn du ausdrücken willst, dass jemand etwas nicht tun kann oder nicht tun darf, verwendest du *can't* oder die Langform *cannot*:

can: Aussagesätze

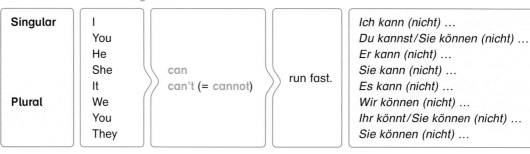

| Singular | I
You
He
She
It | can
can't (= cannot) | run fast. | Ich kann (nicht) ...
Du kannst/Sie können (nicht) ...
Er kann (nicht) ...
Sie kann (nicht) ...
Es kann (nicht) ... |
| Plural | We
You
They | | | Wir können (nicht) ...
Ihr könnt/Sie können (nicht) ...
Sie können (nicht) ... |

b *Can* in Entscheidungsfragen und Kurzantworten

Auf Entscheidungsfragen antwortet man meist nicht mit einem ganzen Satz, sondern mit einer Kurzantwort. Nur mit „*Yes*" oder „*No*" zu antworten ist etwas unhöflich.

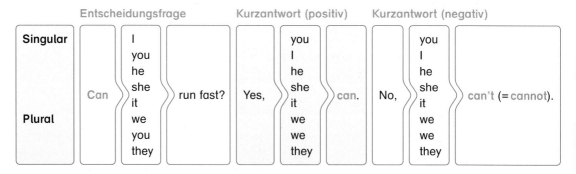

	Entscheidungsfrage			Kurzantwort (positiv)			Kurzantwort (negativ)	
Singular	Can	I you he she it	run fast?	Yes,	you I he she it	can.	No,	you I he she it	can't (= cannot).
Plural		we you they			we we they			we we they	

c *Can* in Fragen mit Fragewort

Bei Fragen mit Fragewort stellst du das Fragewort an den Satzanfang, noch vor *can*.

Where can you play basketball? – You can play basketball in a sports hall.
When can you come? – I can come at 10.30.

LiF7R Fragen – *questions (revision)*

In LiF 1, 2, 4 und 6 hast du schon gesehen, wie man im Englischen Fragen
formulieren kann. Hier gibt es noch einmal eine Zusammenfassung.

a Entscheidungsfragen und Kurzantworten

Entscheidungsfragen sind Fragen, die man mit „Ja" oder „Nein" beantworten
kann. Bei den Verben *be*, *have got* und *can* rückt die jeweilige Form von *be*, *have*
oder *can* an den Satzanfang. In den Kurzantworten wird die entsprechende Form
dann wieder aufgegriffen:

Entscheidungsfragen und Kurzantworten
mit *be, have got, can*   +   –

	+	–
Are you eleven?	Yes, I am.	No, I'm not.
Is he from Hendon?	Yes, he is.	No, he isn't.
Have you got a brother?	Yes, I have.	No, I haven't.
Has she got a pet?	Yes, she has.	No, she hasn't.
Can you play football?	Yes, I can.	No, I can't.

Bei anderen Verben (Vollverben) wie zum Beispiel *play* oder *like* verwendest
du *do* oder *does* am Anfang der Frage.

In den Kurzantworten wird *do* oder *does* aufgegriffen:

Entscheidungsfragen und Kurzantworten
mit *do* + Verb   +   –

	+	–
Do you play football?	Yes, I do.	No, I don't.
Do you like pizza?	Yes, I do.	No, I don't.
Does he like pizza?	Yes, he does.	No, he doesn't.
Do they live in Notting Hill?	Yes, they do.	No, they don't.

Vorsicht bei der 3. Person Singular. Hier verwendest du am Anfang der
Frage *does* und das Verb verliert das *-s*.

    Rajiv plays the guitar.
Does Rajiv play the guitar?

b Fragen mit Fragewort

Who, what, when, where, why und *how* sind Fragewörter.
Wenn du eine Frage mit einem Fragewort stellen möchtest,
stellst du das Fragewort an den Satzanfang.

Who?	–	Wer?
What?	–	Was?
When?	–	Wann?
Where?	–	Wo?
Why?	–	Warum?
How?	–	Wie?

Fragen mit Fragewörtern und *be, have got, can*

Where is Charlie?	*Wo ist Charlie?*
Who has got a pet?	*Wer hat ein Haustier?*
What can we play?	*Was können wir spielen?*

Mit *who* fragst du nach Personen, mit *where* nach Orten.

Ein Merkspruch:
Who, who, who – Wer bist du?
Where, where, where – Wo kommst du her?

Auch bei Fragen mit dem Hilfsverb *do* stellst du das Fragewort
an den Satzanfang:

Fragen mit Fragewörtern und *do/does* + Verb

What do you do after school?	*Was machst du nach der Schule?*
Where do you play football?	*Wo spielt ihr Fußball?*
Why does Charlie like goldfish?	*Warum mag Charlie Goldfische?*
Where do you live?	*Wo wohnst du?*
How do you spell "goal"?	*Wie buchstabiert man „goal"?*

Bei Fragen mit *who* braucht man kein zusätzliches *do*
oder *does*, wenn *who* nach dem Subjekt fragt:

Who lives in Hendon? – *Vanessa* lives in Hendon.
Who likes goldfish? – *Charlie* likes goldfish.

Language in Focus

Theme 4

LiF8 Besitzverhältnisse ausdrücken – *possessives*

a Der s-Genitiv

Wenn du sagen möchtest, wem etwas gehört oder zu wem etwas gehört, kannst du dies mit Hilfe des s-Genitivs ausdrücken. Im **Singular** hängst du bei Nomen einen Apostroph und ein s an ('s):

Rajiv's room is tidy.
The girl's room is big.

Achte auf die unterschiedliche Schreibung im Englischen und im Deutschen: *Vanessa's room – Vanessas Zimmer*

Bei **regelmäßigen Pluralformen** fügst du nur einen Apostroph an das Plural-s an:

The boys' room is very big. – Das Zimmer der Jungen ist sehr groß.

Bei **unregelmäßigen Pluralformen**, die nicht auf -s enden, bildest du den s-Genitiv mit 's:

The children's room is very big. – Das Zimmer der Kinder ist sehr groß.

This is the boy's room.

This is the boys' room.

Der s-Genitiv wird meistens dann verwendet, wenn etwas (zu) einer Person oder einem Tier gehört. Wenn man ausdrücken möchte, dass etwas zu einer Sache gehört, verwendet man meistens eine Konstruktion mit *of*:

The name of the school is Hendon School. – Der Name der Schule ist Hendon School.

b Possessivbegleiter

Possessivbegleiter sind Wörter, die man statt eines Nomens mit s-Genitiv (zum Beispiel *Vanessa's*) verwenden kann, wenn klar ist, worauf sie sich beziehen:

Vanessa lives in a house in Hendon.
Her room is small.
(Vanessa's room is small.)

Possessivbegleiter

Singular			
	My		Mein ...
	Your		Dein/Ihr ...
	His		Sein ...
	Her		Ihr ...
	Its	house is big.	Sein ...
Plural	Our		Unser ...
	Your		Euer/Ihr ...
	Their		Ihr ...

Theme 5

LiF9 Die Verlaufsform der Gegenwart – *present progressive*

Das *present progressive* verwendest du, wenn du sagen möchtest, was jemand gerade tut oder was gerade passiert. Du benutzt es also für Vorgänge, die gerade ablaufen und noch nicht abgeschlossen sind: *Gillian is eating cake. – Charlie is dancing.*

a Aussagesätze im *present progressive*

present progressive: Aussagesätze

Singular	I	am			Ich esse gerade (nicht).
	You	are			Du isst/Sie essen gerade (nicht).
	He	is			Er isst gerade (nicht).
	She	is	(not)	eating.	Sie isst gerade (nicht).
	It	is			Es isst gerade (nicht).
Plural	We	are			Wir essen gerade (nicht).
	You	are			Ihr esst/Sie essen gerade (nicht).
	They	are			Sie essen gerade (nicht).

Im Deutschen gibt es keine Verlaufsform. Um auszudrücken, was jemand gerade tut oder was gerade passiert, kannst du das im Deutschen aber gut mit Wörtern wie *gerade, im Moment* oder *jetzt* wiedergeben, also zum Beispiel:

*David **is opening** presents. –* David macht **gerade** Geschenke auf.

Sprichst du noch eine andere Sprache als Deutsch? Wie wird in dieser Sprache ausgedrückt, dass jemand etwas gerade tut oder etwas gerade passiert?

The girl is reading a book.

So bildest du das *present progressive:*
Form von *be (am, is, are)* + **Grundform des Verbs** + Endung *-ing*:

*He **is drink**ing orange juice.*

! Endet das Verb auf *-e*, dann fällt das *-e* in der Verlaufsform weg.

write	→ *writing*	*Gillian is writing a birthday card.*
dance	→ *dancing*	*Rajiv is dancing.*

! Endet das Verb auf einem kurzen betonten Vokal + Konsonant, wird der Konsonant verdoppelt.

put	→ *putting*	*David is putting food on the table.*
run	→ *running*	*Charlie is running.*

Language in Focus

Für die Verneinung fügst du ein *not* hinter der Form von *be* ein. Hier wird dann oft die Kurzform verwendet:

I am not making pizza.	*I'm not making pizza.*
David is not dancing.	*David isn't dancing.*
They are not watching TV.	*They aren't watching TV.*

b Fragen und Kurzantworten

Entscheidungsfragen im *present progressive* bildest du, indem du die Form von *be* (also *am*, *is* oder *are*) an den Satzanfang stellst. In den Kurzantworten wird die Form von *be* aufgegriffen. In verneinten Kurzantworten verwendet man meistens die Kurzformen.

	Entscheidungsfrage			Kurzantwort (positiv)		Kurzantwort (negativ)
Singular	Am	I		you are.		you aren't.
	Are	you		I am.		I'm not.
	Is	he		he is.		he isn't.
	Is	she	dreaming?	she is.	No,	she isn't.
	Is	it		it is.		it isn't.
Plural	Are	we		we are.		we aren't.
	Are	you		we are.		we aren't.
	Are	they		they are.		they aren't.

Positiv: Yes,

Bei Fragen mit Fragewort stellst du das Fragewort an den Satzanfang:

What are you doing?	– Was machst du (gerade)?
Where are you going?	– Wohin gehst du (gerade)?

Theme 6

[LiF 10] Die einfache Vergangenheit – *simple past*

Das *simple past* verwendest du, wenn du über etwas sprechen willst, das in der Vergangenheit liegt und abgeschlossen ist, zum Beispiel wenn du berichtest, was du erlebt hast, oder wenn du eine Geschichte erzählst: *Last Saturday was the first day of the summer holidays. ...*

a Regelmäßige Formen

Das *simple past* der regelmäßigen Verben bildest du, indem du die Endung *-ed* an den Infinitiv anhängst:

open + ed → opened   Vanessa opened the window.

simple past: regelmäßige Formen

Last Sunday I watched a film. Last Monday Rajiv helped his parents in the shop.	Letzten Sonntag habe ich einen Film gesehen. *(oder: Letzten Sonntag sah ich ...)* Letzten Montag hat Rajiv seinen Eltern im Laden geholfen. *(oder: Letzten Montag half ...)*

Im Deutschen verwendet man in der gesprochenen Sprache statt der Vergangenheitsform eher das Perfekt. Hast du eine andere Muttersprache als Deutsch? Wie ist es da?

! Achte auf folgende Besonderheiten in der Schreibung:
Endet das Verb auf *-e*, dann wird nur *-d* angehängt.

> *like → liked*

Endet das Verb auf einem kurzen betonten Vokal + Konsonant, wird der Konsonant verdoppelt.

> *stop → stopped*

Endet das Verb auf Konsonant + y, dann lautet die Endung im *simple past* -ied.

> *hurry → hurried*

b Unregelmäßige Formen

Unregelmäßige Verben kennst du auch aus dem Deutschen, etwa „gehen":
ich gehe (Gegenwart) – ich ging (Vergangenheit). Auch im Englischen
gibt es unregelmäßige Verben, zum Beispiel:

Infinitiv	*simple past*	
have	had	David had a great holiday.
go	went	He went to Wales with his parents.
do	did	They did lots of things together.

Die unregelmäßigen Verben haben im *simple past* eine eigene Form, die du lernen musst. Eine Liste mit unregelmäßigen Verben, die in diesem Buch vorkommen, findest du auf Seite 264.

Be hat als einziges englisches Verb zwei Formen im *simple past*, *was* und *were*:

I/he/she/it was – *you/we/they* were

simple past von *be*

> I was in London last week.
> They were in London last week.

> Ich war …
> Sie waren …

simple past von *be*: Verneinung

> It wasn't cold last Saturday.
> We weren't at the party.

> Es war letzten Samstag nicht kalt.
> Wir waren nicht auf der Party.

simple past von *be*: Fragen und Kurzantworten

> Were you at the cinema last Saturday?
> Was the film good?

> Yes, we were./No, we weren't.
> Yes it was./No, it wasn't.

c Verneinung mit *didn't*

Sätze im *simple past* verneinst du mit *didn't (did not)*. *Didn't* ist die Vergangenheitsform von *don't* und *doesn't* und ist in allen Personen gleich. Das Verb selbst bleibt im Infinitiv, weil *didn't* schon die Vergangenheit anzeigt.

simple past: bejahter Satz

> Karla talked to Gillian last Sunday.
> I went to London last year.

simple past: verneinter Satz

> Karla didn't talk to Gillian last Sunday.
> I didn't go to London last year.

d Entscheidungsfragen mit *did*

Entscheidungsfragen im *simple past* stellst du mit *did*:

simple past:
Entscheidungsfragen und Kurzantworten   +   –

> Did you go on holiday?
> Did Gillian visit Vanessa in Hendon?

> Yes, I did.
> Yes, she did.

> No, I didn't.
> No, she didn't.

Entscheidungsfragen mit *was* oder *were* stellst du ohne *did*.

e Fragen mit Fragewort und *did*

Das Fragewort steht auch hier am Satzanfang:

What did you do last Sunday?
Where did you go?

> *What did Rajiv do last Sunday? –*
> *He played football.*

Übersicht über in diesem Buch verwendete Arbeitsanweisungen

Act out the dialogue/scene.	Spielt den Dialog/die Szene nach.
Add up all the numbers.	Addiere alle Zahlen.
Ask and answer questions.	Stelle Fragen und beantworte sie.
Ask each other/four more classmates.	Fragt einander/weitere vier Klassenkameraden/Klassenkameradinnen.
Ask the time.	Fragt nach der Uhrzeit.
Ask your partner about …	Frage deinen Partner/deine Partnerin über …
Be a language detective.	Sei ein Sprachendetektiv/eine Sprachendetektivin.
Bring a picture/photo.	Bringe ein Bild/Foto mit.
Check your pairs/sentences/words.	Überprüfe deine Paare/Sätze/Wörter.
Choose a letter/one of the verses.	Wähle einen Buchstaben/eine der Strophen aus.
Collect ideas/information about …	Sammelt Ideen/Informationen über …
Compare with your notes.	Vergleicht mit euren Notizen.
Compare your answers with your partner's answers.	Vergleiche deine Antworten mit denen deines Partners/deiner Partnerin.
Complete the sentences with words from the box.	Vervollständige die Sätze mit Wörtern aus dem Kasten.
Copy the timetable.	Schreibe den Stundenplan ab.
Correct the (wrong) sentences.	Verbessere die (falschen) Sätze.
Describe …	Beschreibe …
Do a class survey/the role play.	Macht eine Umfrage in der Klasse/das Rollenspiel.
Do a project.	Macht ein Projekt.
Draw a picture of …	Zeichne ein Bild von …
Draw this table in your exercise book.	Zeichne diese Tabelle in dein Heft.
Explain in German the difference between …	Erkläre auf Deutsch den Unterschied zwischen …
Fill in …	Trage … ein.
Find a title/more opposites/pairs.	Finde einen Titel/weitere Gegensätze/Paare.
Find words that rhyme with the words above.	Finde Wörter, die sich auf die Wörter oben reimen.
Find out more about …	Finde mehr über … heraus.
Find the "odd one out"/the headwords/matching forms.	Finde das Wort, das nicht zu den anderen passt/die Oberbegriffe/Formen, die zusammen passen.
Get ideas from …	Hole dir Ideen von …
Get into groups of four.	Kommt in Vierergruppen zusammen.
Give a short talk on it.	Halte einen kurzen Vortrag darüber.
Hang the poster up in your classroom.	Hängt das Poster in eurem Klassenzimmer auf.
Have a look at …	Sieh dir … an.
Help out in German.	Hilf auf Deutsch aus.
Interview …	Befrage …
Introduce … to your parents.	Stelle … deinen Eltern vor.
Label the body parts/your classroom.	Beschrifte die Körperteile/dein Klassenzimmer.
Leave out some words.	Lasse ein paar Wörter aus.
Let your partner find the missing words.	Lasse deinen Partner/deine Partnerin die fehlenden Wörter finden.
Listen (again) and read along/sing along.	Höre (noch einmal) zu und lies mit/sing mit.
Listen to the chant/poem/song.	Hört euch den Sprechgesang/das Gedicht/Lied an.
Look at (page) … for help.	Sieh dir zur Hilfe (Seite) … an.
Look at the box/leaflet/photos/pictures.	Sieh dir den Kasten/die Broschüre/Fotos/Bilder an.
Make a character and present him or her.	Bastele ein Wesen und präsentiere es.
Make a collage about …/a fact file/plans.	Mache eine Collage von …/einen Steckbrief/Pläne.
Make a leaflet/list/quiz.	Mache eine Broschüre/eine Liste/ein Quiz.
Make a poster/puzzle piece/recording/story box/table.	Mache ein Poster/Puzzlestück/eine Aufnahme/eine Geschichtenkiste/Tabelle.
Make a word web about …	Erstelle ein Wortnetz über …

Make notes about …	Mache dir Notizen über …
Make up more dialogues / sums / your own chant.	Denke dir mehr Dialoge / Rechenaufgaben / deinen eigenen Sprechgesang aus.
Match the opposites / questions and answers / sentence parts / verb forms.	Ordne die Gegensätze / Fragen und Antworten / Satzteile / Verbformen einander zu.
Mime and guess.	Stellt es pantomimisch dar und ratet.
Mix …	Vermische …
Plan …	Plane …
Play a guessing game / spelling game.	Spielt ein Ratespiel / Buchstabierspiel.
Point at …	Zeige auf …
Practise the dialogue and present it.	Übt den Dialog und führt ihn vor.
Prepare a presentation.	Bereite eine Präsentation vor.
Present …	Stelle … vor.
Put the words in alphabetical order.	Ordne die Wörter in alphabetischer Reihenfolge.
Put the pieces together and …	Bringe die Teile zusammen und …
Put … together to make …	Bringt … zusammen, um … zu machen.
Read about …	Lies über …
Read it to your partner.	Lies es deinem Partner / deiner Partnerin vor.
Read the article / short forms.	Lies den Artikel / die Kurzformen.
Record …	Nimm … auf.
Repeat the words.	Wiederhole die Wörter.
Report to your partner.	Berichte deinem Partner / deiner Partnerin.
Say the chant / tongue twister.	Sprich den Chant / Zungenbrecher.
Say the words for the pictures.	Sage die Wörter für die Bilder.
Send a holiday postcard in English.	Schicke eine Urlaubspostkarte auf Englisch.
Show it to the class.	Zeige es der Klasse.
Sing the song and clap to it.	Singe das Lied und klatsche dazu.
Sort the dialogues / words into the list.	Sortiere die Dialoge / Wörter in die Liste.
Spell your name.	Buchstabiere deinen Namen.
Start your own rhyming dictionary.	Beginne dein eigenes Reimwörterbuch.
Take notes.	Mache dir Notizen.
Take turns.	Wechselt euch ab.
Talk about …	Sprich über … / Sprecht über …
Talk to your classmates like this.	Sprich auf diese Weise mit deinen Klassenkameraden / Klassenkameradinnen.
Tell your class in German.	Sag es deiner Klasse auf Deutsch.
Tell the story in your own words.	Erzähle die Geschichte mit deinen eigenen Worten.
Think about …	Denke über … nach.
Think of more commands.	Denke dir weitere Befehle aus.
Unscramble the commands / questions.	Ordne die Befehle / Fragen.
Use a dictionary.	Benutze ein Wörterbuch.
Use props and gestures / your answers to write a story / your notes.	Verwende Requisiten und Gesten / deine Antworten, um eine Geschichte zu schreiben / deine Notizen.
Use your imagination.	Benutze deine Fantasie.
Walk, stop and talk.	Lauft herum, haltet an und unterhaltet euch.
Watch the video clip(s).	Gucke dir den Videoclip / die Videoclips an.
Work in groups of four / in pairs.	Arbeitet in Vierergruppen / paarweise.
Work with a partner.	Arbeitet mit einem Partner / einer Partnerin zusammen.
Write a dialogue / poem / speech bubble.	Schreibe einen Dialog / ein Gedicht / eine Sprechblase.
Write about …	Schreibe über …
Write down more word groups / the plural forms of the words / more verses.	Schreibe noch mehr Wortgruppen / die Mehrzahlformen der Wörter / weitere Strophen auf.
Write wrong / more sentences for your partner.	Schreibe falsche / weitere Sätze für deinen Partner / deine Partnerin.

Erläuterung der Wortlisten

Es gibt alphabetische Wortlisten und Wortlisten nach Kapiteln.

Alphabetische Wortlisten *(Dictionary)*

Du kannst in der alphabetischen Liste *(Dictionary English-German)* ab Seite 239 nachschlagen, wenn du die Bedeutung eines Wortes wissen möchtest, das im Buch vorgekommen ist. Im *Dictionary German-English* ab Seite 257 kannst du nachschlagen, wenn dir eins der englischen Lernwörter nicht einfällt. Die wichtigsten Arbeitsanweisungen findest du in der Liste auf den Seiten 180–181 und in Kästen innerhalb der Wortlisten nach Kapiteln. Wörter, die im Englischen wie im Deutschen gleich sind, findest du mit ihrer Lautschrift auf Seite 184.

Wortlisten nach Kapiteln *(Words)*

Hier werden die Vokabeln an der Stelle aufgelistet, an der sie zum ersten Mal vorkommen. Manche Vokabeln sind fett gedruckt, die solltest du dir auf jeden Fall merken.

Hier siehst du, wie du diese Wortlisten (ab Seite 185) benutzen kannst.

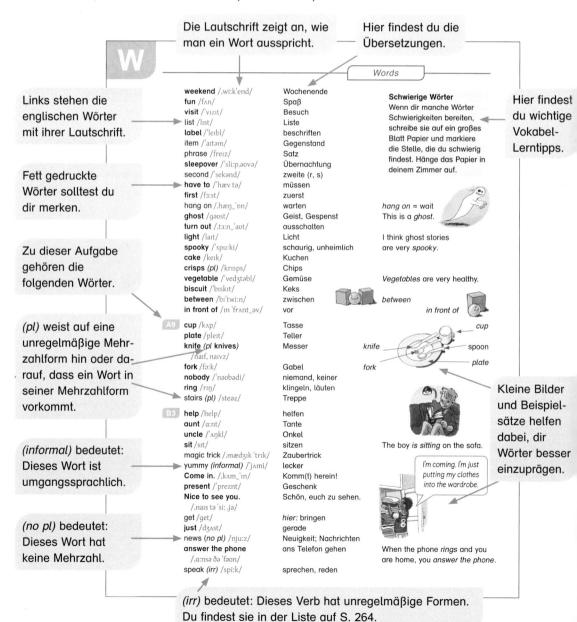

Die Lautschrift zeigt an, wie man ein Wort ausspricht.

Hier findest du die Übersetzungen.

Links stehen die englischen Wörter mit ihrer Lautschrift.

Fett gedruckte Wörter solltest du dir merken.

Zu dieser Aufgabe gehören die folgenden Wörter.

(pl) weist auf eine unregelmäßige Mehrzahlform hin oder darauf, dass ein Wort in seiner Mehrzahlform vorkommt.

(informal) bedeutet: Dieses Wort ist umgangssprachlich.

(no pl) bedeutet: Dieses Wort hat keine Mehrzahl.

Hier findest du wichtige Vokabel-Lerntipps.

Kleine Bilder und Beispielsätze helfen dabei, dir Wörter besser einzuprägen.

(irr) bedeutet: Dieses Verb hat unregelmäßige Formen. Du findest sie in der Liste auf S. 264.

The English alphabet

/eɪ/	/biː/	/siː/	/diː/	/iː/	/ef/	/dʒiː/	/eɪtʃ/	/aɪ/
a	b	c	d	e	f	g	h	i

/dʒeɪ/	/keɪ/	/el/	/em/	/en/	/əʊ/	/piː/	/kjuː/	/aː/
j	k	l	m	n	o	p	q	r

/es/	/tiː/	/juː/	/viː/	/'dʌbljuː/	/eks/	/waɪ/	/zed/
s	t	u	v	w	x	y	z

English sounds

Im Englischen spricht man Wörter oft anders aus, als man sie schreibt. Die Aussprache der Wörter wird mit Hilfe der Lautschrift in jedem Wörterbuch angegeben. Man kann so auch neue Wörter richtig aussprechen, ohne sie vorher gehört zu haben.
Die Lautschrift ist eine Schrift, deren Symbole jeden Laut genau bezeichnen.
Hier ist eine Liste mit den Symbolen dieser Lautschrift zusammen mit Beispielwörtern, in denen der entsprechende Laut vorkommt.

Vokale
/ɑː/ arm
/ʌ/ but
/e/ desk
/ə/ a, an
/ɜː/ girl, bird
/æ/ apple
/ɪ/ in, it
/i/ happy
/iː/ easy, eat
/ɒ/ orange, sorry
/ɔː/ all, call
/ʊ/ look
/u/ January
/uː/ boot

Doppellaute
/aɪ/ eye, by, buy
/aʊ/ our
/eə/ air, there

/eɪ/ take, they
/ɪə/ here
/ɔɪ/ boy
/əʊ/ go, old
/ʊə/ tourist

Konsonanten
/b/ bag, club
/d/ duck, card
/f/ fish, laugh
/g/ get, dog
/h/ hot
/j/ you
/k/ can, duck
/l/ lot, small
/m/ more, mum
/n/ now, sun
/ŋ/ song, long
/p/ present, top
/r/ red, around

/s/ sister, class (stimmlos)
/z/ nose, dogs (stimmhaft)
/t/ time, cat
/ʒ/ television
/dʒ/ sausage
/ʃ/ fresh
/tʃ/ child, cheese
/ð/ these, mother (stimmhaft)
/θ/ bathroom, think (stimmlos)
/v/ very, have
/w/ what, word

/'/ Betonungszeichen für die folgende Silbe (Hauptbetonung)
/ˌ/ Betonungszeichen für die folgende Silbe (Nebenbetonung)

Es gibt auch ...

... viele Wörter, die im Englischen wie im Deutschen gleich sind – außer, dass die meisten von ihnen auf Deutsch groß geschrieben werden. Die meisten dieser Wörter, die im Buch vorkommen, findest du hier. Sie sind nicht in den Wortlisten der einzelnen Kapitel, weil sie dir ja nicht neu sind. Viele von ihnen sprechen wir auch gleich aus. Bei denen, die ein bisschen anders ausgesprochen werden als im Deutschen, haben wir die Lautschrift farbig hervorgehoben.

ABC /ˌeɪbiːˈsiː/
April /ˈeɪprəl/
arm /aːm/
August /ˈɔːgəst/
baby /ˈbeɪbi/
ball /bɔːl/
band /bænd/
basketball /ˈbaːskɪtˌbɔːl/
bingo /ˈbɪŋgəʊ/
bitter lemon /ˌbɪtə ˈlemən/
blind /blaɪnd/
blog /blɒg/
blond /blɒnd/
BMX /ˌbiːemˈeks/
burger /ˈbɜːgə/
bus /bʌs/
butler /ˈbʌtlə/
butter /ˈbʌtə/
café /ˈkæfeɪ/
cartoon /kaːˈtuːn/
CD (player) /ˌsiːˈdiː (ˌpleɪə)/
champion /ˈtʃæmpjən/
chat /tʃæt/
cheddar /ˈtʃedə/
clip /klɪp/
clown /klaʊn/
collage /ˈkɒlaːʒ/
comic /ˈkɒmɪk/
computer /kəmˈpjuːtə/
cool /kuːl/
cornflakes /ˈkɔːnfleɪks/
cyberpet /ˈsaɪbəpet/
dip /dɪp/
doughnut /ˈdəʊˌnʌt/
DVD /ˌdiːviːˈdiː/
email /ˈiːmeɪl/
fan /fæn/
finger /ˈfɪŋgə/
form /fɔːm/
forum /ˈfɔːrəm/
ginger ale /ˌdʒɪndʒərˈeɪl/

giraffe /dʒəˈraːf/
hamster /ˈhæmstə/
hand /hænd/
hey, hi /heɪ, haɪ/
hobby /ˈhɒbi/
hockey /ˈhɒki/
inline skater /ˌɪnlaɪn ˈskeɪtə/
instrument /ˈɪnstrəmənt/
karate /kəˈraːti/
Mars /maːz/
marshmallow /ˈmaːʃˌmæləʊ/
million /ˈmɪljən/
minus /ˈmaɪnəs/
minute /ˈmɪnɪt/
Miss /mɪs/
monster /ˈmɒnstə/
museum /mjuːˈziːəm/
musical /ˈmjuːzɪkl/
name /neɪm/
November /nəʊˈvembə/
oh /əʊ/
OK /ˌəʊˈkeɪ/
online /ˌɒnˈlaɪn/
orange /ˈɒrɪndʒ/
park /paːk/
partner /ˈpaːtnə/
party /ˈpaːti/
person /ˈpɜːsn/
pink /pɪŋk/
pizza /ˈpiːtsə/
plan /plæn/
plural /ˈplʊərəl/
plus /plʌs/
poltergeist /ˈpɒltəgaɪst/
pony /ˈpəʊni/
pool /puːl/
popcorn /ˈpɒpkɔːn/
poster /ˈpəʊstə/
problem /ˈprɒbləm/
quiz /kwɪz/
radio /ˈreɪdiəʊ/

rap /ræp/
rock /rɒk/
rucksack /ˈrʌkˌsæk/
sandwich /ˈsænwɪdʒ/
science fiction /ˌsaɪənsˈfɪkʃn/
September /sepˈtembə/
shampoo /ʃæmˈpuː/
shorts /ʃɔːts/
show /ʃəʊ/
skateboard(er) /ˈskeɪtbɔːd(ə)/
skatepark /ˈskeɪtpaːk/
skater /ˈskeɪtə/
so /səʊ/
sofa /ˈsəʊfə/
sound check /ˈsaʊnd ˌtʃek/
spaghetti /spəˈgeti/
sweatshirt /ˈswetˌʃɜːt/
taxi /ˈtæksi/
team /tiːm/
tennis /ˈtenɪs/
terrarium /təˈreəriəm/
text /tekst/
tiger /ˈtaɪgə/
toast /təʊst/
training /ˈtreɪnɪŋ/
T-shirt /ˈtiː ʃɜːt/
tunnel /ˈtʌnl/
uniform /ˈjuːnɪfɔːm/
update /ˈʌpdeɪt/
USB stick /ˌjuːesˈbiː stɪk/
verb /vɜːb/
video /ˈvɪdiəʊ/
volleyball /ˈvɒlibɔːl/
warm /wɔːm/
whiteboard /ˈwaɪtˌbɔːd/
wind /wɪnd/
wow /waʊ/
yay /jeɪ/
yeah /jeə/
zebra /ˈzebrə/
zoo /zuː/

Words

Welcome

Welcome!

welcome (to) /ˈwelkəm tʊ/	willkommen (in)	

Berry the clown

the /ðə/ — der/die/das

> Listen to … — Höre/Hört … zu..
> What do you understand? — Was verstehst du?

My name is …

My name is … — Ich heiße …
/ˌmaɪ ˈneɪm‿ɪz/
my /maɪ/ — mein(e)
is /ɪz/ — ist

What's your name?

My name is Alice.

> Talk about yourself. — Sprich über dich.

I'm (= I am) /aɪm, ˈaɪ‿æm/ — ich bin, ich heiße
from /frɒm/ — von; aus
eleven /ɪˈlevn/ — elf
year /jɪə/ — Jahr
old /əʊld/ — alt
favourite /ˈfeɪvrət/ — Liebling; Lieblings-
colour /ˈkʌlə/ — Farbe
blue /blu:/ — blau
I /aɪ/ — ich
speak *(irr)* /spi:k/ — sprechen, reden
German /ˈdʒɜ:mən/ — Deutsch; deutsch
Polish /ˈpəʊlɪʃ/ — Polnisch; polnisch
and /ænd/ — und
English /ˈɪŋglɪʃ/ — Englisch; english

The baby is one *year old*.

the *German* flag

> Ask your partner. — Frage deinen Partner/deine Partnerin.

What's your name? — Wie heißt du?
/ˌwɒts jə ˈneɪm/
what's (= what is) — was ist
/ˈwɒts, ˈwɒt‿ɪz/
what /wɒt/ — was; welche(r, s)
your /jɔ:/ — dein(e), euer/eure
How old are you? — Wie alt bist du?
/haʊ‿ˈəʊld‿ɑ: ˌjʊ/
how /haʊ/ — wie
are /ɑ:/ — bist, sind, seid
you /ju:/ — du, dich, dir, man, ihr,
euch; Sie, Ihnen

Hi, I'm eleven years old.
How old are you?

What are your favourite ...? Was sind deine Lieblings- ...?
/ˌwɒt_ə jə ˌfeɪvrət ˈ.../
                                                   A tiger
animal /ˈænɪml/   Tier   is an *animal*.
What languages do you   Welche Sprachen sprichst
  speak? /ˌwɒt ˈlæŋgwɪdʒɪz   du?
  du: ju: ˈspiːk/
language /ˈlæŋgwɪdʒ/   Sprache

> Ask four more classmates.   Frage weitere vier Klassenkameraden/
>   Klassenkameradinnen.

Colourful clothes

colourful /ˈkʌləfl/   farbenfroh, bunt
clothes (*pl*) /kləʊðz/   Kleider, Kleidung   *clothes*

> Listen to the song and sing along.   Höre dir das Lied an und singe mit.
> Act it out.   Spielt es nach.

look around /ˌlʊk_əˈraʊnd/   sich umsehen
circle /ˈsɜːkl/   Kreis
can/can't /kæn/kɑːnt/   können/nicht können   You *can*
see (*irr*) /siː/   sehen   *see* colours
get ready /ˌget ˈredi/   sich fertig machen   in the picture.
if /ɪf/   wenn; falls
you're wearing /jɔː ˈweərɪŋ/ du trägst (gerade)
wear (*irr*) /weə/   tragen
one /wʌn/   eins
two /tuː/   zwei
three /θriː/   drei
stand up /ˌstænd_ˈʌp/   aufstehen
turn around /ˌtɜːn_əˈraʊnd/ sich umdrehen
point (at/to) /pɔɪnt/   deuten (auf), zeigen (auf)
then /ðen/   dann
sit down /ˌsɪt_ˈdaʊn/   sich hinsetzen
back /bæk/   zurück; *hier:* wieder

blue	/bluː/	blau
yellow	/ˈjeləʊ/	gelb
green	/griːn/	grün
black	/blæk/	schwarz
white	/waɪt/	weiß
purple	/ˈpɜːpl/	violett, lila
orange	/ˈɒrɪndʒ/	orange
brown	/braʊn/	braun
red	/red/	rot
grey	/greɪ/	grau

> Talk about Lily's clothes.   Sprich über Lilys Kleidung.

she /ʃiː/   sie
has got /ˌhəz ˈgɒt/   hat
have got /ˌhæv ˈgɒt/   haben
there are /ðeər_ˈɑː/   dort sind; es gibt   *There are* five tomatoes and
there is /ðeər_ˈɪz/   dort ist; es gibt   *there is* one apple.

a/an /ə, eɪ/ən/   ein(e)
cap /kæp/   Mütze
in /ɪn/   in; auf   *She* is 12 years old.
her /hɜː/   ihr/ihre, sie   *Her* name is Claire.
wardrobe /ˈwɔːdrəʊb/   Schrank

Words

Animals

Do you know the animals in the picture?	Kennst du die Tiere auf dem Bild?
Which animals can you find on a farm/in a zoo?	Welche Tiere kannst du auf einem Bauernhof/in einem Zoo finden?
Which animals can be pets?	Welche Tiere können Haustiere sein?

Numbers

| **number** /ˈnʌmbə/ | Zahl; Nummer | One, two and three are *numbers*. |

| Listen to the number rap. | Höre dir den Zahlenrap an. |

this /ðɪs/	diese(r, s)	
be fun /ˌbiː ˈfʌn/	Spaß machen	That's *fun*! Das macht Spaß!
agree /əˈgriː/	zustimmen	Do you *agree*? Stimmst du zu?
in English /ˌɪn ˈɪŋglɪʃ/	auf Englisch	
heaven /ˈhevn/	Himmel	
it's (= it is) /ɪts, ˈɪt‿ɪz/	es ist; es gibt	
time /taɪm/	Zeit	
for /fɔː/	für	
then /ðen/	dann	
up till /ˈʌp tɪl/	bis	
now /naʊ/	jetzt	
we're doing fine /wɪə ˌduːɪŋ ˈfaɪn/	wir machen es gut	
next /nekst/	dann, als Nächstes	
yes /jes/	ja	
we /wiː/	wir	
the best /ðə ˈbest/	der/die/das Beste	
What about ...? /ˌwɒt‿əˌbaʊt ˈ.../	Was ist mit ...?/Wie wäre es mit ...?	
that's (= that is) /ðæts, ˈðæt‿ɪz/	das ist	
at last /ət ˈlɑːst/	endlich, schließlich	
we're rapping /ˌwɪə ˈræpɪŋ/	wir rappen gerade	
very /ˈveri/	sehr	
fast /fɑːst/	schnell	
like /laɪk/	mögen	Charlie *likes* pizza.
rap /ræp/	rappen	
with /wɪð/	mit; bei	
let's (= let us) /lets, ˈlet‿əs/	lass(t) uns ...	
start /stɑːt/	anfangen, beginnen	start ≠ stop
again /əˈgen/	wieder, noch einmal	

1	one	7	seven
2	two	8	eight
3	three	9	nine
4	four	10	ten
5	five	11	eleven
6	six	12	twelve

| Now it is your turn. | Jetzt bist du dran. |
| Talk to your partner. | Sprich mit deinem Partner/deiner Partnerin. |

What's your phone number? /ˌwɒts jə ˈfəʊn‿nʌmbə/	Was ist deine Telefonnummer?
phone /fəʊn/	Telefon
mobile (phone) /ˈməʊbaɪl/	Handy

This is a *mobile phone*.

> Write your partner's phone number down.
>
> Schreibe die Telefonnummer deines Partners / deiner Partnerin auf.

Weather

weather /ˈweðə/	Wetter
spring /sprɪŋ/	Frühling
rain /reɪn/	Regen
jump /dʒʌmp/	springen
into /ˈɪntuː/	in
big /bɪg/	groß
puddle /ˈpʌdl/	Pfütze
summer /ˈsʌmə/	Sommer
hot /hɒt/	heiß
no /nəʊ/	kein(e)
cloud /klaʊd/	Wolke
sit *(irr)* /sɪt/	sitzen
sun /sʌn/	Sonne
eat *(irr)* /iːt/	essen
ice cream /ˈaɪs ˌkriːm/	Eis
autumn /ˈɔːtəm/	Herbst
on /ɒn/	auf; an; in
windy /ˈwɪndi/	windig
day /deɪ/	Tag
fly *(irr)* /flaɪ/	fliegen
kite /kaɪt/	Drachen
winter /ˈwɪntə/	Winter
love /lʌv/	lieben, sehr mögen
snow /snəʊ/	Schnee
build *(irr)* /bɪld/	bauen
snowman *(pl* snowmen) /ˈsnəʊmæn, ˈsnəʊmen/	Schneemann

> *I don't like rain.*

The *sun* is shining.

It's very *windy*.

> *I love snow!*

> Collect weather words.
> What can you do on a hot / cold day?
>
> Sammle Wetterwörter.
> Was kannst du an einem heißen / kalten Tag machen?

In the break

break /breɪk/	Pause

> Look and listen.
> What are the boys talking about?
> Listen and read along.
>
> Schaue und höre zu.
> Worüber reden die Jungen?
> Höre zu und lies mit.

Words

no /nəʊ/	nein	*yes ≠ no*
cheese /tʃiːz/	Käse	

cheese

hate /heɪt/	hassen, nicht ausstehen können	
apple /ˈæpl/	Apfel	
ugh (*informal*) /ʌg/	i, igitt	
Look! /lʊk/	Schau(t) mal!	
give (*irr*) /gɪv/	geben	
(to) me /miː/	mir, mich, ich	This is an *apple*
banana /bəˈnɑːnə/	Banane	and that's a *banana*.

What do you think?	Was hältst du davon?
/ˌwɒt̮_də jə ˈθɪŋk/	
think (*irr*) /θɪŋk/	denken, glauben
sure /ʃɔː/	sicher
great /greɪt/	groß; großartig
idea /aɪˈdɪə/	Idee
swap for /ˈswɒp fɔː/	eintauschen gegen
Sorry. /ˈsɒri/	Es tut mir leid., Entschuldigung.

If you *think* something is a *great idea*, you like it.

Sorry!

but /bʌt/	aber
have (*irr*) /hæv/	haben; essen, trinken
a (little) bit /ə ˌlɪtl ˈbɪt/	ein (kleines) bisschen
of /əv/	von
it /ɪt/	es
Thank you. /ˈθæŋk ju/	Danke.

Act out the dialogue.	Spielt den Dialog nach.

food /fuːd/	Essen
chant /tʃɑːnt/	Sprechgesang

Listen to the chant and say it.	Höre dir den Sprechgesang an und sage ihn.

a lot /ə ˈlɒt/	viel, sehr

Make your own chant.	Mache deinen eigenen Sprechgesang.

Karla

Read about …	Lies über …

hello /həˈləʊ/	hallo
everybody /ˈevriˌbɒdi/	alle; jeder
I've got (= I have got)	ich habe
/ˌaɪv ˈgɒt, ˌaɪ hæv ˈgɒt/	
little /ˈlɪtl/	klein
brother /ˈbrʌðə/	Bruder
his /hɪz/	sein/seine/seiner/seins

I've got a brother.

His brother is wearing a green T-shirt.

he /hiː/	er	*He* is a boy.
football /ˈfʊtˌbɔːl/	Fußball	
like doing something /laɪk ˈduːɪŋ ˌsʌmθɪŋ/	etwas gern tun	
play /pleɪ/	spielen	
wheelchair /ˈwiːltʃeə/	Rollstuhl	
be good at something /biː ˈɡʊd‿æt ˌsʌmθɪŋ/	gut in etwas sein	She *is good at football*.
good /ɡʊd/	gut	
go *(irr)* /ɡəʊ/	gehen; fahren	
to /tʊ/	in, nach, zu	
club /klʌb/	Klub; AG	
at /æt/	an, in, bei, um	
school /skuːl/	Schule	
music /ˈmjuːzɪk/	Musik	They love *music*.
lots of /ˈlɒts‿əv/	viel, jede Menge	
song /sɒŋ/	Lied	
dinosaur /ˈdaɪnəˌsɔː/	Dinosaurier	
too /tuː/	auch	
room /ruːm/	Raum, Zimmer	
pig /pɪɡ/	Schwein	
rabbit /ˈræbɪt/	Kaninchen	This is a *rabbit*.
they /ðeɪ/	sie	
cute /kjuːt/	süß, niedlich	
carrot /ˈkærət/	Möhre, Karotte	
for breakfast /fə ˈbrekfəst/	zum Frühstück	
glass /ɡlɑːs/	Glas	
orange juice /ˈɒrɪndʒ‿ˌdʒuːs/	Orangensaft	
best /best/	beste (r, s)	
friend /frend/	Freund/in	They are *friends*.
Goodbye. /ˌɡʊdˈbaɪ/	Auf Wiedersehen.	

The NHG song

part /pɑːt/	Teil	

Listen to the song.	Höre dir das Lied an.
Then sing along.	Singe dann mit.

come *(irr)* /kʌm/	kommen	
city /ˈsɪti/	Stadt; Innenstadt	London is a *city*.
to /tʊ/	(um) zu	
meet *(irr)* /miːt/	treffen; sich treffen	
a lot (of) /ə ˈlɒt/	viel(e), jede Menge	
nice /naɪs/	schön; nett	
child *(pl* **children)** /tʃaɪld, ˈtʃɪldrən/	Kind	
walk /wɔːk/	gehen	*child* *children*
down /daʊn/	hinunter	

Words

street /striːt/	Straße
some /sʌm/	einige, ein paar; etwas
live /lɪv/	leben, wohnen
perfect /ˈpɜːfɪkt/	perfekt
place /pleɪs/	Ort; Platz
stay /steɪ/	bleiben; wohnen
not /nɒt/	nicht
far /faː/	weit
away /əˈweɪ/	weg
so /səʊ/	deshalb, daher
all /ɔːl/	alle, alles
their /ðeə/	ihr(e)
pet /pet/	Haustier
really /ˈrɪəli/	wirklich
want /wɒnt/	wollen
them /ðem/	sie, ihnen
What about you?	Und du?
/ˌwɒt‿əbaʊt ˈjuː/	

This is a perfect *place* to live in.

This is Rajiv's *pet* Ruby.

They are my friends. Do you want to meet *them*?

Theme 1

I

people /ˈpiːpl/	Leute, Menschen
target task /ˈtaːgɪt ˌtaːsk/	Zielaufgabe
about /əˈbaʊt/	über; an

You can see *people* in the picture.

A1

What can you see?	Was kannst du sehen?
Listen.	Höre zu.
What can you hear?	Was kannst du hören?
Work with a partner.	Arbeitet mit einem Partner / einer Partnerin zusammen.

show *(irr)* /ʃəʊ/	zeigen

A2

new /njuː/	neu

Look at the comic and listen.	Sieh dir den Comic an und hör zu.

look (at) /ˈlʊk‿ət/	(an)sehen, (an)schauen
there's (= there is)	dort ist; es gibt
/ðeəz, ðeər‿ɪz/	
be *(irr)* /biː/	sein
cousin /ˈkʌzn/	Cousin/e
these *(pl of* **this***)* /ðiːz/	diese; das
that /ðæt/	das
again /əˈgen/	wieder, noch einmal
Yes, I am. /ˌjes‿aɪ ˈæm/	Ja.

be	**sein**
I **am**	ich **bin**
you **are**	du **bist** / Sie **sind**
he **is**	er **ist**
she **is**	sie **ist**
it **is**	es **ist**
we **are**	wir **sind**
you **are**	ihr **seid** / Sie **sind**
they **are**	sie **sind**

These children are my friends.
Diese Kinder sind meine Freunde.
These are my friends.
Das sind meine Freunde.

Come on! /ˌkʌm‿ˈɒn/ — Komm(t) jetzt!, Mach(t) schon!

Let's go! /ˌlets ˈgəʊ/ — Lass(t) uns gehen!
let *(irr)* /let/ — lassen
No, it isn't. /ˌnəʊ ɪt‿ˈɪznt/ — Nein.
around /əˈraʊnd/ — um; herum, umher
corner /ˈkɔːnə/ — Ecke — The shop is on the *corner*.

A3

Read what the children say. — Lies, was die Kinder sagen.
Work in groups. — Arbeitet in Gruppen.
Draw the scene in the park. — Zeichne die Szene im Park.
Walk, stop and talk. — Lauft herum, haltet an und unterhaltet euch.
Talk to your classmates like this. — Sprich auf diese Weise mit deinen Klassenkameraden /Klassenkameradinnen.

Where are you from? — Woher kommst du?
/ˌweər‿ə jʊ ˈfrɒm/
where /weə/ — wo; wohin
how /haʊ/ — wie

I'm from London. Where are you from?

A4

Look at the picture. — Sieh dir das Bild an.
Collect words about … — Sammle Wörter über …
Listen to … and read along. — Höre … zu und lies mit.

What does he talk about? — Worüber spricht er?
/ˌwɒt dəz hi ˈtɔːk‿əbaʊt/
parents *(pl)* /ˈpeərənts/ — Eltern
sister /ˈsɪstə/ — Schwester
their /ðeə/ — ihr(e)
chips *(pl)* /tʃɪps/ — Pommes frites — These are *chips*.

ketchup /ˈketʃəp/ — Ketschup
but /bʌt/ — aber
tomato *(pl **tomatoes**)* — Tomate — This is a *tomato*.
/təˈmaːtəʊ, təˈmaːtəʊz/
goldfish *(pl **goldfish**)* — Goldfisch
/ˈgəʊldˌfɪʃ/

He likes *riding* his *bike*.

bike /baɪk/ — Fahrrad
ride a bike /ˌraɪd‿ə ˈbaɪk/ — Fahrrad fahren
big /bɪg/ — groß
think *(irr)* /θɪŋk/ — denken, glauben
best /best/ — beste (r, s)
just like me /ˌdʒʌst laɪk ˈmiː/ — genau wie ich

Write about … — Schreibe über …
Complete the sentences. — Vervollständige die Sätze.
Match the questions and answers. — Ordne die Fragen und Antworten einander zu.

Words

No, they aren't.
/ˌnəʊ ðeɪ‿ˈɑːnt/
No, he isn't. /ˌnəʊ hi ˈɪznt/
Yes, he is. /ˌjes hi‿ˈɪz/
Yes, they are. /ˌjes ðeɪ‿ˈɑː/

Nein.

Nein.
Ja.
Ja.

> Is Adam your brother?

> Yes, he is.

A5 | Look at the pictures and point. | Sieh dir die Bilder an und zeige.

cat /kæt/   Katze
cap /kæp/   Mütze

What have the children got?   Was haben die Kinder?

have got /ˌhæv ˈɡɒt/   haben
also /ˈɔːlsəʊ/   auch
dancing /ˈdɑːnsɪŋ/   Tanzen
I haven't got   ich habe nicht
   /ˌaɪ ˈhævnt ˌɡɒt/

> Dancing is fun!

dog /dɒɡ/   Hund
always /ˈɔːlweɪz/   immer
India /ˈɪndiə/   Indien
at home /ˌæt ˈhəʊm/   zu Hause
cook /kʊk/   Koch / Köchin
play the guitar   Gitarre spielen
   /ˌpleɪ ðə ɡɪˈtɑː/
guitar /ɡɪˈtɑː/   Gitarre
parrot /ˈpærət/   Papagei

Kenny is a *dog*.

I **have got**	ich **habe**
you **have got**	du **hast** / Sie **haben**
he **has got**	er **hat**
she **has got**	sie **hat**
it **has got**	es **hat**
we **have got**	wir **haben**
you **have got**	ihr **habt** / Sie **haben**
they **have got**	sie **haben**

Who has got what?   Wer hat was?

who /huː/   wer; der / die / das

A6   **swim** *(irr)* /swɪm/   schwimmen
all day /ˌɔːl ˈdeɪ/   den ganzen Tag lang
chase /tʃeɪs/   jagen
mouse *(pl **mice**)*   Maus
   /maʊs, maɪs/
nice /naɪs/   schön; nett
learn *(irr)* /lɜːn/   lernen
right away /ˌraɪt‿əˈweɪ/   sofort, gleich

The cat *is chasing* the *mouse*.

A7 | That's me. /ˌðæts ˈmiː/ | Das bin ich.

Watch the video clip.   Gucke dir den Videoclip an.
What has … got?   Was hat … ?
What can you say about …?   Was kannst du über … sagen?
Tell your partner in German.   Sag es deinem Partner / deiner Partnerin
     auf Deutsch.

A8 choose *(irr)* /tʃuːz/   wählen, sich entscheiden

> Draw a picture of your best   Zeichne ein Bild von deinem besten
>   friend and present him or her.   Freund/deiner besten Freundin und stelle
>   ihn oder sie vor.
>
> Make a recording about …   Mache eine Aufnahme über …
> Make a character and present him   Bastele ein Wesen und präsentiere es.
>   or her.

A9 class /klaːs/   Klasse
    puzzle /ˈpʌzl/   Rätsel; *hier:* Puzzle

> Make a puzzle piece about yourself.   Erstelle ein Puzzlestück über dich.

town /taʊn/   Stadt   What's your *age*? =
age /eɪdʒ/   Alter   How old are you?
Germany /ˈdʒɜːməni/   Deutschland
Turkish /ˈtɜːkɪʃ/   Türkisch

> Put the pieces together and make a   Bringe die Teile zusammen und mach ein
>   class puzzle.   Klassenpuzzle.

P1 Practice matters.   *etwa:* Übung macht den
      /ˌpræktɪs ˈmætəz/   Meister.
    explain /ɪkˈspleɪn/   erklären

> Explain what you have to do.   Erkläre, was du tun sollst.
P2   Talk about the friends.   Sprich über die Freunde.

P3 long /lɒŋ/   lang
    short /ʃɔːt/   kurz

> Find the matching forms.   Finde die Formen, die zusammenpassen.
> Write them down in your exercise book. Schreibe sie in dein Heft.
> Be a language detective.   Sei ein Sprachendetektiv/eine
>   Sprachendetektivin.
>
> Look at … again.   Sieh dir noch einmal … an.
> Find sentences with these forms.   Finde Sätze mit diesen Formen.
> Read them out to a partner.   Lies sie einem Partner/einer Partnerin vor.
> Take turns.   Wechselt euch ab.
P4   Read the short forms.   Lies die Kurzformen.
> Write the long forms.   Schreibe die Langformen.
> When do you use "…"?   Wann verwendest du „…"?
P5   You can look at … for help.   Du kannst dir als Hilfe … angucken.

P6 or /ɔː/   oder
    Yes, it is. /ˌjes‿ɪt‿ˈɪz/   Ja.
    Yes, she is. /ˌjes ʃi‿ˈɪz/   Ja.

Words

P7

Listen to the CD and check your questions and answers.	Höre dir die CD an und überprüfe deine Fragen und Antworten.	
Read the text.	Lies den Text.	
Say the words for the pictures.	Sage die Wörter für die Bilder.	
Check your words/ sentences.	Überprüfe deine Wörter/ Sätze.	

I'm	(= I am)	ich bin
you're	(= you are)	du bist
he's	(= he is)	er ist
she's	(= she is)	sie ist
it's	(= it is)	es ist
we're	(= we are)	wir sind
you're	(= you are)	ihr seid
they're	(= they are)	sie sind

B1 area /'eəriə/   Gebiet, Region

Talk about the photos.	Sprich über die Fotos.
What have you got where you live?	Was hast du da, wo du lebst?
What haven't you got?	Was hast du nicht?

we've got (= we have got)   wir haben
/ˌwiːv ˈɡɒt, wiː hæv ˈɡɒt/

we haven't got   wir haben nicht
/ˌwiː ˈhævnt ɡɒt/

We've *got* shops in Notting Hill.

B2

Who is Butterfly?	Wer ist Butterfly?
What do you think the blog is about?	Was glaubst du, worum es in dem Blog geht?
Read the blog.	Lies den Blog.

March /mɑːtʃ/	März	
home /həʊm/	Zuhause; Haus	
now /naʊ/	jetzt	
mum /mʌm/	Mama	
girlfriend /'ɡɜːlˌfrend/	Freundin, Partnerin	
have *(irr)* /hæv/	haben; essen, trinken	
lovely /'lʌvli/	schön	
house /haʊs/	Haus	
saw /sɔː/	sah	

We've got a big *house*.

animal shelter /'ænɪml ˌʃeltə/	Tierheim	
Here I am! /ˌhɪərˌaɪˈæm/	Hier bin ich!	
here /hɪə/	hier; hierher	
miaow /miˈaʊ/	miau	
very /'veri/	sehr	
happy /'hæpi/	glücklich	
know *(irr)* /nəʊ/	wissen, kennen	
our /aʊə/	unsere(r, s)	

Monday	/'mʌndeɪ/	Montag
Tuesday	/'tjuːzdeɪ/	Dienstag
Wednesday	/'wenzdeɪ/	Mittwoch
Thursday	/'θɜːzdeɪ/	Donnerstag
Friday	/'fraɪdeɪ/	Freitag
Saturday	/'sætədeɪ/	Samstag
Sunday	/'sʌndeɪ/	Sonntag

isn't (= is not) /'ɪznt, ɪz ˈnɒt/	ist nicht
garden /'ɡɑːdn/	Garten
yummy /'jʌmi/	lecker
friendly /'frendli/	freundlich
neighbour /'neɪbə/	Nachbar/in
sometimes /'sʌmtaɪmz/	manchmal
cat food /'kæt fuːd/	Katzenfutter

That's *our neighbour*.

they've got (= they have got)   sie haben
  /ˌðeɪv ˈɡɒt, ˌðeɪ hæv ˈɡɒt/
too /tuː/   auch
comment by /ˈkɒment baɪ/   Kommentar von
hope /həʊp/   hoffen
Be careful! /bi ˈkeəfl/   Sei vorsichtig!
careful /ˈkeəfl/   vorsichtig
neighbourhood /ˈneɪbəˌhʊd/   Viertel, Nachbarschaft
want /wɒnt/   wollen
buy (irr) /baɪ/   kaufen
basket /ˈbɑːskɪt/   Korb
market /ˈmɑːkɪt/   Markt
shop /ʃɒp/   Geschäft, Laden
say (irr) /seɪ/   sagen
aren't (= are not) /ˈɑːnt/   sind nicht
sad /sæd/   traurig
tell (irr) /tel/   erzählen

Nur zehn Minuten
Übe die Vokabeln immer nur
5 bis 10 Minuten lang, dafür
aber regelmäßig! Das ist
viel besser, als selten eine
ganze Stunde zu lernen.

This is a *basket*.

happy ≠ sad

What does … say?   Was sagt …?
Find the sentences with "…" in …   Finde die Sätze mit „…" im …
What does the girl talk about?   Worüber spricht das Mädchen?
What is in your area?   Was gibt es in deiner Gegend?
Collect words.   Sammle Wörter.
Ask your partner about his or   Frage deinen Partner/deine Partnerin
  her area.   über seine/ihre Gegend.

---

supermarket /ˈsuːpəˌmɑːkɪt/   Supermarkt
Is there a …? /ˈɪz ðeərˌə/   Gibt es ein/e …?
Are there …? /ˈɑː ðeə/   Gibt es …?
Yes, there is. /ˌjes ðeərˈɪz/   Ja.
No, there isn't.   Nein.
  /ˌnəʊ ðeərˈɪznt/
Yes, there are. /ˌjes ðeərˈɑː/   Ja.
No, there aren't.   Nein.
  /ˌnəʊ ðeərˈɑːnt/
shopping centre /ˈʃɒpɪŋ   Einkaufszentrum
  ˌsentə/
playground /ˈpleɪˌɡraʊnd/   Spielplatz
swimming pool   Schwimmbad
  /ˈswɪmɪŋ puːl/
cinema /ˈsɪnəmə/   Kino

Are there shops in Notting Hill?

Yes, there are.

Is there a *swimming pool* in
your area? – No, *there isn't*.

Talk about …   Sprich über …
Bring a picture and present it.   Bringe ein Bild mit und stelle es vor.

street /striːt/   Straße
quiet /ˈkwaɪət/   leise; ruhig
small /smɔːl/   klein

small ≠ big

Words

Write about …	Schreibe über …

B4 dream /driːm/   Traum

Listen and read about Charlie's dream street.	Höre zu und lies über Charlies Traumstraße.

pond /pɒnd/   Teich
lemonade /ˌleməˈneɪd/   Limonade
fountain /ˈfaʊntɪn/   Brunnen
car /kɑː/   Auto
ride (irr) /raɪd/   fahren; reiten
there /ðeə/   dort, dahin
get (irr) /get/   bekommen
free /friː/   frei; kostenlos
It's great fun. /ˌɪts greɪt ˈfʌn/   Das macht viel Spaß.
fun /fʌn/   Spaß

This is a *fountain*.

I love playing basketball. It's great fun!

What is special about …?	Was ist besonders an …?

B5 **choose** (irr) /tʃuːz/   wählen, sich entscheiden

Draw a picture of … and label it.	Zeichne ein Bild von … und beschrifte es.
Make a collage about …	Mache eine Collage über …
Put your dream streets together to make a dream town.	Bringt eure Traumstraßen zusammen, um eine Traumstadt zu machen.
Look at the words.	Sieh dir die Wörter an.
Put the words together and write them down.	Bringe die Wörter zusammen und schreibe sie auf.

P10 **P12**

computer club /kəmˈpjuːtə ˌklʌb/   Computerklub

P13 boy /bɔɪ/   Junge
girl /gɜːl/   Mädchen

P14 rhyming pair /ˈraɪmɪŋ peə/   Reimpaar

girl   *boy*

Listen to the CD and repeat.	Höre dir die CD an und wiederhole.

stop /stɒp/   aufhören; stehen bleiben   *stop* ≠ start
bring (irr) /brɪŋ/   mitbringen
sing (irr) /sɪŋ/   singen
talk (to) /tɔːk/   sprechen (mit), reden (mit)

Find the rhyming pairs and write them in your exercise book.	Finde die Reimpaare und schreibe sie in dein Heft.
Check your rhyming pairs.	Überprüfe deine Reimpaare.

Theme 2

I

fresh /freʃ/	neu, frisch	
start /stɑːt/	Anfang, Beginn	
Good morning!	Guten Morgen!	
/ˌgʊd ˈmɔːnɪŋ/		

A1

coconut /ˈkəʊkəˌnʌt/	Kokosnuss	
soap /səʊp/	Seife	

soap

> Listen to the song and act it out.   Höre dir das Lied an und spiele es nach.

wash /wɒʃ/	waschen; sich waschen
elbow /ˈelbəʊ/	Ellenbogen
face /feɪs/	Gesicht
neck /nek/	Hals; Nacken
shoulder /ˈʃəʊldə/	Schulter
hair /heə/	Haar
brush one's teeth	sich die Zähne putzen
/ˌbrʌʃ wʌnz ˈtiːθ/	
brush /brʌʃ/	putzen, bürsten
tooth (*pl* **teeth**) /tuːθ, tiːθ/	Zahn
toothpaste /ˈtuːθpeɪst/	Zahnpasta
back /bæk/	Rücken
tummy /ˈtʌmi/	Bauch
chest /tʃest/	Brustkorb
foot (*pl* **feet**) /fʊt, fiːt/	Fuß
knee /niː/	Knie
leg /leg/	Bein

face

You *brush your teeth* with a toothbrush and *toothpaste*.

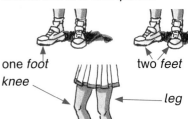

one *foot*   two *feet*

knee   *leg*

A2

hurry (up) /ˌhʌriˈʌp/	sich beeilen

> Look at the comic.   Sieh dir den Comic an.
> Point at body parts and say the words.   Zeige auf Körperteile und sage die Wörter.
> Where is …?   Wo ist …?
> Why does David have to hurry up?   Warum muss sich David beeilen?

o'clock /əˈklɒk/	Uhr
ear /ɪə/	Ohr
dirty /ˈdɜːti/	dreckig, schmutzig
Don't forget …!	Vergiss' nicht …/Vergesst
/ˌdəʊnt fəˈget/	nicht …!
forget (*irr*) /fəˈget/	vergessen
eye /aɪ/	Auge
nose /nəʊz/	Nase
mouth /maʊθ/	Mund
water /ˈwɔːtə/	Wasser
wet /wet/	nass

It's seven *o'clock*.

eyes

nose

mouth

Words

cold /kəʊld/	kalt	*cold* ≠ warm
sea /si:/	Meer, See	
bathroom /ˈbɑ:θˌru:m/	Badezimmer	
quarter /ˈkwɔ:tə/	Viertel	
past /pɑ:st/	nach	It's *quarter past* four.
late /leɪt/	(zu) spät	
just /dʒʌst/	nur, bloß	

Talk about David's morning.	Sprich über Davids Morgen.

still /stɪl/	(immer) noch

Act out the scene.	Spielt die Szene nach.
Tell your partner what to do.	Erzähle deinem Partner/deiner Partnerin, was er/sie tun soll.

A3	mirror /ˈmɪrə/	Spiegel	Who do you see in the *mirror*? – I see Charlie.

Look at the pictures.	Sieh dir die Bilder an.
What does David see in the mirror?	Was sieht David im Spiegel?

long /lɒŋ/	lang	
scary /ˈskeəri/	unheimlich	
haven't got /ˈhævnt gɒt/	habe(n) nicht	
good-looking /ˌgʊdˈlʊkɪŋ/	gut aussehend	
guy /gaɪ/	Kerl, Typ	
tall /tɔ:l/	groß	He is a very *strong* guy!
strong /strɒŋ/	stark	
slim /slɪm/	schlank	
body /ˈbɒdi/	Körper	
short /ʃɔ:t/	kurz	*tall* ≠ *short*
dark /dɑ:k/	dunkel	
Mr /ˈmɪstə/	Herr *(Anrede)*	*Mr* = mister

Which words describe ...?	Welche Wörter beschreiben ...?
Draw a picture of a fantasy character.	Zeichne ein Bild von einer Fantasiegestalt.
Label the body parts.	Beschrifte die Körperteile.
Write a speech bubble.	Schreibe eine Sprechblase.

book /bʊk/	Buch	*book*

Write a text about ...	Schreibe einen Text über ...

A4	grandpa /ˈgrænˌpɑ:/	Opa	
	story /ˈstɔ:ri/	Geschichte	
	bath /bɑ:θ/	Badewanne	*bath*
	bedroom /ˈbedru:m/	Schlafzimmer	

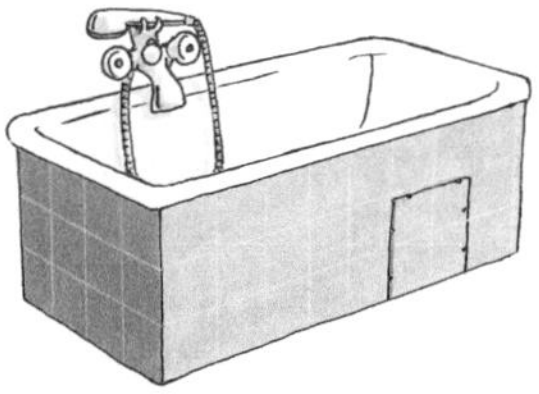

A5	What does the cat do in the story?	Was macht die Katze in der Geschichte?
	What happens to her?	Was passiert ihr?
	Who is who?	Wer ist wer?
	Look at page ... for help.	Sieh dir zur Hilfe Seite ... an.
A6	Describe yourself like this.	Beschreibe dich so.

grey /greɪ/ — grau
curly /ˈkɜːli/ — lockig
sporty /ˈspɔːti/ — sportlich
glasses *(pl)* /ˈglɑːsɪz/ — Brille
freckle /ˈfrekl/ — Sommersprosse

She has *curly* hair and she wears *glasses*.

Write a poem about yourself. — Schreibe ein Gedicht über dich.

smile /smaɪl/ — lächeln
average /ˈævərɪdʒ/ — durchschnittlich

Write about a famous person. — Schreibe über eine berühmte Person.
Read your text but do not say the — Lies deinen Text, sage aber nicht den
  name of the person. — Namen der Person.
Your classmates guess who it is. — Deine Klassenkameraden/Klassen-
 — kameradinnen raten, wer es ist.

A7	**breakfast** /ˈbrekfəst/ — Frühstück	In the picture you can see a
	table /ˈteɪbl/ — Tisch	*table*, a chair and lots of food.

Collect breakfast words. — Sammle Frühstückswörter.
What does David have — Was isst David heute zum
  for breakfast today? — Frühstück?

It's half past eight. — Es ist halb neun.
  /ɪts ˌhɑːf pɑːst ˈeɪt/
half /hɑːf/ — halb
past /pɑːst/ — nach
kitchen /ˈkɪtʃən/ — Küche
you've got (= you have got) — du hast, ihr habt
  /ˈjuːv gɒt, ju ˌhæv ˈgɒt/
only /ˈəʊnli/ — nur, bloß
milk /mɪlk/ — Milch
I don't like ... — Ich mag ... nicht.
  /ˌaɪ ˈdəʊnt laɪk/
every /ˈevri/ — jede (r, s)
I wish it was Sunday! — Ich wünschte, es wäre
  /aɪ ˌwɪʃ ɪt wəz ˈsʌndeɪ/ — Sonntag!
wish /wɪʃ/ — wünschen
cooked /kʊkt/ — gekocht
dad /dæd/ — Papa, Vati

Have you got any sisters?

Yes, but I've only got one. Her name is Charlotte.

David loves a *cooked* Sunday breakfast.

Words

make *(irr)* /meɪk/	machen
baked beans *(pl)*	Bohnen in Tomatensauce
/ˌbeɪkt ˈbiːnz/	
fried egg /ˌfraɪd ˈeg/	Spiegelei
food /fuːd/	Essen
of /əv/	von
sausage /ˈsɒsɪdʒ/	Wurst, Würstchen
extra /ˈekstrə/	zusätzlich
Stop dreaming!	Hör' auf, zu träumen!
/ˌstɒp ˈdriːmɪŋ/	
dream *(irr)* /driːm/	träumen
Hurry up! /ˌhʌriˈʌp/	Beeile dich!
please /pliːz/	bitte
put *(irr)* /pʊt/	setzen, stellen, legen
bowl /bəʊl/	Schüssel, Schale
spoon /spuːn/	Löffel
dishwasher /ˈdɪʃˌwɒʃə/	Spülmaschine
more /mɔː/	mehr; weitere

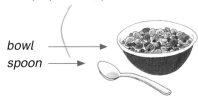

I like *baked beans*, they are my favourite *food*.

sausage

Hurry up David, you're late!

bowl →
spoon →

A8

What do you notice about the verbs?	Was fällt dir an den Verben auf?
Listen to David's dad.	Hör Davids Papa zu.
What do … drink in the morning?	Was trinken … am Morgen?

need /niːd/	brauchen
egg /eg/	Ei
for /fɔː/	für
bean /biːn/	Bohne
what else /ˌwɒtˈels/	was sonst
jam /dʒæm/	Marmelade
a cup of tea /ə ˌkʌp əv ˈtiː/	eine Tasse Tee
tea /tiː/	Tee
us /ʌs/	uns
drink *(irr)* /drɪŋk/	trinken
everything /ˈevriθɪŋ/	alles
know *(irr)* /nəʊ/	wissen, kennen
bacon /ˈbeɪkən/	Schinkenspeck
wait /weɪt/	(er)warten
plate /pleɪt/	Teller
knife *(pl knives)*	Messer
/naɪf, naɪvz/	
fork /fɔːk/	Gabel

In the picture you can see six *eggs*.

I *drink* tea for breakfast. = I have tea for breakfast.

bacon

knife —
fork —

← *cup*
— *spoon*
— *plate*

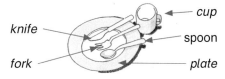

| Find the correct answers. | Finde die richtigen Antworten. |

Yes, he/she does.	Ja.
/ˌjes hiˈ ʃiˈ ˈdʌz/	
No, he/she doesn't.	Nein.
/ˌnəʊ hiˈ ʃiˈ ˈdʌznt/	

Does Vanessa *like* eggs? –
Yes, she does.

What does David have for breakfast on school days and on Sundays?		Was isst David an Schultagen und an Sonntagen zum Frühstück?
Write two lists.		Schreibe zwei Listen.
Write wrong sentences.		Schreibe falsche Sätze.
Your partner corrects them.		Dein Partner / deine Partnerin korrigiert sie.
A9 Say the words in the box and point at the things in the picture.		Sage die Wörter im Kasten und zeige auf die Dinge im Bild.
What is not on the table?		Was ist nicht auf dem Tisch?

cup /kʌp/	Tasse	
A10 healthy /ˈhelθi/	gesund	If you eat a lot of vegetables, you are *healthy*.
morning /ˈmɔːnɪŋ/	Morgen	

Listen to the radio ad.	Hört euch die Anzeige im Radio an.
What is it about?	Worum geht es?
Write and record your own radio ad.	Schreibe deine eigene Radiowerbung und nimm sie auf.
Present ... to the class.	Stelle ... der Klasse vor.
A11 Read Karla's blog entry.	Lies Karlas Blogeintrag.
What does she think about ...?	Was hält sie von ...?

muesli /ˈmjuːzli/ — Müsli
listen (to) /ˈlɪsn/ — zuhören
hear *(irr)* /hɪə/ — hören
that /ðæt/ — dass
honey /ˈhʌni/ — Honig
when /wen/ — wenn; als
sweet /swiːt/ — süß
more /mɔː/ — *hier:* eher

Karla's mum and brother eat *muesli* for breakfast.

Honey is *sweet*.

Who likes what for breakfast?	Wer mag was zum Frühstück?

A12 **time** /taɪm/ — Zeit

What do you find interesting?	Was findest du interessant?
Help out your classmates in German.	Hilf deinen Klassenkameraden / Klassen- kameradinnen auf Deutsch aus.
Talk about breakfast with ...	Sprich mit ... über Frühstück.

eat *(irr)* /iːt/ — essen
before /bɪˈfɔː/ — vor
for breakfast /fə ˈbrekfəst/ — zum Frühstück
at the weekend /ˌæt ðə ˈwiːkend/ — am Wochenende
have breakfast /ˌhæv ˈbrekfəst/ — frühstücken

What do you eat *before* school?
– I always eat cornflakes with milk.
At the weekend David eats a cooked breakfast.

Do a class survey on a poster. | Macht eine Umfrage auf einem Plakat.
Hang it up in your classroom. | Hängt es in eurem Klassenzimmer auf.
What do you like? | Was magst du?
What don't you like? | Was magst du nicht?
What do you have on school days and at the weekend? | Was isst und trinkst du an Schultagen und am Wochenende?

A13 class /klɑːs/   Klasse

Plan a breakfast in your class. | Plant in eurer Klasse ein Frühstück.

write *(irr)* /raɪt/	schreiben	
menu /ˈmenjuː/	Speisekarte	
shopping /ˈʃɒpɪŋ/	Einkaufen; Einkaufs-	
list /lɪst/	Liste	
decide /diˈsaɪd/	entscheiden	
phrase book /ˈfreɪz bʊk/	*Sammlung von Redewendungen*	

Karla and her mum are food *shopping.*

label /ˈleɪbl/	beschriften
take photos /ˌteɪk ˈfəʊtəʊz/	Bilder machen
later /ˈleɪtə/	später
picture dictionary /ˈpɪktʃə ˌdɪkʃənri/	Bildwörterbuch
think of /ˈθɪŋk‿əv/	denken an, sich ausdenken

own /əʊn/	eigene(r, s)
product /ˈprɒdʌkt/	Produkt
during /ˈdjʊərɪŋ/	während
use /juːz/	benutzen

Chocolate is a *product* you can find in a supermarket.

P2

Listen to the words and repeat them. | Höre dir die Wörter an und wiederhole sie.
Which words rhyme? | Welche Wörter reimen sich?
Write them down in pairs. | Schreibe sie paarweise auf.
Listen to the CD and check your pairs. | Höre dir die CD an und überprüfe deine Paare.
Think of more pairs. | Denke dir weitere Paare aus.

P3 weekend /ˌwiːkˈend/   Wochenende   *weekend* = Saturday + Sunday

P4 mime /maɪm/   mimen, pantomimisch darstellen

Unscramble the commands. | Ordne die Befehle.
Tell your partner what to do. | Erzähle deinem Partner/deiner Partnerin, was er/sie tun soll.
Your partner mimes it. | Dein Partner/deine Partnerin stellt es pantomimisch dar.

read *(irr)* /riːd/   lesen

Think of more commands to mime.	Denke dir weitere Befehle aus, die man pantomimisch darstellen kann.

P5 first /fɜːst/ — zuerst

Write about a friend or a family member.	Schreibe über einen Freund/eine Freundin oder ein Familienmitglied.
Look at ... for help.	Sieh dir zur Hilfe ... an.

P6

P7
What does Rajiv do on Sundays? — Was macht Rajiv sonntags?
What doesn't he do? — Was macht er nicht?

work /wɜːk/ — arbeiten

P8 Do you like ...? /ˌduː jə ˈlaɪk/ — Magst du ...?

Ask and answer questions.	Stelle Fragen und beantworte sie.

Yes, I do. /ˌjes‿aɪ ˈduː/ — Ja.
No, I don't. /ˌnəʊ‿aɪ ˈdəʊnt/ — Nein.

P9 scrambled /ˈskræmbld/ — durcheinander gebracht
question /ˈkwestʃn/ — Frage

I	ich
you	du; Sie
he	er
she	sie
we	wir
you	ihr; Sie
they	sie

Unscramble the questions.	Ordne die Fragen.

when /wen/ — wann

Check your questions.	Überprüfe deine Fragen.
Write answers to the questions.	Schreibe Antworten für die Fragen.

B1
classroom /ˈklɑːsˌruːm/ — Klassenzimmer
open /ˈəʊpən/ — öffnen, aufmachen
window /ˈwɪndəʊ/ — Fenster
rubber /ˈrʌbə/ — Radiergummi
in German /ˌɪn ˈdʒɜːmən/ — auf Deutsch
spell (irr) /spel/ — buchstabieren
oh dear /əʊ ˈdɪə/ — oje
funny /ˈfʌni/ — lustig, komisch
pen /pen/ — Stift
It isn't a pen. — Das ist kein Stift.
  /ɪt‿ˈɪznt‿ə ˌpen/
by /baɪ/ — von; mit
hungry /ˈhʌŋgri/ — hungrig
Would you like ...? — Hättest du ... gern?
  /ˌwʊd ju ˈlaɪk/
thanks /θæŋks/ — danke
What time is it? — Wie spät ist es?
  /wɒt‿ˈtaɪm ɪz‿ɪt/

There are two *windows* and a door in the picture.

What is "pen" in German?

It's "Stift". You spell it S-T-I-F-T.

no /nəʊ/   kein(e)

homework /'həʊmwɜːk/   Hausaufgaben

Point at the things in the picture.   Zeige auf die Gegenstände im Bild.

blackboard /'blæk,bɔːd/   Tafel

calendar /'kælɪndə/   Kalender

chair /tʃeə/   Stuhl

pinboard /'pɪn,bɔːd/   Pinnwand

desk /desk/   Schreibtisch

bin /bɪn/   Abfalleimer

map /mæp/   Karte

cupboard /'kʌbəd/   Schrank

sponge /spʌndʒ/   Schwamm

chalk /tʃɔːk/   Kreide

wall /wɔːl/   Wand

clock /klɒk/   Uhr

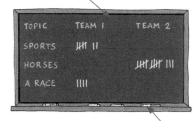

blackboard

sponge   *chalk*

B2

Listen to the dialogues and point to the pupils.   Höre dir die Dialoge an und zeige auf die Schüler/innen.

Then act them out.   Spiele sie dann nach.

Write more dialogues.   Schreibe mehr Dialoge.

B3   Listen to the German teacher.   Höre dem Deutschlehrer zu.

What does he say?   Was sagt er?

Tell your partner in English.   Sag es deinem Partner/deiner Partnerin auf Englisch.

B4   **thing** /θɪŋ/   Ding, Gegenstand

Here is a list of things you can find in a classroom.   Hier ist eine Liste der Gegenstände, die du in einem Klassenzimmer finden kannst.

Listen to the CD and say the words.   Höre dir die CD an und sage die Wörter.

---

pencil /'pensl/   Bleistift

ruler /'ruːlə/   Lineal

pencil case /'pensl ,keɪs/   Federmäppchen

bookshelf (*pl* bookshelves)   Bücherregal
   /'bʊk,ʃelf, 'bʊk,ʃelvz/

schoolbag /'skuːl,bæg/   Schultasche

door /dɔː/   Tür

exercise book   Heft
   /'eksəsaɪz ,bʊk/

overhead projector   Overheadprojektor
   /,əʊvəhed prə'dʒektə/

lunchbox /'lʌntʃbɒks/   Frühstücksdose

I have got a *rubber*, a *pencil* and a *ruler* in my *pencil case*.

exercise book

Write words from the box on cards and label your classroom. — Schreibe Wörter aus dem Kasten auf Karten und beschrifte dein Klassenzimmer.

Look at the box again. — Sieh dir den Kasten noch einmal an.

Make two lists. — Mache zwei Listen.

Write down the plural forms. — Schreibe die Pluralformen.

B5 Put the words from ... in alphabetical order. — Ordne die Wörter aus ... in alphabetischer Reihenfolge.

Make a list of the things in your classroom. — Mache eine Liste der Gegenstände in deinem Klassenzimmer.

B6 Who is she? — Wer ist sie?

Why does ... say "ouch"? — Warum sagt ... „aua"?

Match the sentence parts and write down the sentences. — Ordne die Satzteile einander zu und schreibe die Sätze auf.

ink /ɪŋk/	Tinte	
best /best/	am liebsten	Penny likes green pencils *best*.
inside /ɪnˈsaɪd/	innen, drinnen	
important /ɪmˈpɔːtnt/	wichtig	
out of /ˈaʊt‿əv/	aus	

B7 Look at the clock. — Seht euch die Uhr an.

How do you say the phrases in German? — Was sagst du auf Deutsch für die Ausdrücke?

quarter /ˈkwɔːtə/	Viertel	
half (past) /ˈhɑːf pɑːst/	halb	It's *half past* 12. Es ist halb 1.
to /tʊ/	*hier:* vor	

Ask the time. — Frage nach der Uhrzeit.

What's the time, please? /ˌwɒts ðə ˈtaɪm pliːz/	Wie spät ist es, bitte?	
answer /ˈɑːnsə/	(be)antworten	
ten thirty /ten ˈθɜːti/	zehn Uhr dreißig	
or /ɔː/	oder	
half past ten /ˌhɑːf pɑːst ˈten/	halb elf	*Is it* two twenty? – No, it's half
Is it ...? /ˈɪz‿ɪt/	Ist es ...?	past two.

Now answer these questions. — Beantworte nun diese Fragen.

Then ask your partner. — Frage dann deinen Partner / deine Partnerin.

when /wen/	wann	
get up /ˌget‿ˈʌp/	aufstehen	
in the morning /ˌɪn ðə ˈmɔːnɪŋ/	am Morgen	It's eight o'clock *in the morning*.
leave *(irr)* /liːv/	verlassen; abfahren	

B8 What does ... do when? — Was macht ... wann?

B9 **alphabet** /ˈælfəˌbet/ Alphabet

| Then sing it and clap to it. | Singe dann das Lied und klatsche dazu. |

Come on, sing out with me!

sing out /ˌsɪŋˈaʊt/ laut singen
sing *(irr)* /sɪŋ/ singen
loud /laʊd/ laut
so far /ˌsəʊ ˈfɑː/ bisher
once more /ˌwʌns ˈmɔː/ noch einmal
as /əz/ als; wie
we've done /ˌwiːv ˈdʌn/ wir haben getan

Write a letter on your partner's back with your finger.	Schreibe einen Buchstaben mit deinem Finger auf den Rücken deines Partners / deiner Partnerin.
Spell your name.	Buchstabiere deinen Namen.
Think of a word.	Denk dir ein Wort aus.
Play a spelling game.	Spielt ein Buchstabierspiel.

word /wɜːd/ Wort
right /raɪt/ richtig *right ≠ wrong*

B10 **Here you are.** /ˌhɪə juˈɑː/ Hier, bitte!
cartridge /ˈkɑːtrɪdʒ/ Patrone Use a *dictionary* to
dictionary /ˈdɪkʃənri/ Lexikon find the right word.

B11

Do you speak a language other than English or German?	Sprichst du eine andere Sprache als Englisch oder Deutsch?
Say the alphabet in this language.	Sage das Alphabet in dieser Sprache.
Compare the alphabets.	Vergleicht die Alphabete.

letter /ˈletə/ Buchstabe

Choose a letter.	Wähle einen Buchstaben aus.
Write down all the words you know that start with this letter.	Schreibe alle Wörter auf, die du kennst, die mit diesem Buchstaben anfangen.
You have five minutes.	Du hast fünf Minuten Zeit.
Make a quiz about school things (for example words with missing letters, scrambled words or matching words and pictures).	Mache ein Quiz über Schulgegenstände (zum Beispiel Wörter mit fehlenden Buchstaben, durcheinander gebrachte Wörter oder Wörter und Bilder, die zusammen passen).
Compare your classroom to …	Vergleiche dein Klassenzimmer mit …

B12 poem /ˈpəʊɪm/ Gedicht

| What is special about this classroom? | Was ist besonders an diesem Klassenzimmer? |
| What is the only problem? | Was ist das einzige Problem? |

stairs *(pl)* /steəz/	Treppe
because /bɪˈkɒz/	weil, da
open-air /ˌəʊpənˈeə/	im Freien
grass /grɑːs/	Gras, Wiese
tree /triː/	Baum
flower /ˈflaʊə/	Blume
sky /skaɪ/	Himmel
above /əˈbʌv/	über
do *(irr)* /duː/	tun, machen
fall *(irr)* /fɔːl/	fallen

Draw the open-air classroom.	Zeichne das Klassenzimmer im Freien.
Label it.	Beschrifte es.
Get into groups of four.	Kommt in Vierergruppen zusammen.
Choose one of the verses.	Wähle eine der Strophen aus.
Each pupil learns one line by heart.	Jede/r Schüler/in lernt eine Zeile auswendig.
Present your verse.	Präsentiert eure Strophe.
Make a list of what the open-air classroom hasn't got.	Mache eine Liste der Dinge, die das Klassenzimmer im Freien nicht hat.
What has it got instead?	Was hat es stattdessen?
Use your imagination and describe the classroom in more detail.	Benutze deine Fantasie und beschreibe das Klassenzimmer ausführlicher..

B13 improve /ɪmˈpruːv/   verbessern, verschönern

Look around your classroom.	Seht euch in eurem Klassenzimmer um.
What don't you like?	Was magst du nicht?
Talk about how to improve your classroom.	Sprecht darüber, wie ihr euer Klassenzimmer verschönern könnt.
What changes would you like to make?	Welche Veränderungen würdest du gerne machen?
Make notes.	Mach dir Notizen.
You can use your dictionary.	Du kannst dein Lexikon benutzen.
Now talk in class.	Sprecht nun in der Klasse.
What changes can you really make?	Welche Veränderungen könnt ihr wirklich machen?
Make a plan.	Macht einen Plan.
P11 Find the words and write them down.	Finde die Wörter und schreibe sie auf.

teacher /ˈtiːtʃə/   Lehrer/in

P12 Complete these words with the missing letters.	Vervollständige diese Wörter mit den fehlenden Buchstaben.
Sort the words into the list.	Sortiere die Wörter in die Liste ein.
What have you got in your pencil case?	Was hast du in deinem Federmäppchen?
Make a list.	Mache eine Liste.
P13 What can you see in the picture?	Was kannst du auf dem Bild sehen?
Write it down.	Schreibe es auf.

Words

P14
P15

P16

What do … do when?	Was machen … wann?
Write down the names.	Schreibe die Namen auf.
Listen and check your names.	Höre zu und überprüfe deine Namen.
Ask and answer questions with a partner.	Stellt mit einem Partner / einer Partnerin Fragen und beantwortet sie.

Theme 3

I

free time /friː ˈtaɪm/ — Freizeit

club /klʌb/ — Klub; AG — Badminton and volleyball are *sports*.

sport /spɔːt/ — Sport, Sportart

A1

What's on? /ˌwɒts ˈɒn/ — Was ist los?

What clubs are there at Holland Park School?	Welche AGs gibt es in der Holland Park School?

table tennis /ˈteɪbl ˌtenɪs/ — Tischtennis

lunchtime /ˈlʌntʃtaɪm/ — Mittagszeit, Mittagspause

pm (= post meridiem) /ˌpiːˈem, ˌpəʊst məˈrɪdiəm/ — nachmittags, abends *(nur hinter Uhrzeit zwischen 12 Uhr mittags und Mitternacht)*

gym (= gymnasium) /dʒɪm, dʒɪmneɪziəm/ — Turnhalle

visit /ˈvɪzɪt/ — besuchen

library /ˈlaɪbrəri/ — Bücherei — *library*

sports hall /ˈspɔːts ˌhɔːl/ — Sporthalle

singer /ˈsɪŋə/ — Sänger/in

look for /ˈlʊk fə/ — suchen nach

is looking for /ˌɪz ˈlʊkɪŋ fə/ — sucht nach

after /ˈɑːftə/ — nach

anybody /ˈenibɒdi/ — irgendjemand; jede (r, s)

join /dʒɔɪn/ — mitmachen

cooking /ˈkʊkɪŋ/ — Kochen; Koch-

ready-steady- … /ˌredi ˌstedi ˈ…/ — auf die Plätze, fertig, …

how to /ˈhaʊ tʊ/ — wie man

meal /miːl/ — Mahlzeit, Essen

have something left /ˌhæv sʌmθɪŋ ˈleft/ — etwas übrig haben

sign up /ˌsaɪn ˈʌp/ — sich einschreiben — Anybody can *sign up* for *drama club*.

drama /ˈdrɑːmə/ — Theater

The Lion King /ðə ˈlaɪən ˌkɪŋ/ — *Der König der Löwen*

Mon = **Monday**	Montag
Tue = **Tuesday**	Dienstag
Wed = **Wednesday**	Mittwoch
Thu = **Thursday**	Donnerstag
Fri = **Friday**	Freitag
Sat = **Saturday**	Samstag
Sun = **Sunday**	Sonntag

studio /ˈstjuːdiəʊ/	Atelier, Studio
Mrs /ˈmɪsɪz/	Frau (Anrede)
boy /bɔɪ/	Junge
girl /gɜːl/	Mädchen
for /fɔː/	hier: zu
kickabout /ˈkɪkəˌbaʊt/	Kicken
sports field /ˈspɔːts ˌfiːld/	Sportplatz
football boots (pl)	Fußballschuhe
/ˈfʊtˌbɔːl buːts/	

He's a *boy*.
She's a *girl*.

Listen to the CD and point.	Höre dir die CD an und zeige.
Which posters are the children talking about?	Über welche Poster reden die Kinder?
Which club would you like to join?	Bei welcher AG würdest du gern mitmachen?
What clubs and activities have you got at your school?	Welche AGs und Aktivitäten habt ihr an eurer Schule?

A2

teacher /ˈtiːtʃə/	Lehrer/in

A3

talk about /ˈtɔːkˌəbaʊt/	sprechen über
What are they talking about?	Worüber reden sie?
/ˌwɒt ə ðeɪ ˈtɔːkɪŋ əˌbaʊt/	
which /wɪtʃ/	welche(r, s); was

pupils   *teacher*

A4

cup /kʌp/	Pokal, Cup
cup final /ˈkʌp ˌfaɪnl/	Pokalendspiel, Cupfinale
which /wɪtʃ/	welche(r, s); was
final /ˈfaɪnl/	Endspiel, Finale
versus /ˈvɜːsəs/	gegen
October /ɒkˈtəʊbə/	Oktober
am (= ante meridiem)	morgens, vormittags
/ˌeɪˈem, ˌænti məˈrɪdiəm/	(nur hinter Uhrzeit zwischen Mitternacht und 12 Uhr mittags)

cup

cheer for somebody	jemanden anfeuern
/ˈtʃɪə fə ˌsʌmbədi/	
bring (irr) /brɪŋ/	mitbringen
scarf (pl scarfs or scarves)	Schal
/skɑːf, skɑːfs, skɑːvz/	
family /ˈfæmli/	Familie
hooray /hʊˈreɪ/	hurra
understand (irr)	verstehen
/ˌʌndəˈstænd/	
I don't understand.	Ich verstehe es nicht.
/ˌaɪ ˌdəʊnt ˌʌndəˈstænd/	

They love football and *cheer for* their team. Their *scarves* are red and white.

Sorry, I don't understand.

Words

friendly match /ˈfrendli mætʃ/	Freundschaftsspiel	
talk (to) /tɔ:k/	sprechen (mit), reden (mit)	Karla *is talking to* Charlie.
sports teacher /ˈspɔ:ts ˌti:tʃə/	Sportlehrer/in	
match /mætʃ/	Spiel	
funny /ˈfʌni/	lustig, komisch	A clown is *funny*.

Listen to the children and read along.	Höre den Kindern zu und lies mit.
Help … to understand the poster.	Hilf …, das Poster zu verstehen.
Explain it in German.	Erkläre es auf Deutsch.
What do you think?	Was glaubst du?
Is it true that … ?	Stimmt es, dass … ?
Can … help the girls?	Kann … den Mädchen helfen?

A5

What's up? *(informal)* /ˌwɒtsˈʌp/	Was ist los?	
news *(no pl)* /nju:z/	Neuigkeit; Nachrichten	
goalkeeper /ˈgəʊlˌki:pə/	Tormann/Torfrau	*I'm the goalkeeper on Holland Park boys' team.*
well /wel/	nun	
cold /kəʊld/	Erkältung	
She doesn't like … /ʃi ˈdʌznt ˌlaɪk/	Sie mag … nicht.	
run *(irr)* /rʌn/	laufen, rennen	*See you soon!*
why /waɪ/	warum	
ask /ɑ:sk/	fragen; bitten	
till /tɪl/	bis	
bye /baɪ/	tschüs(s)	*Bye!*
See you soon! /ˌsi: ju: ˈsu:n/	Bis bald!	

What do you know about …?	Was weißt du über …?
Correct the sentences.	Verbessere die Sätze.
… calls …	… ruft … an.
Collect ideas and write a dialogue.	Sammle Ideen und schreibe einen Dialog.
Listen to the radio report.	Höre dir den Radiobericht an.

A6

winner /ˈwɪnə/	Gewinner/in	
the boys' match /ðə ˈbɔɪz ˌmætʃ/	das Spiel der Jungen	The *winner* of *the boys' match* is Hendon School!
score /skɔ:/	Punktestand	
fantastic /fænˈtæstɪk/	fantastisch, super	*fantastic* = super
beat *(irr)* /bi:t/	schlagen	
score /skɔ:/	ein Tor schießen	
scored /skɔ:d/	schoss ein Tor	*Well done* Holland Park girls!
What a …! /ˈwɒt‿ə/	Was für ein/eine …!	The team won the match at the weekend!
well done /ˌwel ˈdʌn/	gut gemacht	

Read the article.	Lies den Artikel.

final /ˈfaɪnl/	letzte(r, s), endgültig	
the girls' match /ðə ˈgɜːlz ˌmætʃ/	das Spiel der Mädchen	Rajiv *is scoring a goal.*
score a goal /ˌskɔːr‿ə ˈgəʊl/	ein Tor schießen	

A7

stadium /ˈsteɪdiəm/	Stadion	Lots of people
chant /tʃɑːnt/	Sprechgesang anstimmen	sing and *chant* in the *stadium.*

Listen and sing along.	Höre zu und sing mit.

a game of football = a football match

game /geɪm/	Spiel
together /təˈgeðə/	zusammen
winning /ˈwɪnɪŋ/	Gewinnen
aim /eɪm/	Ziel
cheer somebody on /ˈtʃɪə ˌsʌmbədiˌˈɒn/	jemanden anfeuern
through /θruː/	durch
'cause (= because) /kɔːz, bɪˈkɒz/	weil, da

cheer somebody on = cheer for somebody

What football songs or chants do you know?	Welche Fußballlieder oder Sprechgesänge kennst du?
What team do you like best?	Welches Team magst du am liebsten?

A8

do *(irr)* /duː/	tun, machen

Play a guessing game.	Spielt ein Ratespiel.
Mime and guess sports.	Stellt eine Sportart pantomimisch dar und erratet sie.

ski /skiː/	Ski fahren, Ski laufen
do gymnastics /ˌduː dʒɪmˈnæstɪks/	Turnen
skate /skeɪt/	inlineskaten
ride a horse /ˌraɪd‿ə ˈhɔːs/	reiten
horse /hɔːs/	Pferd
Yes, I can. /ˌjesˌaɪˌˈkæn/	Ja.
No, I can't. /ˌnəʊˌaɪ ˈkɑːnt/	Nein.

In her free time, Caroline *rides* her *horse.*

Write about what you can and can't do.	Schreibe darüber, was du kannst und nicht kannst.
Where can you do the sports?	Wo kannst du die Sportarten ausüben?

A9

go swimming /ˌgəʊ ˈswɪmɪŋ/	Schwimmen gehen
go skating /ˌgəʊ ˈskeɪtɪŋ/	Skaten gehen
on /ɒn/	auf; an; in
playing field /ˈpleɪɪŋ ˌfiːld/	Sportplatz
sports centre /ˈspɔːtsˌsentə/	Sportcenter

You play hockey on a *playing field.*

Words

tennis court /ˈtenɪs kɔːt/	Tennisplatz	
at home /ˌæt ˈhəʊm/	zu Hause	
in the street /ˌɪn ðə ˈstriːt/	auf der Straße	
gym (= gymnasium)	Turnhalle	
/dʒɪm, dʒɪmneɪziəm/		
mountain /ˈmaʊntɪn/	Berg	

A10 penguin /ˈpeŋgwɪn/   Pinguin

penguin

> Why is the cartoon funny?   Warum ist der Cartoon lustig?

imagine /ɪˈmædʒɪn/   sich etwas vorstellen

A11

What sports do the children do?	Welche Sportarten üben die Kinder aus?
Now watch the video clips and find out.	Schau dir nun die Videoclips an und finde es heraus.
What do you need for your sport?	Was brauchst du für deine Sportart?
Use a dictionary and tell your partner.	Benutze ein Wörterbuch und erzähle es deinem Partner / deiner Partnerin.
What is your favourite sport?	Was ist dein Lieblingssport?
Make a word web.	Erstelle ein Wortnetz.
Read what … write about their sport.	Lies, was … über ihre Sportart schreiben.

A12 (in margin)

shirt /ʃɜːt/	Hemd	*shirt*
captain /ˈkæptɪn/	Mannschaftsführer/in	
own /əʊn/	eigene(r, s)	
practise /ˈpræktɪs/	üben	

> Now write about your sport.   Schreibe nun über deine Sportart.

A13   **present (to)** /priˈzent/   präsentieren

> Choose a sport.   Wählt eine Sportart aus.
> Prepare a presentation.   Bereite eine Präsentation vor.

collect /kəˈlekt/	sammeln	How do you play hockey?
picture /ˈpɪktʃə/	Bild	Can you *teach* me the *rules*,
rule /ruːl/	Regel	please?
action /ˈækʃn/	Handlung	
teach *(irr)* /tiːtʃ/	unterrichten	
another /əˈnʌðə/	noch ein/e	*another* = one more

P2
P3
P4

Write questions and answer them.	Schreibe Fragen auf und beantworte sie.
Match the sentences.	Ordne die Sätze einander zu.
Find the "odd one out".	Finde das Wort, das nicht zu den anderen passt.

P5	What can the children do?	Was können die Kinder machen?
What can't they do?	Was können sie nicht machen?
P6	Find the pairs and write them in your exercise book.	Finde die Paare und schreibe sie in dein Heft.

P7 | page /peɪdʒ/ | Seite

B1

Look at the market scene. | Sieh dir die Marktszene an.

it's (= it is) /ɪts, 'ɪt‿ɪz/ — *hier:* es kostet
pound /paʊnd/ — Pfund
that's (= that is) — *hier:* das kostet
/ðæts, 'ðæt‿ɪz/

> How much is that blue T-shirt?

> It's 6 pounds.

You've got 15 pounds. | Ihr habt 15 Pfund.
What can you buy? | Was kannst du kaufen?
What do the people buy? | Was kaufen die Leute?

B2 | **other** /'ʌðə/ | andere(r, s)

Write the numbers in your exercise book. | Schreibe die Zahlen in dein Heft.
Start with one. | Fange mit eins an.
Listen to the sums and read along / write them down. | Höre dir die Rechenaufgaben an und lies mit / schreibe sie auf.

times /taɪmz/ | multipliziert mit
divided by /dɪ'vaɪdɪd baɪ/ | geteilt durch
equal /'iːkwəl/ | ergeben, sein

B3

Add up all the … numbers. | Addiere alle … Zahlen.
Make up sums for your partner. | Denke dir Rechenaufgaben für deinen Partner / deine Partnerin aus.
Play … in your group. | Spiele … in deiner Gruppe.

B4 | buying /'baɪɪŋ/ | Kaufen
| selling /'selɪŋ/ | Verkaufen | *buying ≠ selling*

Read the dialogue with a partner. | Lies den Dialog mit einem Partner / einer Partnerin.

> Can I help you?

seller /'selə/ | Verkäufer/in
Can I help you? | Kann ich dir / Ihnen helfen?
/ˌkæn‿aɪ 'help juː/
help /help/ | helfen
customer /'kʌstəmə/ | Kunde/Kundin
son /sʌn/ | Sohn
game /geɪm/ | Spiel

customer   *seller*

Words

any /'eni/	(irgend)ein(e)
new ones /'nju: ˌwʌnz/	neue(r, s)
Have you got any new ones? /ˌhæv jə ˌgɒt‿eni 'nju: ˌwʌnz/	Haben Sie irgendwelche neuen?
How about ...? /'haʊ‿əˌbaʊt/	Wie wäre es mit ...?
this one /'ðɪs ˌwʌn/	dieses
look /lʊk/	aussehen
interesting /'ɪntrəstɪŋ/	interessant
How much is it? /ˌhaʊ mʌtʃ 'ɪz‿ɪt/	Wie viel kostet es?
too /tu:/	zu
much /mʌtʃ/	viel
all right /ˌɔ:l 'raɪt/	in Ordnung
call /kɔ:l/	nennen, rufen
I'll take it. /ˌaɪl 'teɪk‿ɪt/	Ich nehme es.
I'll (= I will) /aɪl, 'aɪ wɪl/	
will /wɪl/	werden
take *(irr)* /teɪk/	nehmen, bringen

> I'm looking for a computer game. Have you got any?

How about ...? =
   What about ...?

> 25 pounds for a T-shirt? Oh, that's too much.

take ≠ give

> Practise the dialogue and present it.
> Write your own shopping dialogue.
>
> Übe den Dialog und führe ihn vor.
> Schreibe deinen eigenen Einkaufsdialog.

B5 | **collection** /kə'lekʃn/ | Sammlung |

> Listen and point at the things.
> What things can you collect?
>
> Höre zu und zeige auf die Dinge.
> Welche Dinge kannst du sammeln?

mug /mʌg/	Becher
sticker /'stɪkə/	Aufkleber
toy car /ˌtɔɪ 'ka:/	Spielzeugauto
marble /'ma:bl/	Murmel
cuddly toy /ˌkʌdli 'tɔɪ/	Kuscheltier
card /ka:d/	Karte
stone /stəʊn/	Stein
postcard /'pəʊstˌka:d/	Postkarte, Ansichtskarte
elf *(pl* elves) /elf, elvz/	Elfe
dragon /'drægən/	Drache
seashell /'si:ˌʃel/	Muschel

This is a *marble collection*.

> I collect seashells. What do you collect?

> Interview ...
> Take notes.
>
> Befrage ...
> Mach dir Notizen.

You *take notes* when you listen to somebody and write down parts of what they are saying.
You *make notes* when you write down your own ideas.

how many /haʊ 'meni/	wie viele
model train /ˌmɒdl 'treɪn/	Modelleisenbahn
train /treɪn/	Zug

B6 | at Gillian's (house) /æt‿'dʒɪliənz/ | bei Gillian (zu Hause) |

What do they talk about?　　　　Worüber reden sie?

listen (to) /ˈlɪsn/	zuhören	
at the moment	im Moment	*at the moment* = now
/ˌæt‿ðə ˈməʊmənt/		
turn on /ˌtɜːn‿ˈɒn/	einschalten	
today /təˈdeɪ/	heute	
for /fɔː/	*hier:* nach	
here's (= here is)	hier ist	
/hɪəz. hɪər‿ˈɪz/		
guest /gest/	Gast	
Hi, guys! *(informal)* /ˈhaɪ gaɪz/	Hallo Leute!	
yourself *(pl* **yourselves)**	dich	You look at *yourself* in a mirror.
/jɔːˈself, jɔːˈselvz/		
also /ˈɔːlsəʊ/	auch	*also* = too
describe /dɪˈskraɪb/	beschreiben	
don't say /ˌdəʊnt ˈseɪ/	sag(t) nicht	
something /ˈsʌmθɪŋ/	etwas	She likes to *buy*
buy *(irr)* /baɪ/	kaufen	lots of clothes.
corner shop /ˈkɔːnə ʃɒp/	Tante-Emma-Laden	
story /ˈstɔːri/	Geschichte	
easy /ˈiːzi/	leicht, einfach	
that /ðæt/	der, die, das	
find *(irr)* /faɪnd/	finden	Seashells are *easy* to *find*
beach /biːtʃ/	Strand	on a *beach*.
I don't know. /ˌaɪ ˌdəʊnt ˈnəʊ/	Ich weiß es nicht.	
Over to you. /ˌəʊvə tə ˈjuː/	Jetzt bist du dran.	
special /ˈspeʃl/	besondere(r, s)	
tail /teɪl/	Schwanz	When you listen to the radio,
listener /ˈlɪsnə/	Zuhörer/in	you are a *listener*.
Good luck! /ˌgʊd ˈlʌk/	Viel Glück!	
answer /ˈɑːnsə/	Antwort	*answer* ≠ question
call /kɔːl/	anrufen	

What are the answers?　　　　Was sind die Antworten?
Listen to … and find out.　　　Höre … zu und finde es heraus.

B7
why /waɪ/	warum
telephone /ˈtelɪˌfəʊn/	Telefon

B8

Read the forum.　　　　Lies das Forum.

everyone /ˈevriwʌn/	alle; jeder
next /nekst/	nächste (r, s)
chill *(informal)* /tʃɪl/	sich entspannen, chillen
kind /kaɪnd/	Art, Sorte
play the piano	Klavier spielen
/ˌpleɪ ðə piˈænəʊ/	

The girl *is playing the piano*.

love doing sth /lʌv ˈduːɪŋ ˌsʌmθɪŋ/	etw sehr gern tun
trick /trɪk/	Trick, Kunststück

If you *love doing something* you really like doing it.

What do you like doing after school? — Was machst du gerne nach der Schule?

watch TV /ˌwɒtʃ tiː ˈviː/	Fernsehen gucken
swimming /ˈswɪmɪŋ/	Schwimmen
B9 like best /ˌlaɪk ˈbest/	am liebsten mögen
guinea pig /ˈgɪni ˌpɪg/	Meerschweinchen

This is my *pet* dog Rocky. *He's got* brown *spots*.

B10 spinach /ˈspɪnɪdʒ/	Spinat
spot /spɒt/	Fleck
often /ˈɒfn/	oft, häufig
feed *(irr)* /fiːd/	füttern
him /hɪm/	ihn, ihm
dog food /ˈdɒg fuːd/	Hundefutter
bone /bəʊn/	Knochen
information *(no pl)* /ˌɪnfəˈmeɪʃn/	Informationen

David often *feeds* Kenny *dog food* and gives him a *bone*.

B11
Make a fact file for …	Mache einen Steckbrief über …
Present … to your class.	Stelle … deiner Klasse vor.
Collect words for your hobby and make a word web.	Sammle Wörter für dein Hobby und mache ein Wortnetz.

reading /ˈriːdɪŋ/	Lesen
adventure /ədˈventʃə/	Abenteuer
take out /ˌteɪk ˈaʊt/	*hier:* ausleihen
like doing something /laɪk ˈduːɪŋ ˌsʌmθɪŋ/	etwas gern tun

If you love reading you can go to the library and *take out* lots of books.

I *like meeting* my friends.

Write about … on a piece of paper.	Schreibe auf einem Blatt Papier über …
Now put your products together and make a class exhibition.	Bringt nun eure Produkte zusammen und macht eine Ausstellung in der Klasse.
Are you looking for a new hobby?	Suchst du nach einem neuen Hobby?
Get ideas from your classmates.	Hole dir Ideen von deinen Klassenkameraden/Klassenkameradinnen.

P10 article /ˈaːtɪkl/	Artikel

What do you notice about the "i" sounds?	Was fällt dir am Klang des Buchstabens „i" auf?

P11 classmate /ˈklaːsˌmeɪt/	Klassenkamerad/in
P12 swap /swɒp/	tauschen
P13 opposite /ˈɒpəzɪt/	Gegenteil

"Start" is the *opposite* of "stop".

Match the opposites.	Ordne die Gegensätze einander zu.
Write them in your exercise book.	Schreibe sie in dein Heft.

boring /ˈbɔːrɪŋ/   langweilig

 P14

Find more opposites and ask your partner.	Finde mehr Gegensätze und frage deinen Partner/deine Partnerin.
Write the correct questions for the answers.	Schreibe die richtigen Fragen für die Antworten auf.

at the market /ˌæt‿ðə ˈmaːkɪt/	auf dem Markt	*At the market* Charlie can buy a cool poster for his sister.
in the afternoon /ˌɪn ði‿aːftəˈnuːn/	am Nachmittag	

Theme 4

A1

duvet /ˈduːveɪ/	Steppdecke, Daunendecke	
lamp /læmp/	Lampe	
pillow /ˈpɪləʊ/	Kissen	
cage /keɪdʒ/	Käfig	
shelf *(pl* **shelves)** /ʃelf, ʃelvz/	Regal	There are some books on the *shelf*.
bed /bed/	Bett	This is a *bed*.

A2

Compare the two rooms.	Vergleiche die zwei Zimmer.

Vanessa's room /vəˌnesəz ˈruːm/	Vanessas Zimmer	
Rajiv's room /raːˌdʒiːvz ˈruːm/	Rajivs Zimmer	
tidy /ˈtaɪdi/	ordentlich, aufgeräumt *tidy*	
untidy /ʌnˈtaɪdi/	unordentlich, unaufgeräumt	

A3

Where are the things in …?	Wo sind die Sachen in …?
Listen to … and point.	Höre … zu und zeige.
Tell …	Sag es …

under /ˈʌndə/	unter	*under*
next to /ˈnekst‿tə/	neben	*next to*
behind /bɪˈhaɪnd/	hinter	*behind*
floor /flɔː/	Fußboden	

A4

Write sentences.
Read about ... and find the missing
words.

Schreibe Sätze.
Lies über ... und finde die fehlenden Wörter.

like /laɪk/ — wie

sleep *(irr)* /sliːp/ — schlafen

comfortable /ˈkʌmftəbl/ — bequem

crocodile /ˈkrɒkədaɪl/ — Krokodil

fish (*pl* fish *or* fishes) — Fisch
/fɪʃ, fɪʃ, fɪʃɪz/

spider /ˈspaɪdə/ — Spinne

TV /ˌtiːˈviː/ — Fernseher; Fernsehen

in the middle of — in der Mitte von
/ˌɪn ðə ˈmɪdl̩ əv/

read *(irr)* /riːd/ — lesen

there /ðeə/ — dort, dahin

machine /məˈʃiːn/ — Maschine, Apparat

Emma loves *sleeping*
in her big bed. It is
really *comfortable*.

A dishwasher is a *machine*.

A5

Draw, label and describe ...
Write about ... and let your partner find
the missing words.

Leave out some words and let your
partner find them.
Your partner asks you ten questions
about ...
How much can you remember?

Bring a photo of your room.
Present it.
Interview your partner about ...

Zeichne, beschrifte und beschreibe ...
Schreibe über ... und lass deinen Partner/
deine Partnerin die fehlenden Wörter
finden.
Lass ein paar Wörter aus und lass sie
deinen Partner/deine Partnerin finden.
Dein Partner/deine Partnerin stellt
dir zehn Fragen über ...
An wie viel kannst du dich
erinnern?
Bringe ein Foto von deinem Zimmer mit.
Stelle es vor.
Befrage deinen Partner/deine
Partnerin über ...

A6 **busy** /ˈbɪzi/ — arbeitsreich; beschäftigt

He is *busy* because
he has lots of homework.

Why does Vanessa help her dad with
the shopping?

Warum hilft Vanessa ihrem Papa mit dem
Einkaufen?

Vanessa's dad — Vanessas Papa
/vəˌnesəz ˈdæd/

often /ˈɒfn/ — oft, häufig

do the cooking — kochen
/ˌduː ðə ˈkʊkɪŋ/

sometimes /ˈsʌmtaɪmz/ — manchmal

him /hɪm/ — ihn, ihm

morning /ˈmɔːnɪŋ/ — Morgen

clean /kliːn/ — sauber machen

Gillian often
does the cooking.

never /ˈnevə/	nie, niemals	
do the washing up	abspülen	
/ˌduː ðə ˌwɒʃɪŋ ˈʌp/		
job /dʒɒb/	Aufgabe	
tidy /ˈtaɪdi/	aufräumen	
living room /ˈlɪvɪŋ ˌruːm/	Wohnzimmer	On Saturdays
vacuum /ˈvækjuəm/	staubsaugen	she *vacuums* the floor.
do the shopping	einkaufen	
/ˌduː ðə ˈʃɒpɪŋ/		
usually /ˈjuːʒuəli/	gewöhnlich, normalerweise	

Mime and guess jobs at home.	Stellt eine Aufgabe zu Hause pantomimisch dar und erratet sie.
Who does what on Saturdays?	Wer macht was an den Samstagen?

Vanessa's mum	Vanessas Mama
/vəˌnesəz ˈmʌm/	

A7 life (*pl* lives) /laɪf, laɪvz/ — Leben

What are … talking about?	Worüber reden …?
How do you think they feel?	Wie, glaubst du, fühlen sie sich?
Do boys really have an easy life?	Haben Jungen wirklich ein einfaches Leben?
A8 Unscramble the sentences.	Ordne die Sätze.
Complete the sentences with a word from the box.	Vervollständige die Sätze mit einem Wort aus dem Kasten.

feed *(irr)* /fiːd/	füttern

A9
empty /ˈempti/	ausleeren; ausräumen
take out /ˌteɪk ˈaʊt/	hinausbringen
rubbish /ˈrʌbɪʃ/	Müll

Chores are jobs that you do around the house, like cleaning your room.

A10
chore /tʃɔː/	lästige Aufgabe, Hausarbeit
much /mʌtʃ/	sehr
hurt *(irr)* /hɜːt/	wehtun, schmerzen
head /hed/	Kopf
hard /hɑːd/	hart, anstrengend
work hard /ˌwɜːk ˈhɑːd/	schwer arbeiten

Oh, I have lots of homework to do. It hurts my head!

A11 week /wiːk/ — Woche

7 days = one *week*

afternoon /ˌɑːftəˈnuːn/	Nachmittag
ballet /ˈbæleɪ/	Ballett
wait for /ˈweɪt fɔː/	warten auf
get *(irr)* /get/	bekommen
dance /dɑːns/	tanzen
evening /ˈiːvnɪŋ/	Abend
them /ðem/	sie, ihnen
dance /dɑːns/	Tanz
step /step/	Schritt

They are practising some *dance steps*.

be good fun /bi: ˌgʊd ˈfʌn/	viel Spaß machen
president /ˈprezɪdənt/	Vorsitzende/r
member /ˈmembə/	Mitglied
article /ˈɑːtɪkl/	Artikel
magazine /ˌmægəˈziːn/	Zeitschrift
on /ɒn/	hier: über
science /ˈsaɪəns/	Naturwissenschaft
boring /ˈbɔːrɪŋ/	langweilig
look after somebody /ˌlʊkˈɑːftə ˌsʌmbədi/	sich um jemanden kümmern
back /bæk/	zurück

Reimwörter

Manche Wörter kannst du dir gut merken, wenn du sie gemeinsam mit anderen, die ähnlich ausgesprochen werden, lernst. Du wirst aber merken, dass sie nicht immer gleich geschrieben werden.

read – need   shoe – do

A12

What do you think his favourite days are?	Was sind deiner Meinung nach seine Lieblingstage?
Why?	Warum?
What do you do on Mondays, ...?	Was machst du montags, ...?
Think about jobs at home and activities.	Denke an Aufgaben im Haushalt und Aktivitäten.
You can make a collage, draw pictures, write a text, make a recording, ...	Ihr könnt eine Collage machen, Bilder zeichnen, einen Text schreiben, eine Aufnahme machen, ...
Present your product to the class.	Stelle dein Produkt der Klasse vor.

draw *(irr)* /drɔː/	zeichnen

P4
P5

Unscramble the texts about ...	Entwirre die Texte über ...
What does ... do on Sundays?	Was macht ... sonntags?
What doesn't she do?	Was macht sie nicht?
What do you do on Sundays?	Was machst du sonntags?
What don't you do?	Was machst du nicht?

P6

Look at ... again and complete the sentences with the words in the box.	Sieh dir noch einmal ... an und vervollständige die Sätze mit den Wörtern aus dem Kasten.

P9

Write down who the things or animals belong to.	Schreibe auf, wem die Dinge oder Tiere gehören.

Schwierige Wörter

Wenn dir manche Wörter Schwierigkeiten bereiten, schreibe sie auf ein großes Blatt Papier und markiere die Stelle, die du schwierig findest. Hänge das Papier in deinem Zimmer auf.

B1

weekend /ˌwiːkˈend/	Wochenende
fun /fʌn/	Spaß
visit /ˈvɪzɪt/	Besuch
sleepover /ˈsliːpˌəʊvə/	Übernachtung
second /ˈsekənd/	zweite (r, s)
have to /ˈhæv tə/	müssen
first /fɜːst/	zuerst
hang on /ˌhæŋ ˈɒn/	warten
ghost /gəʊst/	Geist, Gespenst
turn out /ˌtɜːn ˈaʊt/	ausschalten

hang on = wait
This is a *ghost*.

Theme 4

light /laɪt/	Licht	I think ghost stories
spooky /ˈspuːki/	schaurig, unheimlich	are very *spooky*.
chocolate /ˈtʃɒklət/	Schokolade	
pick somebody up	jemanden abholen	
/ˌpɪk ˌsʌmbədiˈʌp/		
station /ˈsteɪʃn/	U-Bahn-Station, Bahnhof	
be one's turn /ˌbiː wʌnz ˈtɜːn/	an der Reihe sein	
It's my turn. /ˌɪts ˈmaɪ tɜːn/	Ich bin dran.	
dinner /ˈdɪnə/	Abendessen	
sound /saʊnd/	klingen, sich anhören	

> *Now it's my turn.*

Are the sentences true or false? Sind die Sätze richtig oder falsch?
Correct the sentences. Korrigiere die Sätze.

---

talk about /ˈtɔːk_əˌbaʊt/	sprechen über
watch /wɒtʃ/	beobachten, ansehen

B2

Act out the dialogue with your partner. Spielt den Dialog mit deinem Partner/deiner Partnerin nach.

Make your own dialogue. Mache deinen eigenen Dialog.

Make a list of things you can do at the weekend. Mache eine Liste von Dingen, die man am Wochenende machen kann.

B3

way /weɪ/	Weg; Art, Weise	Gillian usually *takes the tube*
take the tube /ˌteɪk ðə ˈtjuːb/	die U-Bahn nehmen	to Vanessa's house.
the tube *(informal)* /ðə ˈtjuːb/	(Londoner) U-Bahn	
because /bɪˈkɒz/	weil, da	
walk /wɔːk/	gehen	Look at *line* number 5 of the
line /laɪn/	Linie; Zeile	poem. There are many *lines* in
change /tʃeɪndʒ/	wechseln; umsteigen	the London tube system.
get out /ˌget_ˈaʊt/	aussteigen	

B5

Find the things in the picture. Finde die Gegenstände auf dem Bild.
Show me … Zeige mir …

cake /keɪk/	Kuchen	a birthday *cake*
crisps *(pl)* /krɪsps/	Chips	
vegetable /ˈvedʒtəbl/	Gemüse	*Vegetables* are very healthy.
biscuit /ˈbɪskɪt/	Keks	
fruit /fruːt/	Frucht, Obst	
between /bɪˈtwiːn/	zwischen	*between*
in front of /ɪn ˈfrʌnt_əv/	vor	*in front of*

B6

Listen and point at …. Höre zu und zeige auf …

shopkeeper /ˈʃɒpˌkiːpə/	Ladeninhaber/in	Excuse me, I can't find the milk.
over there /ˌəʊvə ˈðeə/	dort (drüben)	– Oh, it's *over there*.
Is there …? /ˈɪz ðeər/	Gibt es …?	
anything else /eniˌθɪŋ_ˈels/	noch etwas	

how much /haʊ ˈmʌtʃ/	wie viel	*How much is the cheese?*
those *(pl of that)* /ðəʊz/	diese, jene	*Wie viel kostet der Käse?*
p (= penny, pence)	Pence	*How much are the cakes?*
/piː, ˈpeni, pens/		*Wie viel kosten die Kuchen?*
each /iːtʃ/	jede (r, s)	
could /kʊd/	könnte, könntest, könntet, könnten	
Of course! /əv ˈkɔːs/	Natürlich!	*Could I have two apples, please?*
Here you go. /ˌhɪə ju ˈgəʊ/	Hier, bitte!	– Of course, *here you go.*
Anything else?	Sonst noch etwas?, Darf	
/eni,θɪŋ ˈels/	es noch etwas sein?	*So, you have eggs, orange*
everything /ˈevriθɪŋ/	alles	*juice and sausages. That's 4*
altogether /ˌɔːltəˈgeðə/	insgesamt	*pounds 20 altogether, please.*
change /tʃeɪndʒ/	Wechselgeld	

Read the dialogue in groups of three.	Lest den Dialog in Dreiergruppen.
Use props and gestures.	Benutzt Requisiten und Gesten.
Write your own shopping dialogue in your group and act it out.	Schreibe deinen eigenen Einkaufsdialog in deiner Gruppe und spielt ihn nach.
What else do they buy?	Was kaufen sie sonst noch?

B7

B8 tongue twister /ˈtʌŋ ˌtwɪstə/ Zungenbrecher

Listen to the tongue twister and say it.	Höre dir den Zungenbrecher an und sprich ihn.
Explain in German the difference between …	Erkläre auf Deutsch den Unterschied zwischen …

B9

Nice to meet you. /ˌnaɪs tə ˈmiːt jə/	Schön, dich / Sie zu treffen.	
How are you? /ˌhaʊ ˈɑː ˌjʊ/	Wie geht es dir? / Wie geht es Ihnen?	*How are you?*
I'm fine, thanks. /aɪm ˈfaɪn ˌθæŋks/	Es geht mir gut, danke.	
Don't call me …! /ˌdəʊnt ˈkɔːl me/	Nenn' mich nicht …!	
mister /ˈmɪstə/	Herr	*mister,* Mr ≠ Mrs
fine /faɪn/	in Ordnung, gut	
mean *(irr)* /miːn/	meinen	
anyway /ˈeniweɪ/	jedenfalls	
… isn't it? /ˈɪznt ˌɪt/	… nicht wahr?	*It's cold today, isn't it?*
Would you like …? /ˌwʊd ju ˈlaɪk/	Hättest du gern …? / Hättet ihr gern …?	
hot chocolate /hɒt ˈtʃɒklət/	(heißer) Kakao	*They like hot chocolate.*
hungry /ˈhʌŋgri/	hungrig	
special /ˈspeʃl/	*hier:* Spezialgericht	
tonight /təˈnaɪt/	heute Abend	
Why don't you …? /ˈwaɪ ˌdəʊnt juː/	Warum … du nicht …?	

	Work in groups of four.	Arbeitet in Vierergruppen.
	Two of you play the …	Zwei von euch spielen die …
	Introduce … to your parents.	Stelle … deinen Eltern vor.
B10	What do you remember about Gillian and Vanessa's plans for the evening?	An welche Pläne für den Abend von Vanessa und Gillian erinnerst du dich?
	Compare with your notes.	Vergleicht mit euren Notizen.
	What is right?	Was ist richtig?
	Listen again and take notes.	Höre noch einmal zu und mach dir Notizen.
	Correct the sentences.	Verbessere die Sätze.

ghost story /ˈgəʊst ˌstɔːri/   Gespenstergeschichte

thank /θæŋk/   danken, sich bedanken

switch on /ˌswɪtʃˈɒn/   einschalten   *switch on* = turn on

torch (*pl* **torches**)   Taschenlampe   This is a *torch*.
/tɔːtʃ, ˈtɔːtʃɪz/

kind /kaɪnd/   Art, Sorte

nerves (*pl*) /nɜːvz/   Nerven

B11   voice /vɔɪs/   Stimme

dark /dɑːk/   Dunkelheit

Record spooky words and sounds.	Nimm unheimliche Wörter und Geräusche auf.
What is the story about?	Worum geht es in der Geschichte?
What do you like about the story?	Was magst du an der Geschichte?
Write an ending to the story.	Schreibe ein Ende für die Geschichte.

B12   **fun** /fʌn/   lustig, witzig   *fun* = funny

Plan a fun evening with …	Plane einen lustigen Abend mit …
Present your ideas on a piece of paper.	Stelle deine Ideen auf einem Blatt Papier vor.
Collect your ideas to make a book.	Sammelt eure Ideen, um ein Buch zu machen.

think about /ˈθɪŋk_əˌbaʊt/   nachdenken über

P11   plan /plæn/   planen

This is my favourite kind of drink!

Write down questions.	Schreibe Fragen auf.

P12   drink /drɪŋk/   Trinken; Getränk

Write down the words in alphabetical order.	Schreibe die Wörter in alphabetischer Reihenfolge auf.
Write down where Ruby is.	Schreibe auf, wo Ruby ist.
Sort the dialogues.	Sortiere die Dialoge.

P13
P14

P15   price /praɪs/   Preis

P17   Listen to … and repeat the words.   Höre dir … an und wiederhole die Wörter.

Theme 5

I   day by day /ˌdeɪ baɪ ˈdeɪ/   Tag für Tag

A1

Now watch the video clip.	Schau dir nun den Videoclip an.
What do the children talk about?	Worüber reden die Kinder?

A2   **tie** /taɪ/   Krawatte   We have to wear a *tie* to school.

Where do Gillian and David want to go?	Wohin wollen Gillian und David gehen?

history /ˈhɪstri/	Geschichte	
last /lɑːst/	letzte(r, s)	first ≠ *last*
lesson /ˈlesn/	Stunde, Unterricht	
subject /ˈsʌbdʒɪkt/	Schulfach	
maths /mɑːθs/	Mathe	*maths*
terrible /ˈterəbl/	schrecklich	
lunch /lʌntʃ/	Mittagessen	
art /ɑːt/	Kunst	Mr King is our *art* teacher.
by the way /ˌbaɪ ðə ˈweɪ/	übrigens	
You're lucky. /ˌjɔː ˈlʌki/	Du bist ein Glückspilz.	
You're right about that.	Damit hast du recht.	
/jɔː ˈraɪt əˌbaʊt ˌðæt/		I'm good at maths
better /ˈbetə/	besser	but I'm *better* at English.
I'd rather ... /ˌaɪd ˈrɑːðə/	Ich würde lieber ...	
at all /ətˈɔːl/	überhaupt	
You're right. /jɔː ˈraɪt/	Du hast recht.	
miss /mɪs/	verpassen	
I missed lunch.	Ich habe das Mittagessen	
/aɪ ˌmɪst ˈlʌntʃ/	verpasst.	You can buy and eat food in
canteen /kænˈtiːn/	Kantine, Mensa	the school *canteen*.
for lunch /fɔː ˈlʌntʃ/	zum Mittagessen	

What is the best thing about Fridays?	Was ist das Beste an Freitagen?
Tell your class what you like about ...	Erzähle deiner Klasse, was du an ... magst.
What does ... like about ...?	Was mag ... an ...?
Copy Gillian's timetable for Friday and fill in the subjects.	Schreibe Gillians Stundenplan für Freitag ab und trage die Fächer ein.
When is it?	Wann findet es statt?
What does ... like?	Was mag ...?
What doesn't ... like?	Was mag ... nicht?
Collect information about ...	Sammle Informationen über ...
Think about ...	Denke an ...
Then write about ...	Schreibe dann über ...

A3   **timetable** /ˈtaɪmteɪbl/   Stundenplan

Words

> Point at these subjects in David's timetable.
>
> Zeige auf diese Fächer in Davids Stundenplan.

year /jɪə/ — Schuljahr, Klasse
registration /ˌredʒɪ'streɪʃn/ — *Überprüfung der Anwesenheit*
assembly /ə'sembli/ — (Schüler)versammlung
ICT (= Information and Communication Technology) /ˌaɪˌsiː'tiː, ˌɪnfə'meɪʃn̩ən kəˌmjuːnɪ'keɪʃn tek'nɒlədʒi/ — Informationstechnologie, IT

My favourite subject is *ICT*.

RE (= religious education) /ˌaːr'iː, reˌlɪdʒəs edjʊ'keɪʃn/ — Religion
geography /dʒi'ɒgrəfi/ — Erdkunde
PE (= physical education) /ˌpiː'iː, ˌfɪzɪkl̩ edjʊ'keɪʃn/ — Sport

In *PE* we play football and tennis.

a /ə/ — pro, in/im
first /fɜːst/ — erste (r, s)
second /'sekənd/ — zweite (r, s)
third /θɜːd/ — dritte (r, s)
fourth /fɔːθ/ — vierte (r, s)
fifth /fɪfθ/ — fünfte (r, s)

We have 26 lessons *a* week.

← *first*

> Write your timetable in English.
> Make a word web of school words.
>
> Schreibe deinen Stundenplan auf Englisch.
> Erstelle ein Wortnetz von Schulwörtern.

end /end/ — enden; beenden — *end ≠ start*

> Compare your timetable with David's timetable.
>
> Vergleiche deinen Stundenplan mit Davids Stundenplan.

A4

> When do the things happen – before or after school?
>
> Wann passieren die Dinge – vor oder nach der Schule?
>
> Put the pictures in the correct order.
>
> Bringe die Bilder in die richtige Reihenfolge.

go by bus /ˌgəʊ baɪ 'bʌs/ — mit dem Bus fahren
walk the dog /ˌwɔːk ðə 'dɒg/ — den Hund ausführen

He is *walking the dog*.

> Listen to Gillian on her way to school.
> When is the next bus?
> What does she decide?
>
> Höre Gillian auf dem Weg zur Schule zu.
> Wann kommt der nächste Bus?
> Wofür entscheidet sie sich?

to /tʊ/ — bis
about /ə'baʊt/ — ungefähr

A5 **half past six** /ˌhɑːf pɑːst 'sɪks/ — halb sieben
juice /dʒuːs/ — Saft

orange *juice*

half past seven /ˌhaːf paːst ˈsevn/	halb acht	
night /naɪt/	Nacht, Abend	It's dark at *night*.

Sing the song and act it out. — Singe das Lied und spiele es nach.
Act out your day. — Spielt euren Tag nach.
Mime and guess. — Stellt es pantomimisch dar und ratet.
Write down all the questions in the song. — Schreibt alle Fragen in dem Lied auf.
Then write answers about your day. — Schreibe dann Antworten über deinen Tag.
Ask your partner about … — Frage deinen Partner/deine Partnerin über …
Write more verses. — Schreibe weitere Strophen.

A6

Make a fact file about … — Mache einen Steckbrief über …
What do you do/need? — Was machst du/brauchst du?
Who is your teacher? — Wer ist dein/e Lehrer/in?
Make notes about your dream subject and give a short talk on it. — Mach dir Notizen über dein Traumfach und halte einen kurzen Vortrag darüber.
Write your dream timetable and present it to your classmates. — Schreibe deinen Traumstundenplan und präsentiere ihn deinen Klassenkameraden.
You can think of new subjects if you want to. — Du kannst dir neue Fächer ausdenken, wenn du möchtest.

A7

take part in /ˌteɪk ˈpaːt̬ɪn/	teilnehmen an	Why not *take part in* the
eTwinning /ˈiːˌtwɪnɪŋ/	*Schulpartnerschaft per Email*	*eTwinning project?* – OK, that sounds like a good idea.
project /ˈprɒdʒekt/	Projekt	
world /wɜːld/	Welt	

Read the email they get from … — Lies die Email, die sie von … bekommt.
What are Karlotta's favourites? — Was mag Karlotta am liebsten?

Denmark /ˈdenmaːk/	Dänemark	
by bike /ˌbaɪ ˈbaɪk/	mit dem Fahrrad	Gillian is
by bus /ˌbaɪ ˈbʌs/	mit dem Bus	going *by bus*.
to /tʊ/	*hier:* bis	
June /dʒuːn/	Juni	
finish /ˈfɪnɪʃ/	beenden, enden	*finish* = end
pupil /ˈpjuːpl/	Schüler/in	
work /wɜːk/	arbeiten	
photography /fəˈtɒɡrəfi/	Fotografie	
course /kɔːs/	Kurs	I often meet my friends at the
youth club /ˈjuːθ ˌklʌb/	Jugendzentrum	*youth club* after school.

What does … write about in her email? — Worüber schreibt … in ihrer Email?
Talk about it in German. — Sprecht auf Deutsch darüber.
Write an email about your school day. — Schreibe eine Email über deinen Schultag.

A8

school day /ˈskuːl ˌdeɪ/	Schultag	Karlotta's *school day* starts at 9.

What is your dream school day like?	Wie ist dein Traumschultag?
You can draw pictures, make a poster or make a recording.	Du kannst Bilder malen, ein Poster oder eine Aufnahme machen.
These questions can help you.	Diese Fragen können dir helfen.

get to school /ˌget̬ tə ˈskuːl/   zur Schule kommen

Present your dream school day.	Stelle deinen Traumschultag vor.
Here is an example.	Hier ist ein Beispiel.
You can make notes like this.	Du kannst so Notizen machen.

fly *(irr)* /flaɪ/   fliegen
by helicopter /ˌbaɪ ˈheliˌkɒptə/ mit dem Hubschrauber   This is a *helicopter*.

You can listen to an example of a presentation on the CD.	Du kannst dir auf der CD ein Beispiel einer Präsentation anhören.
P2 What do you notice?	Was fällt dir auf?
P3 Choose at least five words and use them to write sentences.	Wähle mindestens fünf Wörter aus und verwende sie, um Sätze zu bilden.
P5 Find the headwords.	Finde die Oberbegriffe.
Write down more word groups.	Schreibe noch mehr Wortgruppen auf.
Your partner has to …	Dein Partner / deine Partnerin muss …
P6 Draw this table in your exercise book.	Zeichne diese Tabelle in dein Heft.
Add more subjects.	Füge weitere Fächer hinzu.
Report to your partner.	Berichte deinem Partner / deiner Partnerin.
P7 Complete the text with the correct forms of the verbs in the box.	Vervollständige den Text mit den richtigen Formen der Verben im Kasten.

home /həʊm/   nach Hause
salad /ˈsæləd/   Salat   Let's make a
for dinner /fə ˈdɪnə/   zum Abendessen   *salad for dinner*!

B1 **Happy birthday (to you)!**   Herzlichen Glückwunsch
    /ˌhæpi ˈbɜːθdeɪ (tʊ ˈjuː)/   zum Geburtstag!

| Stand up when you hear your birthday month. | Stehe auf, wenn du deinen Geburtstags- monat hörst. |

B2 **birthday** /ˈbɜːθdeɪ/   Geburtstag
    is planning /ˌɪz ˈplænɪŋ/   er/sie/es plant (gerade)
    invite /ɪnˈvaɪt/   einladen

What does … check on the Internet?	Was guckt … im Internet nach?
What do … decide?	Was entscheiden …?
B3 Who is at the party?	Wer ist auf der Party?

aunt /ɑːnt/   Tante   The boy
uncle /ˈʌŋkl/   Onkel   *is sitting*
sit *(irr)* /sɪt/   sitzen   on the sofa.

Words

magic trick /ˌmædʒɪk ˈtrɪk/	Zaubertrick	
nobody /ˈnəʊbədi/	niemand, keiner	everyone, everybody ≠ *nobody*
arrive /əˈraɪv/	ankommen	
come in /ˌkʌmˈɪn/	hereinkommen	
Come in. /ˌkʌmˈɪn/	Komm(t) herein!	
present /ˈpreznt/	Geschenk	
Nice to see you.	Schön, euch zu sehen.	
/ˌnaɪs tə ˈsiː ˌjə/		
get *(irr)* /get/	*hier:* bringen	
just /dʒʌst/	gerade	
ring *(irr)* /rɪŋ/	klingeln, läuten	
answer the phone	ans Telefon gehen	
/ˌɑːnsə ðə ˈfəʊn/		

I'm coming. I'm just putting my clothes into the wardrobe.

When the phone *rings* and you are home, you *answer the phone*.

Say what the people are doing. Sage, was die Leute machen.

In picture number … Auf Bild Nummer …
/ˌɪn ˈpɪktʃə ˌnʌmbə/

Make an ABC of … Mach ein Alphabet mit …

balloon /bəˈluːn/ Luftballon These are *balloons*.

Right or wrong? Richtig oder falsch?
Write the end of the story. Schreibe das Ende der Geschichte.

on the phone /ˌɒn ðə ˈfəʊn/	am Telefon	Look, she is *on the phone*.
happen /ˈhæpən/	geschehen, passieren	
phone call /ˈfəʊn kɔːl/	Telefonanruf	

B4
B5

Listen and answer the questions. Höre zu und beantworte die Fragen.
What is everyone doing? Was macht jeder gerade?

pour /pɔː/	gießen, eingießen	The girl *is pouring*
drink /drɪŋk/	Trinken; Getränk	a *drink*.

B6

Write down what the people are doing. Schreibe auf, was die Leute gerade machen.
What do the children/do you like about Was mögen die Kinder/magst du an
  birthdays? Geburtstagen?

B7 **family tree** /ˌfæmli ˈtriː/ Familienstammbaum

Point at these people. Zeige auf diese Leute.

mother /ˈmʌðə/	Mutter
grandparent	Großelternteil
/ˈɡrænˌpeərənt/	
father /ˈfɑːðə/	Vater

father   *mother*

Can you say it the other way round, too? Kannst du es auch andersherum sagen?

woman (pl **women**) /ˈwʊmən, ˈwɪmɪn/	Frau
man (pl **men**) /mæn, men/	Mann
daughter /ˈdɔːtə/	Tochter
grandmother /ˈɡrænˌmʌðə/	Großmutter
granddaughter /ˈɡrænˌdɔːtə/	Enkelin
wife (pl **wives**) /waɪf, waɪvz/	Ehefrau
niece /niːs/	Nichte
son /sʌn/	Sohn
grandfather /ˈɡrænˌfaːðə/	Großvater
grandson /ˈɡrænˌsʌn/	Enkel
husband /ˈhʌzbənd/	Ehemann
nephew /ˈnefjuː/	Neffe

Jan	= **January** /ˈdʒænjuəri/	Januar
Feb	= **February** /ˈfebruəri/	Februar
Mar	= **March** /maːtʃ/	März
Apr	= **April** /ˈeɪprəl/	April
May	= **May** /meɪ/	Mai
Jun	= **June** /dʒuːn/	Juni
Jul	= **July** /dʒʊˈlaɪ/	Juli
Aug	= **August** /ˈɔːɡəst/	August
Sep	= **September** /sepˈtembə/	September
Oct	= **October** /ɒkˈtəʊbə/	Oktober
Nov	= **November** /nəʊˈvembə/	November
Dec	= **December** /dɪˈsembə/	Dezember

Write sentences for your partner to check.
Make a quiz for your class about …

Schreibe Sätze, die dein Partner/deine Partnerin überprüfen soll.
Mache für deine Klasse ein Quiz über …

wrong /rɒŋ/	falsch
whose /huːz/	wessen
first name /ˈfɜːst ˌneɪm/	Vorname

wrong ≠ right, correct
Whose first name starts with a 'G'? – Gillian's.

B8 Present the words for family members in that language.
Stelle die Wörter für Familienmitglieder in dieser Sprache vor.

in this photo /ˌɪn ðɪs ˈfəʊtəʊ/	auf diesem Foto
photo /ˈfəʊtəʊ/	Foto

This is Emma's school *photo*.

Choose photos and present them.
Draw your own family tree.

Suche Fotos aus und zeige sie.
Zeichne deinen eigenen Familienstammbaum.

B9

sixth /sɪksθ/	sechste (r, s)
seventh /ˈsevnθ/	siebte (r, s)
eighth /eɪtθ/	achte (r, s)
ninth /naɪnθ/	neunte (r, s)
tenth /tenθ/	zehnte (r, s)
eleventh /ɪˈlevnθ/	elfte (r, s)
twelfth /twelfθ/	zwölfte (r, s)
thirteenth /ˌθɜːˈtiːnθ/	dreizehnte (r, s)
fourteenth /ˌfɔːˈtiːnθ/	vierzehnte (r, s)
fifteenth /ˌfɪfˈtiːnθ/	fünfzehnte (r, s)
sixteenth /ˌsɪksˈtiːnθ/	sechzente (r, s)
seventeenth /ˌsevnˈtiːnθ/	siebzehnte (r, s)
eighteenth /ˌeɪˈtiːnθ/	achtzehnte (r, s)
nineteenth /ˌnaɪnˈtiːnθ/	neunzehnte (r, s)
twentieth /ˈtwentiəθ/	zwanzigste (r, s)

twenty-first /ˌtwentiˈfɜːst/	einundzwanzigste (r, s)
twenty-second /ˌtwentiˈsekənd/	zweiundzwanzigste (r, s)
twenty-third /ˌtwentiˈθɜːd/	dreiundzwanzigste (r, s)
twenty-fourth /ˌtwentiˈfɔːθ/	vierundzwanzigste (r, s)
twenty-fifth /ˌtwentiˈfɪfθ/	fünfundzwanzigste (r, s)
twenty-sixth /ˌtwentiˈsɪksθ/	sechsundzwanzigste (r, s)
twenty-seventh /ˌtwentiˈsevnθ/	siebenundzwanzigste (r, s)
twenty-eighth /ˌtwentiˈeɪtθ/	achtundzwanzigste (r, s)
twenty-ninth /ˌtwentiˈnaɪnθ/	neunundzwanzigste (r, s)
thirtieth /ˈθɜːtiəθ/	dreißigste (r, s)
thirty-first /ˌθɜːtiˈfɜːst/	einunddreißigste (r, s)

Ask each other.	Fragt einander.
Make a birthday calendar for your class.	Mache einen Geburtstagskalender für deine Klasse.

B10 grandma /ˈɡrænˌmɑː/   Oma   *grandma* = grandmother

Listen to the poem and read along.	Höre dir das Gedicht an und lies mit.
What is the poem about?	Worum geht es in dem Gedicht?
What problem is the person in the poem talking about?	Über welches Problem spricht die Person in dem Gedicht?
What should the person do if Grandma asks?	Was sollte die Person machen, wenn Oma fragt?
Lie?	Lügen?
Tell the truth?	Die Wahrheit sagen?

shouldn't (= should not) /ˈʃʊdnt, ˈʃʊd nɒt/	sollte/solltest/sollten/ solltet nicht	You *shouldn't* be late for school.
lie /laɪ/	lügen	When you *lie* you don't tell the
truth /truːθ/	Wahrheit	*truth*.
if /ɪf/	ob	
sweater /ˈswetə/	Pullover	This is a green *sweater*.

B11

Make a word web about your birthday.	Erstelle ein Wortnetz über deinen Geburtstag.
Now choose.	Wähle nun aus.
Tell your class about …	Erzähle deiner Klasse von …
Make notes first.	Mach dir zuerst Notizen.
Draw a picture and label it.	Zeichne ein Bild und beschrifte es.
Show it to a classmate.	Zeige es einem Klassenkameraden/ einer Klassenkameradin.

have a picnic /ˌhæv ə ˈpɪknɪk/	ein Picknick machen	Karla *is*
when /wen/	wenn; als	*blowing*
blow out /ˌbləʊ ˈaʊt/	ausblasen	*out* the
candle /ˈkændl/	Kerze	*candles*.
such /sʌtʃ/	so	

B12

How can you celebrate your birthdays in your class?	Wie könnt ihr eure Geburtstage in eurer Klasse feiern?
Collect ideas.	Sammelt Ideen.

decoration /ˌdekəˈreɪʃn/	Dekoration, Schmuck	
recipe /ˈresəpi/	Rezept	
many /ˈmeni/	viele	*many* = a lot
like best /ˌlaɪk ˈbest/	am liebsten mögen	

P11 activity /ækˈtɪvəti/ — Aktivität

What are they doing now?	Was machen sie gerade?
P12 Write down the text and complete it.	Schreibe den Text auf und vervollständige ihn.

P13 ready /ˈredi/ — fertig, bereit

Make up more dialogues with …	Denke dir mehr Dialoge mit … aus.
P14 Who is it?	Wer ist es?
Write more sentences for …	Schreibe weitere Sätze für …

Theme 6

I out and about /ˌaʊt‿ən‿əˈbaʊt/	unterwegs
summertime /ˈsʌmətaɪm/	Sommerzeit

A1 trip /trɪp/	Reise, Fahrt	There are lots of animals on the *farm*.
farm /fɑːm/	Bauernhof	
holiday /ˈhɒlɪdeɪ/	Ferien, Urlaub	

Look at the picture of the farm.	Sieh dir das Bild des Bauernhofs an.
What animals can you see?	Welche Tiere kannst du sehen?
Listen to … and point.	Hört euch … an und zeigt.

sheep (*pl* sheep) /ʃiːp/	Schaf	
goat /ɡəʊt/	Ziege	This is a *goat*.
chicken /ˈtʃɪkɪn/	Huhn	
dear /dɪə/	liebe(r) *(Anrede)*	
Excuse me! /ɪkˈskjuːz ˌmi/	Entschuldigen Sie bitte!, Entschuldigung!	
disabled toilet /dɪsˈeɪbld‿ˌtɔɪlət/	Behindertentoilette	
cross /krɒs/	überqueren	*Excuse me,* is there a *toilet* here? – Yes, the *toilets* are in the café.
bridge /brɪdʒ/	Brücke	
toilet /ˈtɔɪlət/	Toilette	

Words

on the left /ˌɒn ðə ˈleft/	links, auf der linken Seite
beautiful /ˈbjuːtəfl/	schön
tractor /ˈtræktə/	Traktor
lamb /læm/	Lamm
get on well /ˌget ɒn ˈwel/	sich gut verstehen
What's going on? /ˌwɒts gəʊɪŋˌˈɒn/	Was passiert hier gerade?
bite *(irr)* /baɪt/	beißen
Don't worry. /ˌdəʊnt ˈwʌri/	Mach dir keine Sorgen.
picnic area /ˈpɪknɪkˌeəriə/	Picknickbereich

There is a *tractor* at Kentish Town City Farm.

I was	ich war
you were	du warst/ Sie waren
he/she was	er/sie war
we were	wir waren
you were	ihr wart/ Sie waren
they were	sie waren

A2

there was /ðeərˌˈwɒz/	dort war; es gab
there were /ðeərˌˈwɜː/	dort waren; es gab
duck /dʌk/	Ente
cow /kaʊ/	Kuh
bull /bʊl/	Stier, Bulle
information stand /ˌɪnfəˈmeɪʃn stænd/	Informationsstand
field /fiːld/	Feld
hen house /ˈhen haʊs/	Hühnerstall

two *cows*

I loved	ich mochte … sehr
I had	ich hatte
I saw	ich sah
I rode	ich ritt
I liked	ich mochte

A3

out /aʊt/	heraus, hinaus; *hier:* aus
sunny /ˈsʌni/	sonnig
be on holiday /ˌbiː ɒn ˈhɒlɪdeɪ/	Urlaub haben
It's fun having you here. /ˌɪts ˈfʌn ˌhævɪŋ juː ˈhɪə/	Es ist schön, dass du hier bist.
far away /ˌfɑːrˌəˈweɪ/	weit weg
until /ənˈtɪl/	bis
month /mʌnθ/	Monat
glad /glæd/	glücklich, froh
move /muːv/	umziehen
suddenly /ˈsʌdnli/	plötzlich
land /lænd/	landen
jump up /ˌdʒʌmpˌˈʌp/	aufspringen, hochspringen
look out /ˌlʊkˌˈaʊt/	hinausschauen
outside /ˌaʊtˈsaɪd/	vor, außerhalb
wave (at/to somebody) /weɪv/	jemandem zuwinken
look up /ˌlʊkˌˈʌp/	hochschauen
so /səʊ/	*hier:* also
off /ɒf/	weg
search /sɜːtʃ/	suchen
for a while /ˌfɔːrˌəˈwaɪl/	eine Weile
finally /ˈfaɪnli/	schließlich, endlich
onto /ˈɒntə/	auf, in
There's a good parrot! /ˈðeəzˌəˌɡʊdˌpærət/	Das ist ein guter Papagei!

When playing basketball, you sometimes have to *jump up*.

she opened	sie öffnete
Ruby landed	Ruby landete
Ruby flew	Ruby flog
she jumped up	sie sprang auf
she looked out	sie sah hinaus
they were	sie waren
she waved	sie winkte
they went	sie gingen
they searched	sie suchten
they found	sie fanden

Theme 6

Write about the first day of the summer holidays.
What does Gillian write in her diary?

Schreibe über den ersten Tag der Sommerferien.
Was schreibt Gillian in ihr Tagebuch?

this morning /ðɪs ˈmɔːnɪŋ/ — heute Morgen

A4 end /end/ — Ende, Schluss
outside /ˌaʊtˈsaɪd/ — draußen
true /truː/ — wahr
plane /ˈeərəˌpleɪn/ — Flugzeug

Planes fly around the world.

What do you like best about the song? — Was gefällt dir an dem Lied am besten?

A5 have a crush on /ˌhævˍə ˈkrʌʃˍɒn/ — verknallt sein in — If you *have a crush* on somebody, you like him or her a lot.

Listen to the story.
Does Charlie like Duncan?

Höre dir die Geschichte an.
Mag Charlie Duncan?

(a pair of) skates /ə ˌpeərˍəv ˈskeɪts/ — (ein Paar) Inliner — She is wearing a *pair of skates*.

skating /ˈskeɪtɪŋ/ — Inlineskaten
hire /ˈhaɪə/ — mieten
brilliant /ˈbrɪljənt/ — genial, klasse
next door /ˌnekst ˈdɔː/ — nebenan

Mr Coleman lives in the house *next door*. – He is our neighbour.

Did you have a good time? /ˌdɪd juː ˌhævˍə gʊdˍˈtaɪm/ — Hattet Ihr Spaß?

have a good time /ˌhævˍə gʊdˍˈtaɪm/ — Spaß haben, eine gute Zeit haben — Did you *have a good time*? Yes, we had fun.

for an hour /ˌfɔːrˍənˍˈaʊə/ — eine Stunde lang

championship /ˈtʃæmpiənʃip/ — Meisterschaft

we hired	wir mieteten
we skated	wir fuhren Inliner
they shouted	sie riefen

What about ...? /ˈwɒtˍəˌbaʊt/ — *hier:* Was war mit ...?

audience /ˈɔːdiəns/ — Publikum
shout /ʃaʊt/ — rufen, schreien

Football fans sometimes *shout* loud chants at matches.

appreciate /əˈpriːʃiˌeɪt/ — schätzen
silly /ˈsɪli/ — albern, dumm
vanilla /vəˈnɪlə/ — Vanille

Work in groups of three.
Read the dialogue.
What does he tell him?
Write it down.
Here are some ideas to help you.

Arbeitet in Dreiergruppen.
Lies / Lest den Dialog.
Was erzählt er ihm?
Schreibe es auf.
Hier sind ein paar Ideen für dich als Hilfe.

Words

A6 paradise /ˈpærədaɪs/   Paradies
     only /ˈəʊnli/   einzige(r, s)
     indoor /ˌɪnˈdɔː/   drinnen, im Haus   *indoor ≠ outdoor*
     road /rəʊd/   Straße
     beginner /bɪˈɡɪnə/   Anfänger/in   *professional ≠ beginner*
     professional /prəˈfeʃnəl/   Profi
     biker /ˈbaɪkə/   Fahrradfahrer/in   The
     offer /ˈɒfə/   anbieten   *opening*
     opening hours (*pl*)   Öffnungszeiten   *hours*
       /ˈəʊpənɪŋˌaʊəz/   *are from*
     membership /ˈmembəʃɪp/   Mitgliedschaft   *9 am to*
     per /pɜː/   pro   *6 pm.*
     session /ˈseʃn/   (Kurs)stunde

Look at the leaflet.	Sieh dir die Broschüre an.
How can you get to the indoor skatepark and what can you do there?	Wie kannst du zum Indoor Skatepark kommen und was kannst du dort machen?
Tell a classmate in German.	Sag es einem Klassenkameraden/einer Klassenkameradin auf Deutsch.
Is there a place like this in your town?	Gibt es einen solchen Ort in deiner Stadt?
Make a leaflet for English-speaking visitors.	Mache eine Broschüre für englischsprachige Besucher/Besucherinnen.

A7   Collect holiday words.   Sammle Urlaubswörter.
     Sort the words.   Sortiere die Wörter.

A8   Listen to Grandpa Phil.   Hört Opa Phil zu.
     What happens in Blackpool?   Was passiert in Blackpool?
     Have you got a funny family story?   Hast du eine lustige Familiengeschichte?

A9   What are your favourite holiday activities?   Was sind deine Lieblingsaktivitäten in den Ferien?

rainy /ˈreɪni/   regnerisch   *rainy ≠ sunny*

Compare your answers with your partner's answers.	Vergleiche deine Antworten mit denen deines Partners/deiner Partnerin.
What is the same?	Was ist gleich?
What is different?	Was ist anders?

A10   Do the role play.   Macht das Rollenspiel.

inline skating   Inlinerfahren
   /ˌɪnlaɪn ˈskeɪtɪŋ/

Make plans for …	Mache Pläne für …
Write a dialogue and present it to the class.	Schreibe einen Dialog und stelle ihn der Klasse vor.

A11   What can you do in your area?   Was kannst du in deiner Gegend machen?
     Make a page for a class holiday booklet.   Mache eine Seite für eine Urlaubsbroschüre in der Klasse.

event /ɪˈvent/	Ereignis	A birthday party is a fun *event*.

Now put your pages together to make a class holiday booklet.	Bringt nun eure Seiten zusammen, um eine Urlaubsbroschüre für die Klasse zu machen.

P2 How many words can you make out of "ice creams"?
Wie viele Wörter kannst du aus "ice creams" machen?

Compare with your partner.
Vergleiche mit deinem Partner/deiner Partnerin.

P4 What does Rajiv tell his family?
Was erzählt Rajiv seiner Familie?

P5 Check your words with a partner and say them.
Überprüfe deine Wörter mit einem Partner/einer Partnerin und sage sie.

You can talk in German.
Du kannst auf Deutsch reden.

P6 Match the verb forms and write them in your exercise book.
Ordne die Verbformen einander zu und schreibe sie in dein Heft.

P8 Find the rhyming pairs for these words from …
Finde die Reimpaare für diese Wörter aus …

pair /ˈpeə/	Paar	
rhyme /raɪm/	sich reimen	*"Pair" rhymes* with "hair".

Find other words that rhyme with the words above.	Finde andere Wörter, die sich auf die Wörter oben reimen.
Start your own rhyming dictionary.	Beginne dein eigenes Reimwörterbuch.

B1

castle /ˈkaːsl/	Burg, Schloss
the coolest /ðə ˈkuːl ɪst/	die coolste, die tollste
be about /ˌbi ə ˈbaʊt/	handeln von
near /nɪə/	nahe, in der Nähe von
carry /ˈkæri/	tragen
laugh /laːf/	lachen
I love reading. /aɪ ˌlʌv ˈriːdɪŋ/	Ich lese sehr gern.

He is watching TV and *laughing*.

What do you like to read?	Was liest du gerne?
Write about what you like to read.	Schreibe darüber, was du gerne liest.

B2 survey /ˈsɜːveɪ/   Umfrage

What do the children like to read?	Was lesen die Kinder gern?
Find out more about …	Finde mehr über … heraus.
Now report to your class in German.	Berichte nun deiner Klasse auf Deutsch.

B3

up /ʌp/	nach oben, hinauf, oben	*up* ≠ down
high /haɪ/	hoch	
model plane /ˌmɒdl ˈpleɪn/	Modellflugzeug	
close /kləʊs/	zumachen, schließen	*close* ≠ open

pick something up /ˌpɪk ˌsʌmθɪŋ‿ˈʌp/	etwas aufheben	
take off /ˌteɪk‿ˈɒf/	abheben; *hier:* wegfliegen	*take off* ≠ land
higher /ˈhaɪə/	höher	
below /bɪˈləʊ/	unten, unter	
river /ˈrɪvə/	Fluss	The *Thames* is a big *river* in
Thames /temz/	Themse	London.
right /raɪt/	genau	
push /pʊʃ/	schieben, stoßen	
give *(irr)* /gɪv/	*hier:* verursachen	
rock /rɒk/	Stein, Fels	
crawl /krɔːl/	krabbeln; kriechen	A *keeper* feeds the animals at
keeper /ˈkiːpə/	(Zoo)wärter/in	the zoo.
elephant /ˈelɪfənt/	Elefant	
be scared /ˌbiː ˈskeəd/	Angst haben	
all over /ˌɔːl‿ˈəʊvə/	überall	
monkey /ˈmʌŋki/	Affe	This is a *monkey*.
closer /ˈkləʊsə/	näher	
Help! /help/	Hilfe!	

Draw a picture for one of the stories.	Zeichne ein Bild für eine der Geschichten.
Which story do you like best?	Welche Geschichte gefällt dir am besten?
Read it to your partner.	Lies sie deinem Partner/deiner Partnerin vor.
What does the keeper say?	Was sagt der Zoowärter/die Zoowärterin?
Complete one of the stories.	Vervollständige eine der Geschichten.
Write another story.	Schreibe noch eine Geschichte.
You can record it.	Du kannst sie aufnehmen.

Theme 6

B4

exciting /ɪkˈsaɪtɪŋ/	aufregend	I think	ich denke nach
volunteer /ˌvɒlənˈtɪə/	ehrenamtliche/r Mitarbeiter/in	I thought	ich dachte nach
farmer /ˈfaːmə/	Bauer/Bäuerin	I want	ich will
quick /kwɪk/	schnell	I wanted	ich wollte
kid /kɪd/	Kind		
foal /fəʊl/	Fohlen	I watch	ich sehe (zu)
excited /ɪkˈsaɪtɪd/	aufgeregt	I watched	ich sah (zu)
think hard /ˌθɪŋk ˈhaːd/	angestrengt nachdenken		
early /ˈɜːli/	früh	*early* ≠ late	
surprised /səˈpraɪzd/	überrascht, erstaunt		

Tell the story in your own words.	Erzähle die Geschichte mit deinen eigenen Worten.

B5

island /ˈaɪlənd/	Insel

Use your imagination.	Benutze deine Fantasie.

feel *(irr)* /fiːl/   sich fühlen
treasure /ˈtreʒə/   Schatz   What is in the
box /bɒks/   Kasten, Kiste   *treasure box?*
noise /nɔɪz/   Geräusch
jungle /ˈdʒʌŋgl/   Dschungel, Urwald

B6

Use your notes.	Verwende deine Notizen.
Use your answers to write a story.	Verwende deine Antworten, um eine Geschichte zu schreiben.
Find a title.	Finde einen Titel.
Make a story box.	Mache / Macht eine Geschichtenkiste.
Everyone gets three pieces of paper.	Jede/r bekommt drei Blätter Papier.
Write one word on each piece of paper.	Schreibe auf jedes Blatt ein Wort.
Put the pieces of paper in the box.	Stecke die Blätter in die Kiste.
Mix them.	Mische sie.
Then take them out.	Nimm sie dann heraus.
Look at the words and make up a story.	Sieh dir die Wörter an und erfinde eine Geschichte.
Record your story and present it to the class.	Nimm deine Geschichte auf und stelle sie der Klasse vor.

Hier findest du die Wörter, die in deinem Buch vorkommen.

5/A3 bedeutet: Dieses Wort kommt das erste Mal in *Theme* 5, Aufgabe A3, vor oder wird erst an dieser Stelle fett gesetzt. Die **fett gedruckten** Wörter solltest du dir merken.

BS markiert Wörter aus den *Book stop*-Texten, O markiert Wörter aus den *Optionals*. Diese Wörter sind zusätzlich mit einem ° versehen.

WB markiert Wörter aus den *Wordbanks*.

sth = something, sb = somebody, etw = etwas, jd = jemand, jdm = jemandem, jdn = jemanden

A

a /ə/ pro, in/im 5/A3

a/an /ə, eɪ /ən/ ein(e) Welcome

a lot /ə ˈlɒt/ viel, sehr Welcome

a lot (of) /ə ˈlɒt əv/ viel(e), jede Menge Welcome

about /əˈbaʊt/ ungefähr 5/A4

about /əˈbaʊt/ über; an 1/I

be about /ˌbi‿əˈbaʊt/ handeln von 4/B11

out and about /ˌaʊt‿ən‿əˈbaʊt/ unterwegs 6/I

above /əˈbʌv/ über 2/B12; oben 6/P8

°acrobat /ˈækrəbæt/ Akrobat/in 1/O

act out /ˌækt‿ˈaʊt/ nachspielen Welcome

action /ˈækʃn/ Handlung 3/A13

activity /ækˈtɪvəti/ Aktivität 3/A1

ad (= advertisement) /æd, ədˈvɜːtɪsmənt/ Anzeige 2/A10

add /æd/ hinzufügen 5/P6

add up /ˌæd‿ˈʌp/ addieren, zusammenzählen 3/B3

adventure /ədˈventʃə/ Abenteuer 3/B11

after /ˈɑːftə/ nach 3/A1

°after that /ˌɑːftə ˈðæt/ danach 2/O2

afternoon /ˌɑːftəˈnuːn/ Nachmittag 4/A11

in the afternoon /ˌɪn ðiˌɑːftəˈnuːn/ am Nachmittag 3/P14

again /əˈgen/ wieder; noch einmal 1/A2

age /eɪdʒ/ Alter 1/A9

agree /əˈgriː/ zustimmen Welcome

aim /eɪm/ Ziel 3/A7

°air /eə/ Luft BS/4

°airport /ˈeəpɔːt/ Flughafen BS/5

all /ɔːl/ alle, alles Welcome

all /ɔːl/ ganz, völlig BS/1

°all around /ˌɔːl‿əˈraʊnd/ überall BS/4

all day /ˌɔːl ˈdeɪ/ den ganzen Tag lang 1/A6

all over /ˌɔːl‿ˈəʊvə/ überall 6/B4

all right /ˌɔːl ˈraɪt/ in Ordnung 3/B4

°alone /əˈləʊn/ allein BS/4

°along /əˈlɒŋ/ entlang BS/1

alphabet /ˈælfəbet/ Alphabet 2/B9

alphabetical /ˌælfəˈbetɪkl/ alphabetisch 2/B5

also /ˈɔːlsəʊ/ auch 3/B6

altogether /ˌɔːltəˈgeðə/ insgesamt 4/B6

always /ˈɔːlweɪz/ immer 1/A5

am (= ante meridiem) /ˌeɪˈem, ˌænti məˈrɪdiəm/ morgens, vormittags *(nur hinter Uhrzeit zwischen Mitternacht und 12 Uhr mittags)* 3/A4

and /ænd/ und Welcome

°angry /ˈæŋgri/ verärgert BS/6

animal /ˈænɪml/ Tier Welcome

animal shelter /ˈænɪml ˌʃeltə/ Tierheim 1/B2

°anonymous /əˈnɒnɪməs/ anonym BS/1

another /əˈnʌðə/ noch ein/e 3/A13

answer /ˈɑːnsə/ Antwort 3/B6

answer /ˈɑːnsə/ (be)antworten 2/B7

answer the phone /ˌɑːnsə ðə ˈfəʊn/ ans Telefon gehen 5/B3

any /ˈeni/ (irgend)ein(e) 3/B4

anybody /ˈenibɒdi/ irgendjemand; jede (r, s) 3/A1

°anything /ˈeniˌθɪŋ/ irgendetwas 3/O

anything else /eniˌθɪŋ‿ˈels/ noch etwas 4/B6

Anything else? /eniˌθɪŋ‿ˈels/ Sonst noch etwas?, Darf es noch etwas sein? 4/B6

anyway /ˈeniweɪ/ jedenfalls 4/B9

apple /ˈæpl/ Apfel Welcome

appreciate /əˈpriːʃiˌeɪt/ schätzen 6/A5

April /ˈeɪprəl/ April 5/B7

are /ɑː/ bist, sind, seid Welcome

°are going /ˌɑː ˈgəʊɪŋ/ gehen (gerade) BS/7

Are there …? /ˈɑː ðeə/ Gibt es …? 1/B3

area /ˈeəriə/ Gebiet, Region 1/B1

aren't (= are not) /ˈɑːnt/ sind nicht 1/B2

around /əˈraʊnd/ um; herum, umher 1/A2

arrive /əˈraɪv/ ankommen 5/B3

art /ɑːt/ Kunst 5/A2

article /ˈɑːtɪkl/ Artikel 4/A11

as /əz/ als; wie 2/B9

ask /ɑːsk/ fragen; bitten 3/A5

ask questions /ˌɑːsk ˈkwestʃnz/ Fragen stellen 2/B7

°be asleep /ˌbi‿əˈsliːp/ schlafen BS/8

assembly /əˈsembli/ (Schüler)versammlung 5/A3

at /æt/ an, in, bei, um Welcome

at all /ˌæt‿ˈɔːl/ überhaupt 5/A2

at Gillian's (house) /ˌæt‿ˈdʒɪliənz/ bei Gillian (zu Hause) 3/B6

at home /ˌæt ˈhəʊm/ zu Hause 3/A9

at last /ˌæt ˈlɑːst/ endlich; schließlich Welcome

at least /ˌæt ˈliːst/ mindestens; wenigstens 5/P3

at the market /ˌæt‿ðə ˈmɑːkɪt/ auf dem Markt 3/P14

at the moment /ˌæt‿ðə ˈməʊmənt/ im Moment 3/B6

at the weekend /ˌæt ðə ˈwiːkend/ am Wochenende 2/A12

audience /ˈɔːdiəns/ Publikum 6/A5

August /ˈɔːgəst/ August 5/B7

aunt /aːnt/ Tante 5/B3

autumn /ˈɔːtəm/ Herbst Welcome

average /ˈævərɪdʒ/ durchschnittlich 2/A6

away /əˈweɪ/ weg Welcome

B

back /bæk/ Rücken 2/A1; zurück 4/A11

back /bæk/ zurück; *hier:* wieder Welcome

°**backwards** /ˈbækwədz/ rückwärts BS/2

bacon /ˈbeɪkən/ Schinkenspeck 2/A8

°**bad** /bæd/ schlecht 6/O

°**bag** /bæg/ Tasche BS/8

baked beans *(pl)* /ˌbeɪkt ˈbiːnz/ Bohnen in Tomatensauce 2/A7

ballet /ˈbæleɪ/ Ballett 4/A11

balloon /bəˈluːn/ Luftballon 5/B3

banana /bəˈnɑːnə/ Banane Welcome

°**bang** /bæŋ/ Knall BS/10

basket /ˈbɑːskɪt/ Korb 1/B2

bat /bæt/ Fledermaus WB

bath /bɑːθ/ Badewanne 2/A4

bathroom /ˈbɑːθˌruːm/ Badezimmer 2/A2

be *(irr)* /biː/ sein 1/A2

be about /ˌbi əˈbaʊt/ handeln von 1/B2

°**be asleep** /ˌbi əˈsliːp/ schlafen BS/8

be born /ˌbiː ˈbɔːn/ geboren werden WB

Be careful! /ˌbiː ˈkeəfl/ Sei vorsichtig! 1/B2

be fun /ˌbiː ˈfʌn/ Spaß machen Welcome

be good at something /ˌbiː ˈgʊd æt ˌsʌmθɪŋ/ gut in etwas sein Welcome

be on holiday /ˌbi ɒn ˈhɒlideɪ/ Urlaub haben 6/A3

be one's turn /ˌbiː wʌnz ˈtɜːn/ an der Reihe sein 4/B1

beach /biːtʃ/ Strand 3/B6

bean /biːn/ Bohne 2/A8

baked beans *(pl)* /ˌbeɪkt ˈbiːnz/ Bohnen in Tomatensauce 2/A7

beat *(irr)* /biːt/ schlagen 3/A6

beautiful /ˈbjuːtəfl/ schön 6/A1

because /bɪˈkɒz/ weil, da 4/B3

°**because of** /bɪˈkɒz əv/ wegen 4/O

bed /bed/ Bett 4/A1

bedroom /ˈbedruːm/ Schlafzimmer 2/A4

before /bɪˈfɔː/ vor 2/A12

°**before** /bɪˈfɔː/ bevor 2/O1

°**begin** *(irr)* /bɪˈgɪn/ anfangen, beginnen 3/O

beginner /bɪˈgɪnə/ Anfänger/in 6/A6

behind /bɪˈhaɪnd/ hinter 4/A3

belong (to) /bɪˈlɒŋ/ gehören 4/P9

below /bɪˈləʊ/ unten, unter 6/B3

best /best/ beste (r, s) 1/A4

best /best/ am liebsten 2/B6

the best /ðə ˈbest/ der/die/das Beste Welcome

like best /ˌlaɪk ˈbest/ am liebsten mögen 3/B9

better /ˈbetə/ besser 5/A2

between /bɪˈtwiːn/ zwischen 4/B5

big /bɪg/ groß 1/A4

bike /baɪk/ Fahrrad 1/A4

by bike /ˌbaɪ ˈbaɪk/ mit dem Fahrrad 5/A7

ride a bike /ˌraɪd ə ˈbaɪk/ Fahrrad fahren 1/A4

biker /ˈbaɪkə/ Fahrradfahrer/in 6/A6

bin /bɪn/ Abfalleimer 2/B1

bird /bɜːd/ Vogel WB

birthday /ˈbɜːθdeɪ/ Geburtstag 5/B2

biscuit /ˈbɪskɪt/ Keks 4/B5

a (little) bit /ə ˌlɪtl ˈbɪt/ ein (kleines) bisschen Welcome

°**a bit** /ə ˈbɪt/ ein bisschen 3/O

bite *(irr)* /baɪt/ beißen 6/A1

black /blæk/ schwarz Welcome

blackboard /ˈblækˌbɔːd/ Tafel 2/B1

°**the blind** /ðə ˈblaɪnd/ die Blinden BS/5

blow out /ˌbləʊ ˈaʊt/ ausblasen 5/B11

blue /bluː/ blau Welcome

body /ˈbɒdi/ Körper 2/A3

body part /ˈbɒdi ˌpaːt/ Körperteil 2/A2

boil /bɔɪl/ kochen WB

°**boiled** /bɔɪld/ gekocht 2/O2

°**boiling** /ˈbɔɪlɪŋ/ kochend 2/O2

bone /bəʊn/ Knochen 3/B10

book /bʊk/ Buch 2/A3

exercise book /ˈeksəsaɪz ˌbʊk/ Heft 2/B4

phrase book /ˈfreɪz bʊk/ *Sammlung von Redewendungen* 2/A13

booklet /ˈbʊklət/ Broschüre 6/A11

bookshelf (*pl* bookshelves) /ˈbʊkˌʃelf, ˈbʊkˌʃelvz/ Bücherregal 2/B4

boot /buːt/ Stiefel WB

football boots *(pl)* /ˈfʊtˌbɔːl buːts/ Fußballschuhe 3/A1

°**bored** /bɔːd/ gelangweilt BS/10

boring /ˈbɔːrɪŋ/ langweilig 4/A11

be born /ˌbiː ˈbɔːn/ geboren werden WB

°**bottom** /ˈbɒtəm/ Boden, Grund 2/O1

bowl /bəʊl/ Schüssel, Schale 2/A7

box /bɒks/ Kasten, Kiste 2/A9

boy /bɔɪ/ Junge 3/A1

the boys' match /ðə ˈbɔɪz ˌmætʃ/ das Spiel der Jungen 3/A6

°**brave** /breɪv/ mutig BS/10

break /breɪk/ Pause Welcome

breakfast /ˈbrekfəst/ Frühstück 2/A7

for breakfast /fə ˈbrekfəst/ zum Frühstück 2/A12

have breakfast /ˌhæv ˈbrekfəst/ frühstücken 2/A13

bridge /brɪdʒ/ Brücke 6/A1

°**brightly** /ˈbraɪtli/ hell BS/7

brilliant /ˈbrɪljənt/ genial, klasse 6/A5

bring *(irr)* /brɪŋ/ mitbringen 3/A4

brother /ˈbrʌðə/ Bruder Welcome

brown /braʊn/ braun Welcome

brush /brʌʃ/ putzen; bürsten 2/A1

brush one's teeth /ˌbrʌʃ wʌnz ˈtiːθ/ sich die Zähne putzen 2/A1

speech bubble /'spiːtʃˌbʌbl/ Sprechblase 2/A3

budgie /'bʌdʒi/ Wellensittich WB

build (irr) /bɪld/ bauen Welcome

bull /bʊl/ Stier, Bulle 6/A2

°bump /bʌmp/ dumpfer Schlag BS/8

go by bus /ˌgəʊ baɪ 'bʌs/ mit dem Bus fahren 5/A4

busy /'bɪzi/ arbeitsreich; beschäftigt 4/A6

but /bʌt/ aber 1/A4

°butterfly /'bʌtəˌflaɪ/ Schmetterling BS/3

buy (irr) /baɪ/ kaufen 3/B6

buying /'baɪɪŋ/ Kaufen 3/B4

by /baɪ/ von; mit 2/B1; in der Nähe BS/10

by bike /ˌbaɪ 'baɪk/ mit dem Fahrrad 5/A7

by bus /ˌbaɪ 'bʌs/ mit dem Bus 5/A7

by heart /ˌbaɪ 'hɑːt/ auswendig 2/B12

by helicopter /ˌbaɪ 'heliˌkɒptə/ mit dem Hubschrauber 5/A8

by the way /ˌbaɪ ðə 'weɪ/ übrigens 5/A2

bye /baɪ/ tschüs(s) 3/A5

C

cage /keɪdʒ/ Käfig 4/A1

cake /keɪk/ Kuchen 4/B5

calendar /'kælɪndə/ Kalender 2/B1

call /kɔːl/ anrufen 3/B6

call /kɔːl/ nennen; rufen 3/B4

phone call /'fəʊn kɔːl/ Telefonanruf 5/B3

°called /kɔːld/ genannt 1/O

°is called /ɪz 'kɔːld/ heißt, wird genannt 4/O

°calm down /ˌkɑːm 'daʊn/ sich beruhigen BS/6

°came /keɪm/ kam/kamen BS/1

can/can't /kæn/kɑːnt/ können/ nicht können Welcome

Can I help you? /ˌkæn aɪ 'help juː/ Kann ich dir/Ihnen helfen? 3/B4

candle /'kændl/ Kerze 5/B11

canteen /kæn'tiːn/ Kantine, Mensa 5/A2

cap /kæp/ Mütze 1/A5

captain /'kæptɪn/ Mannschaftsführer/in 3/A12

car /kɑː/ Auto 1/B4

toy car /ˌtɔɪ 'kɑː/ Spielzeugauto 3/B5

°caravan /'kærəvæn/ Wohnwagen 1/O

card /kɑːd/ Karte 3/B5

careful /'keəfl/ vorsichtig 1/B2

carrot /'kærət/ Möhre, Karotte Welcome

carry /'kæri/ tragen 6/B1

cartridge /'kɑːtrɪdʒ/ Patrone 2/B10

pencil case /'pensl ˌkeɪs/ Federmäppchen 2/B4

castle /'kɑːsl/ Burg; Schloss 6/B1

cat /kæt/ Katze 1/A5

cat food /'kæt fuːd/ Katzenfutter 1/B2

°catch (irr) /kætʃ/ fangen BS/4

'cause (= because) /kɔːz, bɪ'kɒz/ weil, da 3/A7

celebrate /'seləˌbreɪt/ feiern 5/B12

shopping centre /'ʃɒpɪŋ ˌsentə/ Einkaufszentrum 1/B3

chair /tʃeə/ Stuhl 2/B1

chalk /tʃɔːk/ Kreide 2/B1

championship /'tʃæmpiənʃɪp/ Meisterschaft 6/A5

change /tʃeɪndʒ/ wechseln; umsteigen 4/B3; Wechselgeld 4/B6

change /tʃeɪndʒ/ Veränderung 2/B13

chant /tʃɑːnt/ Sprechgesang Welcome; Sprechgesang anstimmen 3/A7

character /'kærəktə/ Wesen, Charakter 1/A8

chase /tʃeɪs/ jagen 1/A6

check /tʃek/ überprüfen, kontrollieren 1/P6

°cheek /tʃiːk/ Wange BS/3

°cheer /tʃɪə/ Jubel, Freude 5/O1

cheer for sb /'tʃɪə fə ˌsʌmbədi/ jdn anfeuern 3/A4

cheer sb on /ˌtʃɪə ˌsʌmbədi ˈɒn/ jdn anfeuern 3/A7

cheese /tʃiːz/ Käse Welcome

°cherry /'tʃeri/ Kirsche 5/O1

chest /tʃest/ Brustkorb 2/A1

chicken /'tʃɪkɪn/ Huhn WB

child (pl children) /tʃaɪld, 'tʃɪldrən/ Kind Welcome

chill (informal) /tʃɪl/ sich entspannen, chillen 3/B8

°chin /tʃɪn/ Kinn BS/1

chips (pl) /tʃɪps/ Pommes frites 1/A4

chocolate /'tʃɒklət/ Schokolade 4/B1

hot chocolate /hɒt 'tʃɒklət/ (heißer) Kakao 4/B9

choose (irr) /tʃuːz/ wählen; sich entscheiden 1/B5

chore /tʃɔː/ lästige Aufgabe, Hausarbeit 4/A10

cinema /'sɪnəmə/ Kino 1/B3

circle /'sɜːkl/ Kreis Welcome

°circus /'sɜːkəs/ Zirkus 1/O

city /'sɪti/ Stadt; Innenstadt Welcome

clap /klæp/ klatschen 2/B9

class /klɑːs/ Klasse 2/A13

classmate /'klɑːsˌmeɪt/ Klassenkamerad/in Welcome

classroom /'klɑːsˌruːm/ Klassenzimmer 2/B1

clean /kliːn/ sauber machen 4/A6

clock /klɒk/ Uhr 2/B1

close /kləʊs/ zumachen; schließen 6/B3

closer /'kləʊsə/ näher 6/B3

clothes (pl) /kləʊðz/ Kleider, Kleidung Welcome

cloud /klaʊd/ Wolke WB

cloudy /'klaʊdi/ bewölkt, bedeckt WB

club /klʌb/ Klub; AG 3/I

°coat /kəʊt/ Mantel 6/O

°cocktail stick /'kɒkteɪl stɪk/ Cocktailspieß 5/O1

coconut /'kəʊkəˌnʌt/ Kokosnuss 2/A1

cold /kəʊld/ kalt 2/A2; Erkältung 3/A5

°cold /kəʊld/ Kälte BS/2

collect /kə'lekt/ sammeln 3/A13

collection /kə'lekʃn/ Sammlung 3/B5

colour /'kʌlə/ Farbe Welcome

colourful /'kʌləfl/ farbenfroh, bunt Welcome

come *(irr)* /kʌm/ kommen
Welcome

Come in. /ˌkʌmˈɪn/ Komm(t) herein! 5/B3

come in /ˌkʌmˈɪn/ hereinkommen 5/B3; *hier:* vorkommen BS/4

Come on! /ˌkʌmˈɒn/ Komm(t) jetzt!; Mach(t) schon! 1/A2

°come out /ˌkʌmˈaʊt/ herauskommen BS/3

°come true /ˌkʌm ˈtruː/ wahr werden BS/7

comfortable /ˈkʌmftəbl/ bequem 4/A4

command /kəˈmɑːnd/ Befehl 2/P4

comment by /ˈkɒment baɪ/ Kommentar von 1/B2

compare /kəmˈpeə/ vergleichen 2/B11

°competition /ˌkɒmpəˈtɪʃn/ Wettbewerb BS/6

complete /kəmˈpliːt/ vervollständigen 1/A4

complete /mætʃ/ zuordnen 3/B7

computer club /kəmˈpjuːtə ˌklʌb/ Computerklub 1/P12

cook /kʊk/ Koch/Köchin 1/A5; kochen, braten, backen 2/O2

cooked /kʊkt/ gekocht 2/A7

do the cooking /ˌduː ðə ˈkʊkɪŋ/ kochen 4/A6

cooking /ˈkʊkɪŋ/ Kochen; Koch- 3/A1

the coolest /ðə ˈkuːlɪst/ der/die/das coolste/tollste 6/B1

copy /ˈkɒpi/ abschreiben 5/A2

corner /ˈkɔːnə/ Ecke 1/A2

corner shop /ˈkɔːnə ʃɒp/ Tante-Emma-Laden 3/B6

correct /kəˈrekt/ richtig, korrekt; korrigieren 2/A8

could /kʊd/ könnte, könntest, könntet, könnten 4/B6

course /kɔːs/ Kurs 5/A7

cousin /ˈkʌzn/ Cousin/e 1/A2

cow /kaʊ/ Kuh WB

crawl /krɔːl/ krabbeln; kriechen 6/B3

°crazy /ˈkreɪzi/ verrückt, wahnsinnig 3/O

°**criminal** /ˈkrɪmɪnl/ Verbrecher/in BS/5

crisps *(pl)* /krɪsps/ Chips 4/B5

crocodile /ˈkrɒkədaɪl/ Krokodil WB

cross /krɒs/ überqueren 6/A1

have a crush on /ˌhævˌə ˈkrʌʃˌɒn/ verknallt sein in 6/A5

cuddly toy /ˌkʌdli ˈtɔɪ/ Kuscheltier 3/B5

cup /kʌp/ Tasse 2/A9

cup /kʌp/ Pokal, Cup 3/A4

cup final /ˈkʌp faɪnl/ Pokalendspiel, Cupfinale 3/A4

a cup of tea /ə ˌkʌpˌəv ˈtiː/ eine Tasse Tee 2/A8

cupboard /ˈkʌbəd/ Schrank 2/B1

curly /ˈkɜːli/ lockig 2/A6

customer /ˈkʌstəmə/ Kunde/Kundin 3/B4

°**cut** *(irr)* /kʌt/ schneiden 5/O1

cute /kjuːt/ süß, niedlich
Welcome

dad /dæd/ Papa, Vati 2/A7

°**daddy** /ˈdædi/ Vati, Papi BS/6

dance /dɑːns/ tanzen 4/A11

dance /dɑːns/ Tanz 4/A11

dancing /ˈdɑːnsɪŋ/ Tanzen 1/A5

°**dangerous** /ˈdeɪndʒərəs/ gefährlich BS/10

°**dare** /deə/ Mutprobe BS/10

dark /dɑːk/ dunkel 2/A3

dark /dɑːk/ Dunkelheit 4/B11

daughter /ˈdɔːtə/ Tochter 5/B7

day /deɪ/ Tag Welcome

all day /ˌɔːl ˈdeɪ/ den ganzen Tag lang 1/A6

school day /ˈskuːl ˌdeɪ/ Schultag 2/A12

day by day /ˌdeɪ baɪ ˈdeɪ/ Tag für Tag 5/I

day out /ˌdeɪ ˈaʊt/ *Ausflugstag* 6/A10

°**dead** /ded/ tot BS/6

dear /dɪə/ liebe(r) (Anrede) 6/A1

oh dear /əʊ ˈdɪə/ oje 2/B1

December /dɪˈsembə/ Dezember 5/B7

decide /dɪˈsaɪd/ entscheiden 2/A13

decoration /ˌdekəˈreɪʃn/ Dekoration; Schmuck 5/B12

Denmark /ˈdenmɑːk/ Dänemark 5/A7

describe /dɪˈskraɪb/ beschreiben 3/B6

desk /desk/ Schreibtisch 2/B1

detective /dɪˈtektɪv/ Detektiv/in 1/P3

dialogue /ˈdaɪəlɒg/ Gespräch, Dialog Welcome

diary /ˈdaɪəri/ Tagebuch 6/A3

dictionary /ˈdɪkʃənri/ Lexikon 2/B10

picture dictionary /ˈpɪktʃə ˌdɪkʃənri/ Bildwörterbuch 2/A13

Did you have a good time? /ˌdɪd ju ˌhævˌə ɡʊdˈtaɪm/ Hattet Ihr Spaß? 6/A5

°Did you know that ...? /ˌdɪd ju ˈnəʊ ˌðæt/ Wusstest du, dass ...? 4/O

difference /ˈdɪfrəns/ Unterschied 4/B8

different /ˈdɪfrənt/ anders; andere(r, s); verschiedene(r, s) 6/A9

°**difficult** /ˈdɪfɪklt/ schwierig, schwer BS/4

dinner /ˈdɪnə/ Abendessen 4/B1

for dinner /fə ˈdɪnə/ zum Abendessen 5/P7

dinosaur /ˈdaɪnəsɔː/ Dinosaurier Welcome

°**dip** /dɪp/ eintauchen 5/O1

dirty /ˈdɜːti/ dreckig, schmutzig 2/A2

disabled toilet /dɪsˈeɪbldˌtɔɪlət/ Behindertentoilette 6/A1

°**disappear** /ˌdɪsəˈpɪə/ verschwinden 4/O

°**disgusting** /dɪsˈgʌstɪŋ/ widerlich BS/10

dishwasher /ˈdɪʃˌwɒʃə/ Spülmaschine 2/A7

divided by /dɪˈvaɪdɪd baɪ/ geteilt durch 3/B2

divorced /dɪˈvɔːst/ geschieden WB

do *(irr)* /duː/ tun; machen 3/A8

do gymnastics /ˌduː dʒɪmˈnæstɪks/ Turnen 3/A8

do the cooking /ˌduː ðə ˈkʊkɪŋ/ kochen 4/A6

do the shopping /ˌduː ðə ˈʃɒpɪŋ/ einkaufen 4/A6

do the washing up /ˌduː ðə ˌwɒʃɪŋˈʌp/ abspülen 4/A6

Do you like …? /ˌduː jə ˈlaɪk/ Magst du …? 2/P8

dog /dɒg/ Hund 1/A5

walk the dog /ˌwɔːk ðə ˈdɒg/ den Hund ausführen 5/A4

dog food /ˈdɒg fuːd/ Hundefutter 3/B10

Don't call me …! /ˌdəʊnt ˈkɔːl miː/ Nenn' mich nicht …! 4/B9

Don't forget …! /ˌdəʊnt fəˈget/ Vergiss' nicht …/Vergesst nicht …! 2/A2

don't say /ˌdəʊnt ˈseɪ/ sag(t) nicht 3/B6

Don't worry. /ˌdəʊnt ˈwʌri/ Mach dir keine Sorgen. 6/A1

well done /ˌwel ˈdʌn/ gut gemacht 3/A6

door /dɔː/ Tür 2/B4

°**double room** /ˌdʌbl ˈruːm/ Doppelzimmer BS/8

down /daʊn/ hinunter Welcome

°**Dr** (= Doctor) /ˈdɒktə/ BS/6

dragon /ˈdrægən/ Drache 3/B5

drama /ˈdrɑːmə/ Theater 3/A1

draw (irr) /drɔː/ zeichnen 4/A12

dream /driːm/ Traum 1/B4

dream (irr) /driːm/ träumen 2/A7

dress /dres/ Kleid WB

drink /drɪŋk/ Trinken; Getränk 5/B5

drink (irr) /drɪŋk/ trinken 2/A8

°**drug** /drʌg/ Rauschgift BS/5

°**drum** /drʌm/ Trommel 1/O

duck /dʌk/ Ente 6/A2

during /ˈdjʊərɪŋ/ während 2/A13

duvet /ˈduːveɪ/ Steppdecke, Daunendecke 4/A1

E

each /iːtʃ/ jede (r, s) 2/B12

each other /ˌiːtʃ ˈʌðə/ einander 5/B9

ear /ɪə/ Ohr 2/A2

early /ˈɜːli/ früh 6/B4

easy /ˈiːzi/ leicht; einfach 3/B6

eat (irr) /iːt/ essen 2/A12

egg /eg/ Ei 2/A8

fried egg /ˌfraɪd ˈeg/ Spiegelei 2/A7

°**scrambled egg** /ˌskræmbld ˈeg/ Rührei 2/O2

°**egg over easy** /ˌeg ˌəʊvər ˈiːzi/ auf beiden Seiten gebratenes Spiegelei 2/O2

°**egg-white** /ˈegwaɪt/ Eiweiß 2/O1

elbow /ˈelbəʊ/ Ellenbogen 2/A1

elephant /ˈelɪfənt/ Elefant WB

elf (pl elves) /elf, elvz/ Elfe 3/B5

anything else /eniˌθɪŋ ˈels/ noch etwas 4/B6

Anything else? /eniˌθɪŋ ˈels/ Sonst noch etwas?, Darf es noch etwas sein? 4/B6

what else /ˌwɒt ˈels/ was sonst 2/A8

°**email** /ˈiːmeɪl/ mailen 3/O

empty /ˈempti/ ausleeren; ausräumen 4/A9

end /end/ enden; beenden 5/A3

end /end/ Ende; Schluss 5/B3

ending /ˈendɪŋ/ Ende; Schluss 4/B11

English /ˈɪŋglɪʃ/ Englisch; english Welcome

in English /ˌɪn ˈɪŋglɪʃ/ auf Englisch Welcome

English-speaking /ˈɪŋglɪʃˌspiːkɪŋ/ englisch-sprachig 6/A6

°**enter** /ˈentə/ hier: die Bühne betreten BS/6

entry /ˈentri/ Eintrag 2/A11

equal /ˈiːkwəl/ ergeben, sein 3/B2

°**escalator** /ˈeskəˌleɪtə/ Rolltreppe 4/O

eTwinning /ˈiːˌtwɪnɪŋ/ Schulpartnerschaft per Email 5/A7

°**even** /ˈiːvn/ selbst, sogar 3/O

evening /ˈiːvnɪŋ/ Abend 4/A11

in the evening /ˌɪn ðiˈiːvnɪŋ/ am Abend 6/A3

event /ɪˈvent/ Ereignis 6/A11

°**ever** /ˈevə/ jemals BS/10

°**ever so small** /ˌevə səʊ ˈsmɔːl/ so wahnsinnig klein BS/1

every /ˈevri/ jede (r, s) 2/A7

everybody /ˈevriˌbɒdi/ alle; jeder Welcome

everyone /ˈevriwʌn/ alle; jeder 3/B8

everything /ˈevriθɪŋ/ alles 4/B6

°**everywhere** /ˈevriweə/ überall BS/3

example /ɪgˈzɑːmpl/ Beispiel 5/A8

excited /ɪkˈsaɪtɪd/ aufgeregt 6/B4

exciting /ɪkˈsaɪtɪŋ/ aufregend 6/B4

Excuse me! /ɪkˈskjuːz ˌmiː/ Entschuldigen Sie bitte!, Entschuldigung! 6/A1

exercise book /ˈeksəsaɪz ˌbʊk/ Heft 2/B4

exhibition /ˌeksɪˈbɪʃn/ Ausstellung 3/B11

°**exit** /ˈeksɪt/ Abgang BS/6

°**experiment** /ɪkˈsperɪmənt/ Experiment, Versuch 2/O1

explain /ɪkˈspleɪn/ erklären 1/P1

°**explosive** /ɪkˈspləʊsɪv/ Sprengstoff BS/5

extra /ˈekstrə/ zusätzlich 2/A7

eye /aɪ/ Auge 2/A2

F

face /feɪs/ Gesicht 2/A1

fact file /ˈfækt ˌfaɪl/ Steckbrief 3/B10

fall (irr) /fɔːl/ fallen 2/B12

false /fɔːls/ falsch 4/B1

family /ˈfæmli/ Familie 3/A4

family tree /ˌfæmli ˈtriː/ Familienstammbaum 5/B7

famous /ˈfeɪməs/ berühmt 2/A6

fantastic /fænˈtæstɪk/ fantastisch, super 3/A6

fantasy /ˈfæntəsi/ Fantasie 2/A3

far /fɑː/ weit Welcome

far away /ˌfɑːr əˈweɪ/ weit weg 6/A3

farm /fɑːm/ Bauernhof WB

farmer /ˈfɑːmə/ Bauer/Bäuerin 6/B4

fast /fɑːst/ schnell Welcome

°**faster** /ˈfɑːstə/ schneller BS/10

father /ˈfɑːðə/ Vater 5/B7

favourite /ˈfeɪvrət/ Liebling; Lieblings- Welcome

February /ˈfebruəri/ Februar 5/B7

feed (irr) /fiːd/ füttern 4/A8

feel *(irr)* /fi:l/ sich fühlen 4/A7; fühlen, spüren BS/2

feeling /ˈfi:lɪŋ/ Gefühl WB

field /fi:ld/ Feld 6/A2

playing field /ˈpleɪɪŋ ˌfi:ld/ Sportplatz 3/P4

fifth /fɪfθ/ fünfte (r, s) 5/A3

°figure /ˈfɪgə/ Gestalt BS/10

fill in /ˌfɪlˈɪn/ eintragen, ausfüllen 5/A2

cup final /ˈkʌp faɪnl/ Pokalendspiel, Cupfinale 3/A4

final /ˈfaɪnl/ Endspiel, Finale 3/A4; letzte(r, s), endgültig 3/A6

finally /ˈfaɪnli/ schließlich, endlich 6/A3

find *(irr)* /faɪnd/ finden 3/B6

find out /ˌfaɪndˈaʊt/ herausfinden 3/A11

I'm fine, thanks. /aɪm ˈfaɪn ˌθæŋks/ Es geht mir gut, danke. 4/B9

fine /faɪn/ in Ordnung, gut 4/B9

we're doing fine /wɪə ˌdu:ɪŋ ˈfaɪn/ wir machen es gut Welcome

finish /ˈfɪnɪʃ/ beenden; enden 5/A7

°fire /faɪə/ Feuer; Kamin BS/8

first /fɜ:st/ zuerst 4/B1; erste (r, s) 5/A3

first name /ˈfɜ:st ˌneɪm/ Vorname 5/B7

fish *(pl* fish *or* fishes) /fɪʃ, fɪʃ, fɪʃɪz/ Fisch WB

°fizzy water /ˈfɪzi ˌwɔ:tə/ Mineralwasser 2/O2

°float /fləʊt/ oben bleiben 2/O1

floor /flɔ:/ Fußboden 4/A3

flower /ˈflaʊə/ Blume 2/B12

°flutter /ˈflʌtə/ flattern BS/1

fly /flaɪ/ Fliege WB

fly *(irr)* /flaɪ/ fliegen 5/A8

foal /fəʊl/ Fohlen 6/B4

°follow /ˈfɒləʊ/ folgen, verfolgen BS/9

food /fu:d/ Essen 2/A7

dog food /ˈdɒg fu:d/ Hundefutter 3/B10

foot *(pl* feet) /fʊt, fi:t/ Fuß 2/A1

football /ˈfʊtbɔ:l/ Fußball Welcome

football boots *(pl)* /ˈfʊtbɔ:l bu:ts/ Fußballschuhe 3/A1

°footstep /ˈfʊtstep/ Schritt BS/8

for /fɔ:/ für 2/A8

for /fɔ:/ *hier:* zu 3/A1; *hier:* nach 3/B6

°for *(+ Zeitraum)* /fɔ:/ ... lang 2/O2

for a while /ˌfɔ:r_ə ˈwaɪl/ eine Weile 6/A3

for an hour /ˌfɔ:r_ən_ˈaʊə/ eine Stunde lang 6/A5

for breakfast /fə ˈbrekfəst/ zum Frühstück 2/A12

for dinner /fə ˈdɪnə/ zum Abendessen 5/P7

for example /ˌfər_ɪgˈzɑ:mpl/ zum Beispiel 2/B11

for help /ˌfə ˈhelp/ als Hilfe 1/P5

for lunch /fɔ: ˈlʌntʃ/ zum Mittagessen 5/A2

forget *(irr)* /fəˈget/ vergessen 2/A2

fork /fɔ:k/ Gabel 2/A8

fountain /ˈfaʊntɪn/ Brunnen 1/B4

fourth /fɔ:θ/ vierte (r, s) 5/A3

fox /fɒks/ Fuchs WB

freckle /ˈfrekl/ Sommersprosse 2/A6

free /fri:/ frei; kostenlos 1/B4

free time /fri: ˈtaɪm/ Freizeit 3/I

°freezer /ˈfri:zə/ Gefrierschrank BS/3

fresh /freʃ/ neu, frisch 2/I

Friday /ˈfraɪdeɪ/ Freitag 1/B2

fried egg /ˌfraɪdˈeg/ Spiegelei 2/A7

friend /frend/ Freund/in Welcome

friendly /ˈfrendli/ freundlich 1/B2

friendly match /ˈfrendli mætʃ/ Freundschaftsspiel 3/A4

frog /frɒg/ Frosch WB

from /frɒm/ von; aus Welcome

fruit *(no pl)* /fru:t/ Frucht, Obst 4/B5

°fry /fraɪ/ braten 2/O2

°frying pan /ˈfraɪɪŋ ˌpæn/ Bratpfanne 2/O2

°full /fʊl/ voll 3/O

fun /fʌn/ Spaß 4/B1; lustig 4/B12; witzig 4/B12

be good fun /ˌbi: ˌgʊd ˈfʌn/ viel Spaß machen 4/A11

be fun /ˌbi: ˈfʌn/ Spaß machen Welcome

funny /ˈfʌni/ lustig; komisch 3/A4

G

°gallery /ˈgæləri/ Galerie BS/9

game /geɪm/ Spiel 3/B4

guessing game /ˈgesɪŋ ˌgeɪm/ Ratespiel 3/A8

garden /ˈgɑ:dn/ Garten 1/B2

geography /dʒiˈɒgrəfi/ Erdkunde 5/A3

German /ˈdʒɜ:mən/ Deutsch; deutsch Welcome

in German /ˌɪn ˈdʒɜ:mən/ auf Deutsch 2/B1

Germany /ˈdʒɜ:məni/ Deutschland 1/A9

gesture /ˈdʒestʃə/ Handbewegung, Geste 4/B6

°get in /ˌgetˈɪn/ hereinkommen BS/1

get *(irr)* /get/ bekommen 4/A11

get *(irr)* /get/ *hier:* zusammen kommen 2/B12; *hier:* bringen 5/B3; *hier:* kommen, gelangen 6/A6; werden BS/10

get on well /ˌget_ɒn ˈwel/ sich gut verstehen 6/A1

get out /ˌget_ˈaʊt/ aussteigen 4/B3

°get out /ˌget_ˈaʊt/ *hier:* herausnehmen BS/9

get ready /ˌget ˈredi/ sich fertig machen Welcome

get to school /ˌget_tə ˈsku:l/ zur Schule kommen 5/A8

get up /ˌget_ˈʌp/ aufstehen 2/B7

ghost /gəʊst/ Geist; Gespenst 4/B1

ghost story /ˈgəʊst ˌstɔ:ri/ Gespenstergeschichte 4/B10

°ghostel /ˈgəʊstl/ *Herberge für Gespenster* BS/8

giraffe /dʒəˈrɑ:f/ Giraffe WB

girl /gɜ:l/ Mädchen 3/A1

girlfriend /ˈgɜ:lˌfrend/ Freundin, Partnerin 1/B2

the girls' match /ðə ˈgɜ:lz ˌmætʃ/ das Spiel der Mädchen 3/A6

give a talk /ˌgɪv_ə ˈtɔ:k/ eine Rede halten 5/A6

give *(irr)* /gɪv/ geben Welcome

give *(irr)* /gɪv/ *hier:* verursachen 6/B3

glad /glæd/ glücklich, froh 6/A3

glass /glɑːs/ Glas Welcome

glasses *(pl)* /ˈglɑːsɪz/ Brille 2/A6

glove /glʌv/ Handschuh WB

Here you go. /ˌhɪə ju ˈgəʊ/ Hier, bitte! 4/B6

go by bus /ˌgəʊ baɪ ˈbʌs/ mit dem Bus fahren 5/A4

°go for a walk /ˌgəʊ fərˌə ˈwɔːk/ spazieren gehen 6/O

°go in /ˌgəʊ ˈɪn/ hineingehen BS/8

go *(irr)* /gəʊ/ gehen; fahren Welcome

go skating /ˌgəʊ ˈskeɪtɪŋ/ Skaten gehen 3/A9

go swimming /ˌgəʊ ˈswɪmɪŋ/ Schwimmen gehen 3/A9

Let's go! /ˌlets ˈgəʊ/ Lass(t) uns gehen! 1/A2

score a goal /ˌskɔːrˌə ˈgəʊl/ ein Tor schießen 3/A6

goalkeeper /ˈgəʊlˌkiːpə/ Tormann/Torfrau 3/A5

goat /gəʊt/ Ziege 6/A1

goldfish *(pl goldfish)* /ˈgəʊldˌfɪʃ/ Goldfisch 1/A4

good /gʊd/ gut Welcome

be good at something /ˌbiː ˈgʊdˌæt ˌsʌmθɪŋ/ gut in etwas sein Welcome

be good fun /ˌbiː ˌgʊd ˈfʌn/ viel Spaß machen 4/A11

Good luck! /ˌgʊd ˈlʌk/ Viel Glück! 3/B6

Good morning! /ˌgʊd ˈmɔːnɪŋ/ Guten Morgen! 2/I

good-looking /ˌgʊdˈlʊkɪŋ/ gut aussehend 2/A3

Goodbye. /ˌgʊdˈbaɪ/ Auf Wiedersehen. Welcome

°grab /græb/ greifen nach BS/10

granddaughter /ˈgrænˌdɔːtə/ Enkelin 5/B7

grandfather /ˈgrænˌfɑːðə/ Großvater 5/B7

grandma /ˈgrænˌmɑː/ Oma 5/B10

grandmother /ˈgrænˌmʌðə/ Großmutter 5/B7

grandpa /ˈgrænˌpɑː/ Opa 2/A4

grandparent /ˈgrænˌpeərənt/ Großelternteil 5/B7

grandson /ˈgrænˌsʌn/ Enkel 5/B7

°grape /greɪp/ Traube 5/O1

grass /grɑːs/ Gras; Wiese 2/B12

°grave /greɪv/ Grab BS/10

great /greɪt/ groß; großartig Welcome

green /griːn/ grün Welcome

grey /greɪ/ grau 2/A6

group /gruːp/ Gruppe 1/A2

°grow *(irr)* /grəʊ/ wachsen BS/2

guess /ges/ (er)raten 2/A6

guessing game /ˈgesɪŋ ˌgeɪm/ Ratespiel 3/A8

guest /gest/ Gast 3/B6

°guide dog /ˈgaɪdˌdɒg/ Blindenhund BS/5

guinea pig /ˈgɪni ˌpɪg/ Meerschweinchen WB

guitar /gɪˈtɑː/ Gitarre 1/A5

play the guitar /ˌpleɪ ðə gɪˈtɑː/ Gitarre spielen 1/A5

guy /gaɪ/ Kerl, Typ 2/A3

gym (= gymnasium) /dʒɪm, dʒɪmneɪziəm/ Turnhalle 3/A9

do gymnastics /ˌduː dʒɪmˈnæstɪks/ Turnen 3/A8

H

hair /heə/ Haar 2/A1

°hairy /ˈheəri/ haarig BS/4

half /hɑːf/ halb 2/A7

half (past) /ˈhɑːf pɑːst/ halb 2/B7

°hall /hɔːl/ Halle BS/8

°hallway /ˈhɔːlˌweɪ/ Korridor, Flur BS/10

hamster /ˈhæmstə/ Hamster WB

hang on /ˌhæŋ ˈɒn/ warten 4/B1

hang up /ˌhæŋ ˈʌp/ aufhängen 2/A12

happen /ˈhæpən/ geschehen, passieren 2/A4

happy /ˈhæpi/ glücklich 1/B2

Happy birthday (to you)! /ˌhæpi ˈbɜːθdeɪ tʊ juː/ Herzlichen Glückwunsch zum Geburtstag! 5/B1

hard /hɑːd/ hart, anstrengend 4/A10; fest, kräftig 5/O2

°hard-boiled /ˌhɑːdˈbɔɪld/ hart gekocht 2/O2

has got /ˌhəz ˈgɒt/ hat Welcome

hat /hæt/ Hut WB

hate /heɪt/ hassen, nicht ausstehen können Welcome

°be haunted /ˌbiː ˈhɔːntɪd/ spuken BS/8

°It's haunted. /ˌɪts ˈhɔːntɪd/ Es spukt. BS/10

have a good time /ˌhævˌə ˌgʊdˈtaɪm/ Spaß haben, eine gute Zeit haben 6/A5

°have a look at /ˌhævˌə ˈlʊkˌət/ sich ansehen 4/O

have a picnic /ˌhævˌə ˈpɪknɪk/ ein Picknick machen 5/B11

have breakfast /ˌhæv ˈbrekfəst/ frühstücken 2/A13

have got /ˌhæv ˈgɒt/ haben 1/A5

have *(irr)* /hæv/ haben; essen, trinken 1/B2

°have seen /ˌhæv ˈseen/ haben gesehen BS/3

have to /ˈhæv tə/ müssen 4/B1

Have you got any new ones? /ˌhæv jə ˌgɒtˌeni ˈnjuː ˌwʌnz/

haven't got /ˈhævnt gɒt/ haben nicht 2/A3

It's fun having you here. /ˌɪts ˈfʌn ˌhævɪŋ ju: ˈhɪə/ Es ist schön, dass du hier bist. 6/A3

he /hiː/ er Welcome

he's (= he is) /hiːz, ˈhiːˌɪz/ er ist 2/A3

head /hed/ Kopf 4/A10

headword /ˈhedwɜːd/ Stichwort; *hier:* Oberbegriff 5/P5

healthy /ˈhelθi/ gesund 2/A10

hear *(irr)* /hɪə/ hören 1/A1

by heart /ˌbaɪ ˈhɑːt/ auswendig 2/B12

°heart /hɑːt/ Herz BS/1

heaven /ˈhevn/ Himmel Welcome

hedgehog /ˈhedʒˌhɒg/ Igel WB

by helicopter /ˌbaɪ ˈheliˌkɒptə/ mit dem Hubschrauber 5/A8

hello /həˈləʊ/ hallo Welcome

help /help/ helfen 3/B4

help out /ˌhelpˈaʊt/ aushelfen 2/A12

for help /ˌfə ˈhelp/ als Hilfe 1/P5

Help! /help/ Hilfe! 6/B3

hen house /ˈhen haʊs/ Hühner-
stall 6/A2

her /hɜː/ ihr/ihre; sie Welcome

here /hɪə/ hier; hierher 1/B2

Here I am! /ˌhɪərˌaɪˈæm/ Hier
bin ich! 1/B2

Here you are. /ˌhɪə juˈɑː/ Hier,
bitte! 2/B10

Here you go. /ˌhɪə juˈgəʊ/ Hier,
bitte! 4/B6

here's (= here is) /hɪəz,
hɪərˈɪz/ hier ist 3/B6

Hi, guys! (*informal*) /ˈhaɪ gaɪz/
Hallo Leute! 3/B6

high /haɪ/ hoch 6/B3

higher /ˈhaɪə/ höher 6/B3

°hill /hɪl/ Hügel BS/3

him /hɪm/ ihn, ihm 4/A6

hire /ˈhaɪə/ mieten 6/A5

his /hɪz/ sein/seine/seiner/seins
Welcome

history /ˈhɪstri/ Geschichte 5/A2

°hit (*irr*) /hɪt/ treffen, stoßen
gegen BS/10

°hole /həʊl/ Loch BS/1

be on holiday /ˌbiˌɒn ˈhɒlɪdeɪ/
Urlaub haben 6/A3

holiday /ˈhɒlɪdeɪ/ Ferien; Urlaub
6/A1

home /həʊm/ Zuhause;
Haus 1/B2

at home /ˌæt ˈhəʊm/ zu Hause
3/P4

home /həʊm/ nach Hause 5/P7

homework /ˈhəʊmwɜːk/ Hausaufgaben 2/B1

honey /ˈhʌni/ Honig 2/A11

°hood /hʊd/ Kapuze BS/10

hooray /hʊˈreɪ/ hurra 3/A4

hope /həʊp/ hoffen 1/B2

horse /hɔːs/ Pferd 3/A8

ride a horse /ˌraɪdˌə ˈhɔːs/
reiten 3/A8

hot /hɒt/ heiß Welcome

hot chocolate /hɒt ˈtʃɒklət/
(heißer) Kakao 4/B9

for an hour /ˌfɔːrˌən ˈaʊə/ eine
Stunde lang 6/A5

house /haʊs/ Haus 1/B2

at Vanessa's house
/ˌætˌvəˌnesəz ˈhaʊs/ bei
Vanessa zu Hause 4/A6

how /haʊ/ wie 1/A3

How about …? /ˈhaʊˌəˌbaʊt/ Wie
wäre es mit …? 3/B4

How are you? /ˌhaʊˈɑːˌjʊ/
Wie geht es dir?/Wie geht es
Ihnen? 4/B9

how many /haʊ ˈmeni/ wie viele
3/B5

how much /haʊ ˈmʌtʃ/ wie viel
4/B6

How much is it? /ˌhaʊ mʌtʃˈɪzˌɪt/
Wie viel kostet es? 3/B4

How old are you? /haʊˈəʊldˌɑː
ˌjʊ/ Wie alt bist du? Welcome

how to /ˈhaʊ tʊ/ wie man 3/A1

hungry /ˈhʌŋgri/ hungrig 4/B9

hurry (up) /ˌhʌriˈˌʌp/ sich
beeilen 2/A2

Hurry up! /ˌhʌriˈˌʌp/ Beeile
dich! 2/A7

hurt (*irr*) /hɜːt/ wehtun,
schmerzen 4/A10

husband /ˈhʌzbənd/ Ehemann 5/B7

I

I /aɪ/ ich Welcome

I don't know. /ˌaɪ ˌdəʊnt ˈnəʊ/ Ich
weiß es nicht. 3/B6

I don't like … /ˌaɪ ˈdəʊnt laɪk/ Ich
mag … nicht. 2/A7

I don't understand. /ˌaɪ
ˌdəʊntˌʌndəˈstænd/ Ich verstehe
es nicht. 3/A4

°I want to be … /aɪ ˈwɒntə ˌbiː/
Ich möchte … sein. 1/O

I wish it was Sunday! /aɪ ˌwɪʃˌɪt
wəz ˈsʌndeɪ/ Ich wünschte,
es wäre Sonntag. 2/A7

I'd rather … /ˌaɪd ˈrɑːðə/ Ich
würde lieber … 5/A2

I'll (= I will) /aɪl, ˈaɪ wɪl/ ich
werde 3/B4

I'll take it. /ˌaɪl ˈteɪkˌɪt/ Ich
nehme es. 3/B4

I'm (= I am) /aɪm, ˈaɪˌæm/ ich bin,
ich heiße Welcome

I'm fine, thanks.
/aɪm ˈfaɪn ˌθæŋks/ Es geht mir
gut, danke. 4/B9

I've got (= I have got)
/ˌaɪv ˈgɒt, ˌaɪ hæv ˈgɒt/ ich habe
Welcome

°ice /aɪs/ Eis BS/5

ice cream /ˈaɪs ˌkriːm/ Eis
Welcome

ICT (= Information and
Communication Technology)
/ˌaɪˌsiːˈtiː, ˌɪnfəˈmeɪʃnˌən
kəˌmjuːnɪˈkeɪʃn tekˌnɒlədʒi/
Informationstechnologie,
IT 5/A3

°icy /ˈaɪsi/ vereist BS/10

idea /aɪˈdɪə/ Idee Welcome

if /ɪf/ wenn; falls Welcome;
ob 5/B10

imagination /ɪˌmædʒɪˈneɪʃn/
Fantasie, Vorstellungskraft
2/B12

imagine /ɪˈmædʒɪn/ sich etwas
vorstellen 3/A10

important /ɪmˈpɔːtnt/ wichtig
2/B6

improve /ɪmˈpruːv/ verbessern,
verschönern 2/B13

in /ɪn/ in; auf Welcome

in detail /ɪn ˈdiːteɪl/ ausführlich
2/B12

in English /ɪnˈɪŋglɪʃ/ auf Englisch Welcome

in front of /ɪn ˈfrʌntˌəv/ vor 4/B5

in German /ɪn ˈdʒɜːmən/ auf
Deutsch 2/B1

in pairs /ɪn ˈpeəz/ paarweise 2/P2

In picture number … /ɪn ˈpɪktʃə
ˌnʌmbə/ Auf Bild Nummer …
5/B3

in the afternoon
/ɪn ðiˌɑːftəˈnuːn/ am Nachmittag 3/P14

in the middle of /ɪn ðə ˈmɪdlˌəv/
in der Mitte von 4/A4

in the morning /ɪn ðə ˈmɔːnɪŋ/
am Morgen 2/B7

in the street /ɪn ðə ˈstriːt/ auf
der Straße 3/A9

in this photo /ˌɪn ðɪs ˈfəʊtəʊ/ auf
diesem Foto 5/B8

India /ˈɪndiə/ Indien 1/A5

°Indian /ˈɪndiən/ Inder/in;
indisch 1/O

indoor /ˌɪnˈdɔː/ drinnen, im
Haus 6/A6

information (*no pl*) /ˌɪnfəˈmeɪʃn/
Informationen 5/A2

information stand /ˌɪnfəˈmeɪʃn stænd/ Informationsstand 6/A2

ink /ɪŋk/ Tinte 2/B6

inline skating /ˌɪnlaɪn ˈskeɪtɪŋ/ Inlinerfahren 6/A10

°insect /ˈɪnsekt/ Insekt 3/O

inside /ɪnˈsaɪd/ innen, drinnen; hinein 2/B6

instead /ɪnˈsted/ stattdessen 2/B12

interesting /ˈɪntrəstɪŋ/ interessant 3/B4

on the Internet /ˌɒn ðiˈɪntənet/ im Internet 5/B2

interview /ˈɪntəˌvjuː/ interviewen, befragen 3/B5

into /ˈɪntuː/ in Welcome

introduce sb /ˌɪntrəˈdjuːs ˌsʌmbədi/ jdn vorstellen 4/B9

invite /ɪnˈvaɪt/ einladen 5/B2

is /ɪz/ ist Welcome

Is it …? /ˈɪzˌɪt/ Ist es …? 2/B7

Is there …? /ˈɪz ðeər/ Gibt es …? 4/B6

Is there a …? /ˈɪz ðeərˌə/ Gibt es ein/e …? 1/B3

island /ˈaɪlənd/ Insel 6/B5

… isn't it? /ˈɪzntˌɪt/ … nicht wahr? 4/B9

it /ɪt/ es Welcome

It isn't a pen. /ɪtˈɪzntˌə ˌpen/ Das ist kein Stift. 2/B1

it's (= it is) /ɪts, ˈɪtˌɪz/ hier: es kostet 3/B1

it's (= it is) /ɪts, ˈɪtˌɪz/ es ist; es gibt Welcome

It's great fun. /ˌɪts greɪt ˈfʌn/ Das macht viel Spaß. 1/B4

It's half past eight. /ɪts ˌhɑːf pɑːstˌˈeɪt/ Es ist halb neun. 2/A7

It's my turn. /ˌɪts ˈmaɪ tɜːn/ Ich bin dran. 4/B1

°its /ɪts/ sein(e), ihr(e) BS/4

jacket /ˈdʒækɪt/ Jacke WB

jam /dʒæm/ Marmelade 2/A8

January /ˈdʒænjuəri/ Januar 5/B7

job /dʒɒb/ Aufgabe 4/A6

°job /dʒɒb/ hier: Stelle, Job, Beruf 1/O

join /dʒɔɪn/ mitmachen 3/A1

°joke /dʒəʊk/ Spaß, Witz BS/9

°juggle /ˈdʒʌɡl/ jonglieren 3/O

°juggling /ˈdʒʌɡlɪŋ/ Jonglieren 1/O

orange juice /ˈɒrɪndʒˌˌdʒuːs/ Orangensaft Welcome

juice /dʒuːs/ Saft 5/A5

July /dʒʊˈlaɪ/ Juli 5/B7

jump /dʒʌmp/ springen WB

jump up /ˌdʒʌmpˌˈʌp/ aufspringen 6/A3

jumper /ˈdʒʌmpə/ Pullover WB

June /dʒuːn/ Juni 5/B7

jungle /ˈdʒʌŋɡl/ Dschungel, Urwald 6/B5

just /dʒʌst/ gerade 5/B3

just /dʒʌst/ nur, bloß 2/A2

just like me /ˌdʒʌst laɪk ˈmiː/ genau wie ich 1/A4

K

°keep doing sth /ˌkiːp ˈduːɪŋ ˌsʌmθɪŋ/ etw weiter tun 2/O2

keeper /ˈkiːpə/ (Zoo)wärter/in 6/B3

ketchup /ˈketʃəp/ Ketschup 1/A4

kickabout /ˈkɪkəˌbaʊt/ Kicken 3/A1

kid /kɪd/ Kind 6/B4

°kill /kɪl/ töten BS/6

°killed /kɪld/ tötete/töteten BS/6

kind /kaɪnd/ Art; Sorte 4/B10

kitchen /ˈkɪtʃən/ Küche 2/A7

kite /kaɪt/ Drachen Welcome

knee /niː/ Knie 2/A1

knife (pl knives) /naɪf, naɪvz/ Messer 2/A8

°knock (on/at) /nɒk/ klopfen BS/10

know (irr) /nəʊ/ wissen; kennen 2/A8

L

label /ˈleɪbl/ beschriften 2/A13

°lady /ˈleɪdi/ Frau BS/10

lamb /læm/ Lamm 6/A1

lamp /læmp/ Lampe 4/A1

land /lænd/ landen 6/A3

language /ˈlæŋɡwɪdʒ/ Sprache Welcome

last /lɑːst/ letzte(r, s) 5/A2

at last /ət ˈlɑːst/ endlich; schließlich Welcome

late /leɪt/ (zu) spät 2/A2

later /ˈleɪtə/ später 2/A13

laugh /lɑːf/ lachen 6/B1

°laughter /ˈlɑːftə/ Gelächter, Lachen BS/7

leaflet /ˈliːflət/ Prospekt; Broschüre 6/A6

learn (irr) /lɜːn/ lernen 1/A6

leave (irr) /liːv/ verlassen; abfahren 2/B7

leave out /ˌliːvˌˈaʊt/ auslassen 4/A4

have sth left /ˌhæv sʌmθɪŋ ˈleft/ etw übrig haben 3/A1

on the left /ˌɒn ðə ˈleft/ links, auf der linken Seite 6/A1

°left /left/ (nach) links BS/9

°be left /ˌbi ˈleft/ übrig bleiben BS/3

leg /leɡ/ Bein 2/A1

°lemon /ˈlemən/ Zitrone 5/O1

lemonade /ˌleməˈneɪd/ Limonade 1/B4

lesson /ˈlesn/ Stunde; Unterricht 5/A2

let (irr) /let/ lassen 1/A2

let's (= let us) /lets, ˈletˌəs/ lass(t) uns … Welcome

Let's go! /ˌlets ˈɡəʊ/ Lass(t) uns gehen! 1/A2

letter /ˈletə/ Buchstabe 2/B9

library /ˈlaɪbrəri/ Bücherei 3/A1

lie /laɪ/ lügen 5/B10; liegen BS/10

life (pl lives) /laɪf, laɪvz/ Leben 4/A7

light /laɪt/ Licht 4/B1

I don't like … /ˌaɪ ˈdəʊnt laɪk/ Ich mag … nicht. 2/A7

like /laɪk/ mögen Welcome; wie 4/A4

just like me /ˌdʒʌst laɪk ˈmiː/ genau wie ich 1/A4

What is it like? /ˌwɒtˌɪzˌɪt ˈlaɪk/ Wie ist es? 5/A8

like best /ˌlaɪk ˈbest/ am liebsten mögen 5/B12

like doing sth /laɪk ˈduːɪŋ ˌsʌmθɪŋ/ etw gern tun 3/B11

like this /ˌlaɪk ˈðɪs/ so 1/A3

liked /laɪkt/ mochte 6/A2

line /laɪn/ Linie; Zeile 4/B3

lion /ˈlaɪən/ Löwe WB

list /lɪst/ Liste 2/A13

listen (to) /ˈlɪsn/ zuhören 3/B6

listener /ˈlɪsnə/ Zuhörer/in 3/B6

°**litre** /ˈliːtə/ Liter 5/O1

little /ˈlɪtl/ klein Welcome

°**a little** /ə ˈlɪtl/ ein bisschen 2/O2

live /lɪv/ leben, wohnen
Welcome

living room /ˈlɪvɪŋ ˌruːm/ Wohnzimmer 4/A6

°**locked** /lɒkt/ verschlossen
BS/10

long /lɒŋ/ lang 2/A3

°**longer** /ˈlɒŋgə/ länger 2/O2

look /lʊk/ aussehen 3/B4

°**look after** /ˌlʊk ˈɑːftə/ aufpas-
sen auf BS/5

look after sb
/ˌlʊk ˈɑːftə ˌsʌmbədi/ sich um
jdn kümmern 4/A11

look around /ˌlʊk əˈraʊnd/ sich
umsehen Welcome

look (at) /ˈlʊk ət/ (an)sehen,
(an)schauen 1/A2

°**look down** /ˌlʊk ˈdaʊn/ nach
unten schauen BS/9

look for /ˈlʊk fə/ suchen nach
3/A1

look out /ˌlʊk ˈaʊt/ hinaus-
schauen 6/A3

look up /ˌlʊk ˈʌp/ hochschauen
6/A3

Look! /lʊk/ Schau(t) mal!
Welcome

is looking for /ˌɪz ˈlʊkɪŋ fə/ sucht
(gerade) nach 3/A1

°**lose (irr)** /luːz/ verlieren BS/8

a lot (of) /ə ˈlɒt/ viel(e), jede
Menge Welcome

lots of /ˈlɒts əv/ viel, jede
Menge Welcome

loud /laʊd/ laut 2/B9

°**louder** /ˈlaʊdə/ lauter BS/10

love /lʌv/ lieben, sehr mögen
Welcome

love doing sth /lʌv ˈduːɪŋ
ˌsʌmθɪŋ/ etw sehr gern
tun 3/B8

I love reading. /aɪ ˌlʌv ˈriːdɪŋ/ Ich
lese sehr gern. 6/B1

lovely /ˈlʌvli/ schön 1/B2

Good luck! /ˌgʊd ˈlʌk/ Viel
Glück! 3/B6

You're lucky. /ˌjɔː ˈlʌki/ Du bist
ein Glückspilz. 5/A2

lunch /lʌntʃ/ Mittagessen 5/A2

for lunch /fə ˈlʌntʃ/ zum Mittagessen 5/A2

lunchbox /ˈlʌntʃbɒks/ Frühstücksdose 2/B4

lunchtime /ˈlʌntʃtaɪm/ Mittagszeit, Mittagspause 3/A1

°**lyrics (pl)** /ˈlɪrɪks/ Liedtext BS/7

M

machine /məˈʃiːn/ Maschine,
Apparat 4/A4

magazine /ˌmægəˈziːn/ Zeitschrift 4/A11

magic trick /ˌmædʒɪk ˈtrɪk/
Zaubertrick 5/B3

make (irr) /meɪk/ machen 2/A7

make notes /ˌmeɪk ˈnəʊts/ sich
Notizen machen 2/B13

make up /ˌmeɪk ˈʌp/ erfinden,
sich ausdenken 3/B3

man (pl men) /mæn, men/
Mann 5/B7

many /ˈmeni/ viele 5/B12

map /mæp/ Karte 2/B1

marble /ˈmɑːbl/ Murmel 3/B5

March /mɑːtʃ/ März 1/B2

market /ˈmɑːkɪt/ Markt 1/B2

at the market /ˌæt ðə ˈmɑːkɪt/
auf dem Markt 3/P14

match /mætʃ/ Spiel 3/A4

friendly match /ˈfrendli mætʃ/
Freundschaftsspiel 3/A6

match /mætʃ/ zuordnen 1/A4

matching /ˈmætʃɪŋ/ zusammen-
passend 1/P3

maths /mɑːθs/ Mathe 5/A2

May /meɪ/ Mai 5/B7

°**maybe** /ˈmeɪbi/ vielleicht BS/8

(to) me /miː/ mir; mich; ich
Welcome

meal /miːl/ Mahlzeit, Essen 3/A1

mean (irr) /miːn/ meinen 4/B9

Nice to meet you. /ˌnaɪs tə ˈmiːt
jə/ Schön, dich/Sie zu treffen.
4/B9

meet (irr) /miːt/ treffen; sich
treffen Welcome

member /ˈmembə/ Mitglied 2/P6

membership /ˈmembəʃɪp/
Mitgliedschaft 6/A6

menu /ˈmenjuː/ Speisekarte
2/A13

°**metre** /ˈmiːtə/ Meter 4/O

miaow /miˈaʊ/ miau 1/B2

in the middle of /ˌɪn ðə ˈmɪdl əv/
in der Mitte von 4/A4

milk /mɪlk/ Milch 2/A7

mime /maɪm/ mimen, pantomimisch darstellen 2/P4

mirror /ˈmɪrə/ Spiegel 2/A3

miss /mɪs/ verpassen 5/A2

missing /ˈmɪsɪŋ/ fehlend 2/B11

mister /ˈmɪstə/ Herr 4/B9

mix /mɪks/ (ver)mischen 6/B6

mobile (phone) /ˈməʊbaɪl/
Handy Welcome

model plane /ˌmɒdl ˈpleɪn/
Modellflugzeug 6/B3

model train /ˌmɒdl ˈtreɪn/
Modelleisenbahn 3/B5

at the moment /ˌæt ðə
ˈməʊmənt/ im Moment 3/B6

Monday /ˈmʌndeɪ/ Montag 1/B2

°**money** /ˈmʌni/ Geld BS/6

monkey /ˈmʌŋki/ Affe WB

month /mʌnθ/ Monat 5/B1

more /mɔː/ mehr; weitere 2/A7

more /mɔː/ hier: eher 2/A11

Good morning! /ˌgʊd ˈmɔːnɪŋ/
Guten Morgen! 2/I

in the morning /ˌɪn ðə ˈmɔːnɪŋ/
am Morgen 2/B7

morning /ˈmɔːnɪŋ/ Morgen 4/A6

this morning /ðɪs ˈmɔːnɪŋ/ heute
Morgen 6/A3

°**most** /məʊst/ am meisten 4/O;
die meisten 5/O2

°**mostly** /ˈməʊstli/ meistens BS/4

mother /ˈmʌðə/ Mutter 5/B7

motorbike /ˈməʊtəˌbaɪk/ Motor-
rad WB

mountain /ˈmaʊntɪn/ Berg 3/A9

mouse (pl mice) /maʊs, maɪs/
Maus 1/A6

mouth /maʊθ/ Mund 2/A2

move /muːv/ umziehen 6/A3;
sich bewegen BS/10

°**the movies (pl)** /ðə ˈmuːviz/
Kino BS/7

Mr /'mɪstə/ Herr 2/A3

Mrs /'mɪsɪz/ Frau 3/A1

How much is it? /ˌhaʊ mʌtʃˈɪzˌɪt/ Wie viel kostet es? 3/B4

much /mʌtʃ/ viel 3/B4

much /mʌtʃ/ sehr 4/A10

muesli /'mju:zli/ Müsli 2/A11

mug /mʌg/ Becher 3/B5

mum /mʌm/ Mama 1/B2

music /'mju:zɪk/ Musik Welcome

must /mʌst/ müssen 3/A9

my /maɪ/ mein(e) Welcome

My name is … /ˌmaɪ ˈneɪmˌɪz/ Ich heiße … Welcome

near /nɪə/ nahe, in der Nähe von 6/B1

neck /nek/ Hals; Nacken 2/A1

need /ni:d/ brauchen 2/A8

neighbour /'neɪbə/ Nachbar/in 1/B2

neighbourhood /'neɪbəˌhʊd/ Viertel, Nachbarschaft 1/B2

nephew /'nefju:/ Neffe 5/B7

nerves (pl) /nɜ:vz/ Nerven 4/B10

°nervous /'nɜ:vəs/ nervös BS/9

°network /'netˌwɜ:k/ Netz 4/O

never /'nevə/ nie, niemals 4/A6

new /nju:/ neu 1/A2

new ones /'nju: ˌwʌnz/ neue(r, s) 3/B4

news (no pl) /nju:z/ Neuigkeit; Nachrichten 3/A5

°newsagent's shop / 'nju:zˌeɪdʒənts ˌʃɒp/ Zeitschriftengeschäft 1/O

next /nekst/ nächste (r, s) 3/B8

next /nekst/ dann, als Nächstes Welcome

next door /ˌnekstˈdɔ:/ nebenan 6/A5

next to /'nekstˌtə/ neben 4/A3

°nibble /'nɪbl/ knabbern BS/1

nice /naɪs/ schön; nett 1/A6

Nice to meet you. /ˌnaɪs tə ˈmi:tˌjə/ Schön, dich/euch/Sie zu treffen. 4/B9

Nice to see you. /ˌnaɪs tə ˈsi:ˌjə/ Schön, dich/euch/Sie zu sehen. 5/B3

niece /ni:s/ Nichte 5/B7

night /naɪt/ Nacht; Abend 5/A5

nil /nɪl/ Null (bei Spielen) WB

no /nəʊ/ nein Welcome; kein(e) 2/B1

nobody /'nəʊbədi/ niemand, keiner 5/B3

noise /nɔɪz/ Geräusch 6/B5

nose /nəʊz/ Nase 2/A2

not /nɒt/ nicht Welcome

°not at all /ˌnɒtˌətˈɔ:l/ überhaupt nicht BS/1

°nothing /'nʌθɪŋ/ nichts BS/3

notice /'nəʊtɪs/ bemerken; wahrnehmen 2/A7

November /nəʊ'vembə/ November 5/B7

now /naʊ/ jetzt 1/B2

number /'nʌmbə/ Zahl; Nummer Welcome

o'clock /ə'klɒk/ Uhr 2/A2

October /ɒk'təʊbə/ Oktober 5/B7

odd one out /ˌɒd wʌnˈaʊt/ das Wort, das nicht zu den anderen passt 3/P4

of /əv/ von 2/A7

Of course! /əv ˈkɔ:s/ Natürlich! 4/B6

off /ɒf/ weg 6/A3

offer /'ɒfə/ anbieten 6/A6

often /'ɒfn/ oft, häufig 4/A6

oh dear /əʊ ˈdɪə/ oje 2/B1

°oil /ɔɪl/ Öl 2/O2

old /əʊld/ alt Welcome

on /ɒn/ auf; an; in 3/A9

What's on? /ˌwɒtsˈɒn/ Was ist los? 3/A1

on /ɒn/ hier: über 4/A11

on the Internet /ˌɒn ðiˈɪntənet/ im Internet 5/B2

on the left /ˌɒn ðə ˈleft/ links, auf der linken Seite 6/A1

on the phone /ˌɒn ðə ˈfəʊn/ am Telefon 5/B3

once more /ˌwʌns ˈmɔ:/ noch einmal 2/B9

one /wʌn/ eins Welcome

°one night /'wʌn ˌnaɪt/ eines Nachts BS/2

only /'əʊnli/ nur, bloß 2/A7

only /'əʊnli/ einzige(r, s) 2/B12

onto /'ɒntə/ auf, in 6/A3

open /'əʊpən/ öffnen, aufmachen 2/B1

°open /'əʊpən/ sich öffnen BS/10

open-air /ˌəʊpənˈeə/ im Freien 2/B12

°opened /'əʊpənd/ öffnete/ öffneten 4/O

opening hours (pl) /'əʊpənɪŋˌaʊəz/ Öffnungszeiten 6/A6

opposite /'ɒpəzɪt/ Gegenteil 3/P13

or /ɔ:/ oder 2/B7

orange /'ɒrɪndʒ/ orange Welcome

°orange /'ɒrɪndʒ/ Orange; Apfelsine 5/O1

orange juice /'ɒrɪndʒˌdʒu:s/ Orangensaft Welcome

order /'ɔ:də/ Reihenfolge 2/B5

other /'ʌðə/ andere(r, s) 3/B2

our /aʊə/ unsere(r, s) 1/B2

out /aʊt/ heraus, hinaus; hier: aus 6/A3

out and about /ˌaʊtˌənˌəˈbaʊt/ unterwegs 6/I

out of /'aʊtˌəv/ aus 2/B6

outside /ˌaʊtˈsaɪd/ vor 6/A3; draußen; außerhalb 6/A3

°over /'əʊvə/ über 4/O

all over /ˌɔ:lˈəʊvə/ überall 6/B3

over there /ˌəʊvə ˈðeə/ dort (drüben) 4/B6

Over to you. /ˌəʊvə tə ˈju:/ Jetzt bist du dran. 3/B6

overhead projector /ˌəʊvəhed prəˈdʒektə/ Overheadprojektor 2/B4

own /əʊn/ eigene(r, s) 3/A12

p (= penny, pence) /pi:, 'peni, pens/ Pence 4/B6

page /peɪdʒ/ Seite 2/A5

pair /'peə/ Paar 2/P2

rhyming pair /'raɪmɪŋ peə/ Reimpaar 1/P14

°frying pan /'fraɪɪŋ ˌpæn/ Bratpfanne 2/O2

°pan /pæn/ Pfanne 2/O2

piece of paper /ˌpi:sˌəv ˈpeɪpə/ Blatt Papier 6/B6

paradise /ˈpærədaɪs/ Paradies 6/A6

parents (pl) /ˈpeərənts/ Eltern 1/A4

parrot /ˈpærət/ Papagei 1/A5

body part /ˈbɒdi ˌpaːt/ Körperteil 2/A2

part /paːt/ Teil Welcome

°pass /paːs/ vorbeigehen an BS/10

°passenger /ˈpæsɪndʒə/ Fahrgast, Passagier/in 4/O

past /paːst/ nach 2/A7

half past six /ˌhaːf paːst ˈsɪks/ halb sieben 5/A5

°path /paːθ/ Weg, Pfad BS/10

PE (= physical education) /ˌpiː ˈiː, ˌfɪzɪkl̩ ˌedjʊˈkeɪʃn/ Sport 5/A3

°peanut /ˈpiːnʌt/ Erdnuss BS/1

°peel /piːl/ schälen 3/O

pen /pen/ Stift 2/B1

pencil /ˈpensl/ Bleistift 2/B4

pencil case /ˈpensl ˌkeɪs/ Federmäppchen 2/B4

penguin /ˈpeŋgwɪn/ Pinguin WB

people /ˈpiːpl/ Leute, Menschen 1/I

°pepper /ˈpepə/ Pfeffer 2/O2

per /pɜː/ pro 6/A6

perfect /ˈpɜːfɪkt/ perfekt Welcome

°perhaps /pəˈhæps/ vielleicht 3/O

pet /pet/ Haustier WB

answer the phone /ˌaːnsə ðə ˈfəʊn/ ans Telefon gehen 5/B3

on the phone /ˌɒn ðə ˈfəʊn/ am Telefon 5/B3

phone /fəʊn/ Telefon Welcome

phone call /ˈfəʊn kɔːl/ Telefonanruf 5/B3

in this photo /ˌɪn ðɪs ˈfəʊtəʊ/ auf diesem Foto 5/B8

photo /ˈfəʊtəʊ/ Foto 1/B1

photography /fəˈtɒgrəfi/ Fotografie 5/A7

°take photos /ˌteɪk ˈfəʊtəʊz/ Fotos machen 3/O

phrase /freɪz/ Satz; Ausdruck 2/B7

phrase book /ˈfreɪz bʊk/ Sammlung von Redewendungen 2/A13

play the piano /ˌpleɪ ðə piˈænəʊ/ Klavier spielen 3/B8

pick sb up /ˌpɪk ˌsʌmbədiˈʌp/ jdn abholen 4/B1

pick sth up /ˌpɪk ˌsʌmθɪŋˈʌp/ etw aufheben 6/B3

°pick up /ˌpɪkˈʌp/ aufheben 3/O

°pickpocket /ˈpɪkˌpɒkɪt/ Taschendieb/in BS/9

have a picnic /ˌhæv ə ˈpɪknɪk/ ein Picknick machen 5/B11

picnic area /ˈpɪknɪk ˌeəriə/ Picknickbereich 6/A1

picture /ˈpɪktʃə/ Bild 3/A13

picture dictionary /ˈpɪktʃə ˌdɪkʃənri/ Bildwörterbuch 2/A13

piece /piːs/ Stück; Teil 1/A9

piece of paper /ˌpiːs əv ˈpeɪpə/ Blatt Papier 4/B12

pig /pɪg/ Schwein Welcome

guinea pig /ˈgɪni ˌpɪg/ Meerschweinchen 3/B9

pillow /ˈpɪləʊ/ Kissen 4/A1

pinboard /ˈpɪnˌbɔːd/ Pinnwand 2/B1

°pineapple /ˈpaɪnˌæpl/ Ananas 5/O1

place /pleɪs/ Ort; Platz Welcome

plan /plæn/ planen 2/A13

plane /pleɪn/ Flugzeug 6/A4

model plane /ˌmɒdl ˈpleɪn/ Modellflugzeug 6/B3

plate /pleɪt/ Teller 2/A8

play /pleɪ/ spielen Welcome

°play /pleɪ/ Spiel BS/2

play the guitar /ˌpleɪ ðə gɪˈtaː/ Gitarre spielen 1/A5

play the piano /ˌpleɪ ðə piˈænəʊ/ Klavier spielen 3/B8

playground /ˈpleɪˌgraʊnd/ Spielplatz 1/B3

playing field /ˈpleɪɪŋ ˌfiːld/ Sportplatz 3/A9

please /pliːz/ bitte 2/A7

pm (= post meridiem) /ˌpiːˈem, ˌpəʊst məˈrɪdiəm/ nachmittags; abends (nur hinter Uhrzeit zwischen 12 Uhr mittags und Mitternacht) 3/A1

°pocket /ˈpɒkɪt/ Tasche (an Kleidungsstück) BS/9

poem /ˈpəʊɪm/ Gedicht 2/A6

°point /pɔɪnt/ Punkt 5/O2

point (at/to) /pɔɪnt/ deuten (auf), zeigen (auf) 1/A5

°poisonous /ˈpɔɪznəs/ giftig BS/4

polar bear /ˌpəʊlə ˈbeə/ Eisbär WB

°police /pəˈliːs/ Polizei BS/5

°policeman (pl policemen) /pəˈliːsmən/ Polizist BS/9

Polish /ˈpəʊlɪʃ/ Polnisch; polnisch Welcome

pond /pɒnd/ Teich 1/B4

swimming pool /ˈswɪmɪŋ puːl/ Schwimmbad 1/B3

postcard /ˈpəʊstˌkaːd/ Postkarte, Ansichtskarte 3/B5

pound /paʊnd/ Pfund 3/B1

pour /pɔː/ gießen, eingießen 5/B5

°practice /ˈpræktɪs/ Praxis 1/O

°veterinary practice /ˌvetrnri ˈpræktɪs/ Tierarztpraxis 1/O

Practice matters. /ˌpræktɪs ˈmætəz/ etwa: Übung macht den Meister. 1/P1

practise /ˈpræktɪs/ üben 3/A12

prepare /prɪˈpeə/ vorbereiten 3/A13

present /ˈpreznt/ Geschenk 5/B3

present (to) /prɪˈzent/ präsentieren 3/A13

presentation /ˌpreznˈteɪʃn/ Präsentation, Vortrag 3/A13

president /ˈprezɪdənt/ Vorsitzende/r 4/A11

price /praɪs/ Preis 4/P15

product /ˈprɒdʌkt/ Produkt 2/A13

professional /prəˈfeʃnəl/ Profi 6/A6

project /ˈprɒdʒekt/ Projekt 5/A7

overhead projector /ˌəʊvəhed prəˈdʒektə/ Overheadprojektor 2/B4

prop /prɒp/ Requisite 4/B6

puddle /ˈpʌdl/ Pfütze WB

pupil /ˈpjuːpl/ Schüler/in 5/A7

purple /ˈpɜːpl/ violett, lila Welcome

°purse /pɜːs/ Portmonee BS/9

push /pʊʃ/ schieben; stoßen 6/B3

put *(irr)* /pʊt/ setzen, stellen, legen 2/A7

puzzle /ˈpʌzl/ Rätsel; *hier:* Puzzle 1/A9

Q

quarter /ˈkwɔːtə/ Viertel 2/B7

question /ˈkwestʃn/ Frage 1/A4

ask questions /ˌɑːsk ˈkwestʃnz/ Fragen stellen 4/A9

quick /kwɪk/ schnell 6/B4

°**quicker** /ˈkwɪkə/ schneller 4/O

°**quickly** /ˈkwɪkli/ schnell BS/10

quiet /ˈkwaɪət/ leise; ruhig 1/B3

°**quite** /kwaɪt/ ziemlich 1/O

R

rabbit /ˈræbɪt/ Kaninchen Welcome

°**railway** /ˈreɪlweɪ/ Eisenbahn BS/1

°**railway station** /ˈreɪlweɪ ˌsteɪʃn/ Bahnhof BS/5

rain /reɪn/ Regen Welcome

rainy /ˈreɪni/ regnerisch WB

rap /ræp/ rappen Welcome

rat /ræt/ Ratte WB

°**rather** /ˈrɑːðə/ ziemlich BS/1

I'd rather ... /ˌaɪd ˈrɑːðə/ Ich würde lieber ... 5/A2

RE (= religious education) /ˌɑːr ˈiː, reˌlɪdʒəsˌedjʊˈkeɪʃn/ Religion *(Schulfach)* 5/A3

°**reach** /riːtʃ/ erreichen BS/10

read *(irr)* /riːd/ lesen 4/A4

read along /ˌriːd_əˈlɒŋ/ mitlesen Welcome

read out /ˌriːd_ˈaʊt/ (laut) vorlesen 1/P3

read sth to sb /ˈriːd ˌsʌmθɪŋ tə ˌsʌmbədi/ jdm etw vorlesen 6/B3

I love reading. /aɪ ˌlʌv ˈriːdɪŋ/ Ich lese sehr gern. 6/B1

reading /ˈriːdɪŋ/ Lesen 3/B11

ready /ˈredi/ fertig, bereit 5/P13

ready-steady- ... /ˌredi ˌstedi ˈ.../ auf die Plätze, fertig, ... 3/A1

really /ˈrɪəli/ wirklich Welcome

recipe /ˈresəpi/ Rezept 5/B12

record /rɪˈkɔːd/ aufnehmen 2/A10

recording /rɪˈkɔːdɪŋ/ Aufnahme 1/A8

red /red/ rot Welcome

registration /ˌredʒɪˈstreɪʃn/ *Überprüfung der Anwesenheit* 5/A3

remember /rɪˈmembə/ sich erinnern an 4/A5

repeat /rɪˈpiːt/ wiederholen 1/P14

report /rɪˈpɔːt/ Bericht 3/A6

report (to) /rɪˈpɔːt/ berichten 5/P6

°**rescue** /ˈreskjuː/ Rettungs- BS/5

rhyme /raɪm/ sich reimen 2/P2

rhyming dictionary /ˈraɪmɪŋ ˌdɪkʃənri/ Reimwörterbuch 6/P8

rhyming pair /ˈraɪmɪŋ peə/ Reimpaar 1/P14

°**ride** /raɪd/ Fahrt 6/O

ride a bike /ˌraɪd_ə ˈbaɪk/ Fahrrad fahren 1/A4

ride a horse /ˌraɪd_ə ˈhɔːs/ reiten 3/A8

ride *(irr)* /raɪd/ fahren; reiten 1/B4

right /raɪt/ richtig 2/B9

You're right. /jɔː ˈraɪt/ Du hast recht. 5/A2

right /raɪt/ genau 6/B3

You're right about that. /jɔː ˈraɪt_əˌbaʊt ˌðæt/ Damit hast du recht. 5/A2

°**right** /raɪt/ (nach) rechts BS/9

right away /ˌraɪt_əˈweɪ/ sofort, gleich 1/A6

ring *(irr)* /rɪŋ/ klingeln, läuten 5/B3

river /ˈrɪvə/ Fluss 6/B3

road /rəʊd/ Straße 6/A6

rock /rɒk/ Stein; Fels 6/B3

role play /ˈrəʊl pleɪ/ Rollenspiel 6/A10

°**roll** /rəʊl/ rollen BS/3

room /ruːm/ Raum; Zimmer Welcome

°**double room** /ˌdʌbl ˈruːm/ Doppelzimmer BS/8

the other way round /ðiˌʌðə weɪ ˈraʊnd/ anders herum 5/B7

°**round** /raʊnd/ rund BS/2

rubber /ˈrʌbə/ Radiergummi 2/B1

rubbish /ˈrʌbɪʃ/ Müll 4/A9

rule /ruːl/ Regel 3/A13

ruler /ˈruːlə/ Lineal 2/B4

run *(irr)* /rʌn/ laufen; rennen 3/A5

°**run about** /ˌrʌn_əˈbaʊt/ herumrennen BS/1

°**run away** /ˌrʌn_əˈweɪ/ weglaufen BS/9

S

sad /sæd/ traurig 1/B2

°**safe** /seɪf/ sicher, ungefährlich BS/4

salad /ˈsæləd/ Salat 5/P7

°**salt** /sɔːlt/ Salz 2/O1

the same /ðə ˈseɪm/ der/die/das Gleiche 6/A9

°**sat** /sæt/ saß/saßen BS/1

Saturday /ˈsætədeɪ/ Samstag 1/B2

sausage /ˈsɒsɪdʒ/ Wurst, Würstchen 2/A7

°**save** /seɪv/ retten BS/5

saw /sɔː/ sah 1/B2

say *(irr)* /seɪ/ sagen 1/B2

°**scare** /skeə/ erschrecken BS/8

be scared /ˌbiː ˈskeəd/ Angst haben 6/B3

scarf (pl scarfs or scarves) /skɑːf, skɑːfs, skɑːvz/ Schal WB

scary /ˈskeəri/ unheimlich 2/A3

scene /siːn/ Szene 1/A2

school /skuːl/ Schule Welcome

get to school /ˌget_tə ˈskuːl/ zur Schule kommen 5/A8

school day /ˈskuːl ˌdeɪ/ Schultag 5/A8

schoolbag /ˈskuːlˌbæg/ Schultasche 2/B4

science /ˈsaɪəns/ Naturwissenschaft 4/A11

score /skɔː/ einen Punkt machen; Punktestand 3/A6

score a goal /ˌskɔːr_ə ˈgəʊl/ ein Tor schießen 3/A6

scored /skɔːd/ machte einen Punkt, schoss ein Tor 3/A6

°**Scotland** /ˈskɒtlənd/ Schottland 6/O

scrambled /ˈskræmbld/ durcheinander gebracht 2/P9

°**scrambled egg** /ˌskræmbldˈeg/ Rührei 2/O2

°scratch(ing) /ˈskrætʃ(ɪŋ)/ Kratzen BS/10

°scream /skriːm/ schreien BS/8; Schrei BS/10

sea /siː/ Meer, See 2/A2

search /sɜːtʃ/ suchen 6/A3

seashell /ˈsiːˌʃel/ Muschel 3/B5

second /ˈsekənd/ zweite (r, s) 5/A3

°second /ˈsekənd/ Sekunde BS/10

see (irr) /siː/ sehen Welcome

See you (soon)! /ˌsiː juː ˈsuːn/ Bis bald! 3/A5

°seem /siːm/ scheinen BS/1

seller /ˈselə/ Verkäufer/in 3/B4

selling /ˈselɪŋ/ Verkaufen 3/B4

°send (irr) /send/ schicken 6/O

sentence /ˈsentəns/ Satz 1/A4

September /sepˈtembə/ September 5/B7

session /ˈseʃn/ Stunde 6/A6

°shall /ʃæl/ sollen BS/8

°shape /ʃeɪp/ Form, Gestalt 3/O

°sharpener /ˈʃaːpnə/ Bleistiftspitzer 3/O

she /ʃiː/ sie Welcome

She doesn't like … /ʃɪ ˈdʌznt ˌlaɪk/ Sie mag … nicht. 3/A5

she's (= she is) /ʃiːz, ʃɪ ɪz/ sie ist 1/P4

sheep (pl sheep) /ʃiːp/ Schaf WB

°sheepdog /ˈʃiːpdɒg/ Schäferhund; Hütehund BS/5

shelf (pl shelves) /ʃelf, ʃelvz/ Regal 4/A1

°shell /ʃel/ Schale 2/O1

animal shelter /ˈænɪml ʃeltə/ Tierheim 1/B2

°shine (irr) /ʃaɪn/ scheinen BS/7

shirt /ʃɜːt/ Hemd 3/A12

°shiver /ˈʃɪvə/ zittern BS/10

°shocked /ˈʃɒkt/ schockiert, entsetzt BS/10

shoe /ʃuː/ Schuh WB

shop /ʃɒp/ Geschäft, Laden 1/B2

corner shop /ˈkɔːnə ʃɒp/ Tante-Emma-Laden 3/B6

shopkeeper /ˈʃɒpˌkiːpə/ Ladeninhaber/in 4/B6

do the shopping /ˌduː ðə ˈʃɒpɪŋ/ einkaufen 4/A6

shopping /ˈʃɒpɪŋ/ Einkaufen; Einkaufs- 2/A13

shopping centre /ˈʃɒpɪŋ ˌsentə/ Einkaufszentrum 1/B3

short /ʃɔːt/ kurz 2/A3

should /ʃʊd/ sollte/solltest/sollten/solltet 5/B10

shoulder /ˈʃəʊldə/ Schulter 2/A1

shouldn't (= should not) /ˈʃʊdnt, ʃʊd nɒt/ sollte/sollten nicht 5/B10

shout /ʃaʊt/ rufen; schreien 6/A5

show (irr) /ʃəʊ/ zeigen 1/A1

°shut /ʃʌt/ schließen BS/10

sign up /ˌsaɪn ˈʌp/ sich einschreiben 3/A1

°silk /sɪlk/ Seide; hier: Spinnwebe BS/4

silly /ˈsɪli/ albern, dumm 6/A5

sing (irr) /sɪŋ/ singen 2/B9

sing along /ˌsɪŋ əˈlɒŋ/ mitsingen Welcome

sing out /ˌsɪŋ ˈaʊt/ laut singen 2/B9

singer /ˈsɪŋə/ Sänger/in 3/A1

°Sir (Anrede vor Vornamen) /sɜː/ Sir; Herr BS/9

sister /ˈsɪstə/ Schwester 1/A4

sit down /ˌsɪt ˈdaʊn/ sich hinsetzen Welcome

sit (irr) /sɪt/ sitzen 5/B3

skate /skeɪt/ inlineskaten 3/A8

(a pair of) skates /ə ˌpeər əv ˈskeɪts/ (ein Paar) Inliner 6/A5

go skating /ˌgəʊ ˈskeɪtɪŋ/ Skaten gehen 3/A9

ski /skiː/ Ski fahren, Ski laufen 3/A8

skirt /skɜːt/ Rock WB

sky /skaɪ/ Himmel 2/B12

sleep (irr) /sliːp/ schlafen 4/A4

°sleeping /ˈsliːpɪŋ/ schlafend BS/6

sleepover /ˈsliːpˌəʊvə/ Übernachtung 4/B1

slim /slɪm/ schlank 2/A3

°slowly /ˈsləʊli/ langsam BS/3

small /smɔːl/ klein 1/B3

°smell /smel/ riechen BS/10

smile /smaɪl/ lächeln 2/A6

snow /snəʊ/ Schnee Welcome

snowman (pl snowmen) /ˈsnəʊmæn, ˈsnəʊmen/ Schneemann WB

snowy /ˈsnəʊi/ verschneit, schneereich WB

so /səʊ/ deshalb, daher Welcome; hier: also 6/A3

so far /ˈsəʊ faː/ bisher 2/B9

soap /səʊp/ Seife 2/A1

sock /sɒk/ Socke WB

°soft-boiled /ˌsɒftˈbɔɪld/ weich gekocht 2/O2

some /sʌm/ einige, ein paar; etwas Welcome

°someone /ˈsʌmwʌn/ jemand, irgendwer 4/O

something /ˈsʌmθɪŋ/ etwas 3/B6

sometimes /ˈsʌmtaɪmz/ manchmal 4/A6

son /sʌn/ Sohn 5/B7

song /sɒŋ/ Lied Welcome

See you (soon)! /ˌsiː juː ˈsuːn/ Bis bald! 3/A5

°soon /suːn/ bald BS/3

Sorry. /ˈsɒri/ Es tut mir leid., Entschuldigung. Welcome

sort /sɔːt/ sortieren 2/P12

sound /saʊnd/ Geräusch, Klang 3/P10; klingen, sich anhören 4/B1

speak (irr) /spiːk/ sprechen, reden Welcome

special /ˈspeʃl/ besondere(r, s) 1/B4; hier: Spezialgericht 4/B7

speech bubble /ˈspiːtʃ ˌbʌbl/ Sprechblase 2/A3

spell (irr) /spel/ buchstabieren 2/B1

spelling /ˈspelɪŋ/ Buchstabieren; Rechtschreibung 2/B9

spider /ˈspaɪdə/ Spinne 4/A4

spinach /ˈspɪnɪdʒ/ Spinat 3/B10

sponge /spʌndʒ/ Schwamm 2/B1

spooky /ˈspuːki/ schaurig; unheimlich 4/B1

spoon /spuːn/ Löffel 2/A7

sport /spɔːt/ Sport, Sportart 3/I

sports centre /ˈspɔːts ˌsentə/ Sportcenter 3/A9

sports field /'spɔːts ˌfiːld/ Sportplatz 3/A1

sports hall /'spɔːts ˌhɔːl/ Sporthalle 3/A1

sports teacher /'spɔːts ˌtiːtʃə/
Sportlehrer/in 3/A4

sporty /'spɔːti/ sportlich 2/A6

spot /spɒt/ Fleck 3/B10

spring /sprɪŋ/ Frühling Welcome

squirrel /'skwɪrəl/ Eichhörnchen
WB

°St Bernard's dog /sənt 'bɜːnədz
ˌdɒg/ Bernhardiner BS/5

stadium /'steɪdiəm/ Stadion 3/A7

stairs (pl) /steəz/ Treppe 2/B12

°stall /stɔːl/ Stand BS/9

information stand /ˌɪnfə'meɪʃn
stænd/ Informationsstand 6/A2

°stand (irr) /stænd/ stehen BS/2

stand up /ˌstænd‿'ʌp/ aufstehen
Welcome

°stare at /'steər‿æt/ anstarren
3/O

start /staːt/ anfangen, beginnen Welcome

start /staːt/ Beginn 2/I

station /'steɪʃn/ U-Bahn-Station;
Bahnhof 4/B1

stay /steɪ/ bleiben; wohnen
Welcome

°steal (irr) /stiːl/ stehlen BS/9

step /step/ Schritt 4/A11

°cocktail stick /'kɒkteɪl stɪk/
Cocktailspieß 5/O1

°stick /stɪk/ Stock 3/O

sticker /'stɪkə/ Aufkleber 3/B5

still /stɪl/ (immer) noch 2/A2

°stir /stɜː/ rühren 2/O2

stone /stəʊn/ Stein 3/B5

stop /stɒp/ aufhören; stehen
bleiben 1/A3; stoppen BS/9

Stop dreaming! /ˌstɒp 'driːmɪŋ/
Hör' auf, zu träumen! 2/A7

story /'stɔːri/ Geschichte 3/B6

ghost story /'gəʊst ˌstɔːri/
Gespenstergeschichte 6/B1

°strange /streɪndʒ/ sonderbar,
merkwürdig 3/O

°straw /strɔː/ Strohhalm 5/O1

street /striːt/ Straße 1/B3

in the street /ˌɪn ðə 'striːt/ auf
der Straße 3/A9

strong /strɒŋ/ stark 2/A3

studio /'stjuːdiəʊ/ Atelier,
Studio 3/A1

subject /'sʌbdʒɪkt/ Schulfach
5/A2

such /sʌtʃ/ so 5/B11

°suck /sʌk/ saugen 5/O2

suddenly /'sʌdnli/ plötzlich
6/A3

°sugar /'ʃʊgə/ Zucker 5/O1

suitcase /'suːtˌkeɪs/ Koffer
Welcome

summer /'sʌmə/ Sommer
Welcome

summertime /'sʌmətaɪm/
Sommerzeit 6/I

sums (only plural) /sʌmz/
Rechenaufgabe 3/B2

sun /sʌn/ Sonne Welcome

Sunday /'sʌndeɪ/ Sonntag 1/B2

sunglasses (pl) /'sʌnˌglaːsɪz/
Sonnenbrille WB

sunny /'sʌni/ sonnig WB

°sunny side up /ˌsʌni saɪd‿'ʌp/
Spiegelei 2/O2

supermarket /'suːpəˌmaːkɪt/
Supermarkt 1/B3

sure /ʃɔː/ sicher Welcome

°surprise /sə'praɪz/
Überraschung BS/9

surprised /sə'praɪzd/ überrascht,
erstaunt 6/B4

survey /'sɜːveɪ/ Umfrage 2/A12

swap /swɒp/ tauschen 3/P12

swap for /'swɒp fɔː/ eintauschen
gegen Welcome

sweater /'swetə/ Pullover WB

sweet /swiːt/ süß 2/A11

swim (irr) /swɪm/ schwimmen
1/A6

swimming /'swɪmɪŋ/ Schwimmen 3/B8

go swimming /ˌgəʊ 'swɪmɪŋ/
Schwimmen gehen 3/A9

swimming pool /'swɪmɪŋ puːl/
Schwimmbad 1/B3

switch on /ˌswɪtʃ‿'ɒn/ einschalten 4/B10

°Switzerland /'swɪtsələnd/
Schweiz BS/5

T

table /'teɪbl/ Tisch 2/A7

table /'teɪbl/ Tabelle 5/P6

table tennis /'teɪbl ˌtenɪs/ Tisch-
tennnis 3/A1

°tag /tæg/ Schild, Etikett 3/O

tail /teɪl/ Schwanz 3/B6

take (irr) /teɪk/ nehmen;
bringen 3/B4

I'll take it. /ˌaɪl 'teɪk‿ɪt/ Ich
nehme es. 3/B4

take notes /ˌteɪk 'nəʊts/ sich
Notizen machen 3/B5

take off /ˌteɪk‿'ɒf/ abheben; hier:
wegfliegen 6/B3

take out /ˌteɪk‿'aʊt/ hinausbringen 4/A9

take out /ˌteɪk‿'aʊt/ hier: aus-
leihen 3/B11

take part in /ˌteɪk 'paːt‿ɪn/
teilnehmen an 5/A7

take photos /ˌteɪk 'fəʊtəʊz/
Bilder machen 2/A13

take the tube /ˌteɪk ðə 'tjuːb/
die U-Bahn nehmen 4/B3

take turns /ˌteɪk 'tɜːnz/ sich
abwechseln 1/P3

give a talk /ˌgɪv‿ə 'tɔːk/ eine
Rede halten 5/A6

talk about /'tɔːk‿əˌbaʊt/ sprechen
über 3/A3

talk (to) /tɔːk/ sprechen (mit);
reden (mit) 3/A4

tall /tɔːl/ groß 2/A3

target task /'taːgɪt ˌtaːsk/ Zielaufgabe 1/I; Zielaufgabe 1/A9

tea /tiː/ Tee 2/A8

a cup of tea /ə ˌkʌp‿əv 'tiː/ eine
Tasse Tee 2/A8

teach (irr) /tiːtʃ/ unterrichten
3/A13

teacher /'tiːtʃə/ Lehrer/in 3/A2

°tear /tɪə/ Träne BS/3

brush one's teeth
/ˌbrʌʃ wʌnz 'tiːθ/ sich die
Zähne putzen 2/A1

telephone /'telɪˌfəʊn/ Telefon
3/B7

tell (irr) /tel/ erzählen 1/B2

°tell (irr) /tel/ hier: sagen 2/O1

ten thirty /ten 'θɜːti/ zehn Uhr
dreißig 2/B7

tennis court /ˈtenɪs kɔːt/ Tennis-
platz 3/A9

tenth /tenθ/ zehnte (r, s) 5/B9

terrible /ˈterəbl/ schrecklich 5/A2

°terrified /ˈterəfaɪd/ erschrocken,
verängstigt BS/10

°terrifying /ˈterəˌfaɪɪŋ/ Angst
erregend BS/10

Thames /temz/ Themse 6/B3

than /ðæn/ als 2/B11

thank /θæŋk/ danken, sich
bedanken 4/B10

Thank you. /ˈθæŋk ju/ Danke.
Welcome

thanks /θæŋks/ danke 2/B1

I'm fine, thanks.
/aɪm ˈfaɪn ˌθæŋks/ Es geht mir
gut, danke. 4/B9

that /ðæt/ das 1/A2

that /ðæt/ dass 2/A11; der, die,
das 2/B11

that's (= that is) /ðæts, ˈðæt‿ɪz/
das ist Welcome; *hier:* das
kostet 3/B1

That's me. /ˌðæts ˈmiː/ Das bin
ich. 1/A7

°that's why /ˈðæts ˌwaɪ/ deshalb
BS/1

the /ðə/ der/die/das Welcome

The Lion King /ðə ˈlaɪən ˌkɪŋ/ *Der
König der Löwen* 3/A1

the other way round /ði‿ˌʌðə weɪ
ˈraʊnd/ anders herum 5/B7

the tube (*informal*) /ðə ˈtjuːb/ die
(Londoner) U-Bahn 4/B3

their /ðeə/ ihr(e) 1/A4

them /ðem/ sie; ihnen 4/A11

then /ðen/ dann Welcome

there /ðeə/ dort; dahin 4/A4

there are /ðeər‿ˈɑː/ dort sind; es
gibt Welcome

there is /ðeər‿ˈɪz/ dort ist; es
gibt Welcome

there was /ðeə ˈwɒz/ dort war;
es gab 6/A2

there were /ðeə ˈwɜː/ dort waren;
es gab 6/A2

there's (= there is) /ðeəz,
ðeər‿ɪz/ dort ist; es gibt 1/A2

There's a good parrot! /ˈðeəz‿ə
ˌɡʊd ˌpærət/ Das ist ein guter
Papagei! 6/A3

these (*pl* of this) /ðiːz/ diese;
das 1/A2

they /ðeɪ/ sie Welcome

they're (= they are) /ðeə, ðeɪ‿ˈɑː/
sie sind 1/P4

they've got (= they have got)
/ˌðeɪv ˈɡɒt, ˌðeɪ hæv ˈɡɒt/
sie haben 1/B2

°thin /θɪn/ dünn 4/O

thing /θɪŋ/ Ding; Gegenstand
2/B4

think (*irr*) /θɪŋk/ denken;
glauben 1/A4

What do you think? /ˌwɒt‿də jə
ˈθɪŋk/ Was hältst du davon?
Welcome

think about /ˈθɪŋk‿əˌbaʊt/ nachdenken über 4/B12

think hard /ˌθɪŋk ˈhɑːd/ ange-
strengt nachdenken 6/B4

think of /ˈθɪŋk‿əv/ denken an,
sich ausdenken 2/A13

third /θɜːd/ dritte (r, s) 5/A3

this /ðɪs/ diese(r, s) Welcome

this morning /ðɪs ˈmɔːnɪŋ/ heute
Morgen 6/A3

this one /ˈðɪs ˌwʌn/ dieses 3/B4

those (*pl* of that) /ðəʊz/ diese,
jene 4/B6

°thread /θred/ Faden BS/4

through /θruː/ durch 3/A7

°throw (*irr*) /θrəʊ/ werfen 5/O2

°thump /θʌmp/ schlagen BS/10

Thursday /ˈθɜːzdeɪ/ Donnerstag
1/B2

tidy /ˈtaɪdi/ ordentlich, aufgeräumt 4/A2; aufräumen 4/A6

tie /taɪ/ Krawatte 5/A2

tiger /ˈtaɪɡə/ Tiger WB

till /tɪl/ bis 3/A5

time /taɪm/ Zeit 2/A12

free time /friː ˈtaɪm/ Freizeit 3/I

What time is it?
/wɒt‿ˈtaɪm‿ɪz‿ɪt/
Wie spät ist es? 2/B1

have a good time /ˌhæv‿ə
ɡʊd‿ˈtaɪm/ Spaß haben, eine
gute Zeit haben 6/A5

What's the time, please?
/ˌwɒts ðə ˈtaɪm pliːz/ Wie spät ist
es, bitte? 2/B7

times /taɪmz/ multipliziert mit 3/B2

timetable /ˈtaɪmteɪbl/ Stundenplan 5/A3

°tired /ˈtaɪəd/ müde BS/8

title /ˈtaɪtl/ Titel 6/B5

to /tʊ/ in; nach; zu Welcome

to /tʊ/ *hier:* für 4/B11; bis 5/A4;
hier: bis 5/A7; um zu Welcome

today /təˈdeɪ/ heute 3/B6

toe /təʊ/ Zeh WB

together /təˈɡeðə/ zusammen
3/A7

toilet /ˈtɔɪlət/ Toilette 6/A1

disabled toilet /dɪsˈeɪbld‿ˌtɔɪlət/
Behindertentoilette 6/A1

tomato (*pl* tomatoes)
/təˈmɑːtəʊ, təˈmɑːtəʊz/
Tomate 1/A4

tongue twister /ˈtʌŋ ˌtwɪstə/
Zungenbrecher 4/B8

tonight /təˈnaɪt/ heute Abend
4/B9

too /tuː/ auch 1/B2

too /tuː/ zu 3/B4

°toot /tuːt/ hupen, tuten BS/1

tooth (*pl* teeth) /tuːθ, tiːθ/
Zahn 2/A1

toothbrush /ˈtuːθbrʌʃ/ Zahnbürste WB

toothpaste /ˈtuːθpeɪst/ Zahnpasta 2/A1

torch (*pl* torches) /tɔːtʃ, ˈtɔːtʃɪz/
Taschenlampe 4/B10

°touch /tʌtʃ/ berühren BS/1

town /taʊn/ Stadt 1/A9

cuddly toy /ˌkʌdli ˈtɔɪ/ Kuscheltier 3/B5

toy car /ˌtɔɪ ˈkɑː/ Spielzeugauto
3/B5

°track /træk/ Schiene BS/1

tractor /ˈtræktə/ Traktor 6/A1

°traffic /ˈtræfɪk/ Verkehr BS/5

train /treɪn/ Zug 3/B5

model train /ˌmɒdl ˈtreɪn/
Modelleisenbahn 3/B5

trainers /ˈtreɪnəz/ Turnschuhe
WB

°trapped /træpt/ gefangen
BS/10

treasure /ˈtreʒə/ Schatz 6/B5

family tree /ˌfæmli ˈtriː/
Familienstammbaum 5/B7

tree /triː/ Baum 2/B12

magic trick /ˌmædʒɪk ˈtrɪk/ Zaubertrick 5/B3

trick /trɪk/ Trick, Kunststück 3/B8

trip /trɪp/ Reise, Fahrt 4/B3; stolpern BS/10

(a pair of) trousers /ˈtraʊzəz/ Hose WB

true /truː/ wahr 3/A4

truth /truːθ/ Wahrheit 5/B10

°try /traɪ/ probieren; versuchen 5/O3

take the tube /ˌteɪk ðə ˈtjuːb/ die U-Bahn nehmen 4/B3

the tube (informal) /ðə ˈtjuːb/ die (Londoner) U-Bahn 4/B3

Tuesday /ˈtjuːzdeɪ/ Dienstag 1/B2

tummy /ˈtʌmi/ Bauch 2/A1

Turkish /ˈtɜːkɪʃ/ Türkisch 1/A9

be one's turn /ˌbi wʌnz ˈtɜːn/ an der Reihe sein 4/B1

°turn /tɜːn/ werden BS/3; abbiegen BS/9

turn around /ˌtɜːn əˈraʊnd/ sich umdrehen Welcome

turn on /ˌtɜːn ˈɒn/ einschalten 3/B6

turn out /ˌtɜːn ˈaʊt/ ausschalten 4/B1

°turn over /ˌtɜːn ˈəʊvə/ umdrehen 2/O2

take turns /ˌteɪk ˈtɜːnz/ sich abwechseln 1/P3

TV /ˌtiː ˈviː/ Fernseher; Fernsehen 4/A4

watch TV /ˌwɒtʃ tiː ˈviː/ Fernsehen gucken 3/B8

°type /taɪp/ Art BS/5

U

ugh (informal) /ʌg/ i, igitt Welcome

uncle /ˈʌŋkl/ Onkel 5/B3

under /ˈʌndə/ unter 4/A3

°underground /ˈʌndəɡraʊnd/ U-Bahn 4/O

understand (irr) /ˌʌndəˈstænd/ verstehen 3/A4

unscramble /ʌnˈskræmbl/ wieder ordnen 2/P4

untidy /ʌnˈtaɪdi/ unordentlich, unaufgeräumt 4/A2

until /ənˈtɪl/ bis 6/A3

°unusual /ʌnˈjuːʒəl/ ungewöhnlich 3/O

up /ʌp/ nach oben; hinauf; oben 6/B3

up till /ˈʌp tɪl/ bis Welcome

°upstairs /ˌʌpˈsteəz/ (nach) oben BS/8

us /ʌs/ uns 2/A8

use /juːz/ benutzen 2/A13

°usual /ˈjuːʒəl/ gewöhnlich, üblich BS/3

usually /ˈjuːʒəli/ gewöhnlich, normalerweise 4/A6

V

vacuum /ˈvækjuəm/ staubsaugen 4/A6

vanilla /vəˈnɪlə/ Vanille 6/A5

vegetable /ˈvedʒtəbl/ Gemüse 4/B5

verse /vɜːs/ Strophe 2/B12

versus /ˈvɜːsəs/ gegen 3/A4

very /ˈveri/ sehr 1/B2

°veterinary practice /ˌvetrnri ˈpræktɪs/ Tierarztpraxis 1/O

°village /ˈvɪlɪdʒ/ Dorf BS/3

visit /ˈvɪzɪt/ besuchen 3/A1; Besuch 4/B1

visitor /ˈvɪzɪtə/ Besucher/in 6/A6

voice /vɔɪs/ Stimme 4/B11

volunteer /ˌvɒlənˈtɪə/ ehrenamtliche/r Mitarbeiter/in 6/B4

W

wait /weɪt/ (er)warten 2/A8

wait for /ˈweɪt fɔː/ warten auf 4/A11

walk /wɔːk/ gehen 4/B3

°walk /wɔːk/ Spaziergang 6/O

°go for a walk /ˌɡəʊ fər ə ˈwɔːk/ spazieren gehen 6/O

walk the dog /ˌwɔːk ðə ˈdɒg/ den Hund ausführen 5/A4

wall /wɔːl/ Wand 2/B1

want /wɒnt/ wollen 1/B2

wardrobe /ˈwɔːdrəʊb/ Schrank Welcome

warm /wɔːm/ warm WB

°was /wɒz/ war BS/1

wash /wɒʃ/ waschen; sich waschen 2/A1

do the washing up /ˌduː ðə ˌwɒʃɪŋ ˈʌp/ abspülen 4/A6

watch /wɒtʃ/ beobachten; ansehen 4/B1

watch TV /ˌwɒtʃ tiː ˈviː/ Fernsehen gucken 3/B8

water /ˈwɔːtə/ Wasser 2/A2

°fizzy water /ˈfɪzi ˌwɔːtə/ Mineralwasser 2/O2

wave (at/to sb) /weɪv/ jdm zuwinken 6/A3

way /weɪ/ Weg; Art, Weise 4/B3

the other way round /ðiˌʌðə weɪ ˈraʊnd/ anders herum 5/B7

we /wiː/ wir Welcome

wear (irr) /weə/ tragen Welcome

weather /ˈweðə/ Wetter Welcome

°web /web/ Netz BS/4

Wednesday /ˈwenzdeɪ/ Mittwoch 1/B2

week /wiːk/ Woche 4/A11

weekend /ˌwiːkˈend/ Wochenende 4/B1

at the weekend /ˌæt ðə ˈwiːkend/ am Wochenende 2/A12

welcome (to) /ˈwelkəm tʊ/ willkommen (in) Welcome

well /wel/ nun 3/A5

get on well /ˌget ɒn ˈwel/ sich gut verstehen 6/A1

°well /wel/ gut BS/6

well done /ˌwel ˈdʌn/ gut gemacht 3/A6

wellie /ˈweli/ Gummistiefel WB

°were /wɜː/ warst/waren/wart BS/6

°were born /ˌwɜː ˈbɔːn/ sind geboren 1/O

wet /wet/ nass 2/A2

what /wɒt/ was; welche(r, s) Welcome

What a …! /ˈwɒt ə/ Was für ein/eine …! 3/A6

What about …? /ˌwɒt əˌbaʊt ˈ…/ Was ist mit …?/Wie wäre es mit …? Welcome

What about …? /ˌwɒt əˌbaʊt ˈ…/ hier: Was war mit …? 6/A5

What about you? /ˌwɒt əˌbaʊt ˈjuː/ Und du? Welcome

What are they talking about?
/ˌwɒt‿ə ðeɪ ˈtɔːkɪŋ‿əˌbaʊt/
Worüber reden sie? 3/A3

What are your favourite …?
/ˌwɒt‿ə jə ˌfeɪvrət ˈ…/ Was sind
deine Lieblings- …? Welcome

What do you think? /ˌwɒt‿də
jə ˈθɪŋk/ Was hältst du davon?
Welcome

What does he talk about?
/ˌwɒt dəz hi ˈtɔːk‿əbaʊt/
Worüber spricht er? 1/A4

what else /ˌwɒt‿ˈels/ was sonst
2/A8

What is it like? /ˌwɒt‿ɪz‿ɪt ˈlaɪk/
Wie ist es? 5/A8

What languages do you speak?
/ˌwɒt ˈlæŋgwɪdʒɪz duː juː ˈspiːk/
Welche Sprachen sprichst
du? Welcome

What time is it?
/wɒt‿ˈtaɪm‿ɪz‿ɪt/ Wie spät ist
es? 2/B1

what's (= what is) /ˈwɒts,
ˈwɒt‿ɪz/ was ist Welcome

What's going on? /ˌwɒts
gəʊɪŋ‿ˈɒn/ Was passiert hier
gerade? 6/A1

What's on? /ˌwɒts‿ˈɒn/ Was ist
los? 3/A1

What's the time, please?
/ˌwɒts ðə ˈtaɪm pliːz/ Wie spät
ist es, bitte? 2/B7

What's up? *(informal)*
/ˌwɒts‿ˈʌp/ Was ist los? 3/A5

What's your name? /ˌwɒts jə
ˈneɪm/ Wie heißt du? Welcome

What's your phone number?
/ˌwɒts jə ˈfəʊn‿nʌmbə/ Was ist
deine Telefonnummer?
Welcome

wheelchair /ˈwiːltʃeə/ Rollstuhl
1/A5

when /wen/ wann 2/B7; wenn;
als 5/B11

where /weə/ wo; wohin 1/A3

Where are you from?
/ˌweər‿ə jʊ ˈfrɒm/ Woher
kommst du? 1/A3

which /wɪtʃ/ welche(r, s); was
3/A4

°**while** /waɪl/ Weile BS/10

for a while /ˌfɔːr‿ə ˈwaɪl/ eine
Weile 6/A3

white /waɪt/ weiß Welcome

who /huː/ wer; der/die/das 1/A5

who's (= who is) /huːz, ˈhuː‿ɪz/
wer ist 1/P3

whose /huːz/ wessen 5/B7

why /waɪ/ warum 3/B7

Why don't you …? /ˈwaɪ ˌdəʊnt
juː/ Warum … du nicht …? 4/B9

wife *(pl* wives) /waɪf, waɪvz/
Ehefrau 5/B7

will /wɪl/ werden 3/B4

°**win** *(irr)* /wɪn/ gewinnen 5/O2

wind /wɪnd/ Wind WB

window /ˈwɪndəʊ/ Fenster 2/B1

windy /ˈwɪndi/ windig WB

°**wine** /waɪn/ Wein BS/8

winner /ˈwɪnə/ Gewinner/in 3/A6

winning /ˈwɪnɪŋ/ Gewinnen 3/A7

winter /ˈwɪntə/ Winter Welcome

wish /wɪʃ/ wünschen 2/A7

I wish it was Sunday! /aɪ ˌwɪʃ‿ɪt
wəz ˈsʌndeɪ/ Ich wünschte,
es wäre Sonntag. 2/A7

with /wɪð/ mit; bei Welcome

woman *(pl* **women)** /ˈwʊmən,
ˈwɪmɪn/ Frau 5/B7

°**wonder** /ˈwʌndə/ sich fragen
BS/10

°**wonderful** /ˈwʌndəfl/ wunder-
bar, wundervoll BS/3

°**wooden** /ˈwʊdn/ Holz-, hölzern
BS/10

°**woods** *(pl)* /wʊdz/ Wald 3/O

word /wɜːd/ Wort 2/B9

word web /ˈwɜːd web/ Wort-
netz 3/A12

work /wɜːk/ arbeiten 5/A7

work hard /ˌwɜːk ˈhaːd/ schwer
arbeiten 4/A10

°**working** /ˈwɜːkɪŋ/ Arbeits- BS/5;
Arbeiten, Arbeit BS/7

world /wɜːld/ Welt 5/A7

Don't worry. /ˌdəʊnt ˈwʌri/ Mach
dir keine Sorgen. 6/A1

°**worry** /ˈwʌri/ Sorge BS/7

would /wʊd/ würde(st, en,
et) 2/B13

Would you like …? /ˌwʊd juː
ˈlaɪk/ Hättest du … gern? 2/B1
Hättest du gern …?/Hättet ihr
gern …? 4/B9

°**wrap** /ræp/ einwickeln BS/4

write *(irr)* /raɪt/ schreiben
2/A13

write down /ˌraɪt ˈdaʊn/ aufschreiben Welcome

wrong /rɒŋ/ falsch 5/B7

Y

year /jɪə/ Jahr Welcome; Schuljahr, Klasse 5/A3

yellow /ˈjeləʊ/ gelb Welcome

yes /jes/ ja Welcome

yesterday /ˈjestədeɪ/ gestern
WB

°**yolk** /jəʊk/ Eigelb 2/O1

you /juː/ du; dich; dir; man; ihr;
euch; Sie; Ihnen Welcome

you're (= you are) /jɔː, juː‿ˈɑː/
du bist, ihr seid 1/P4

You're lucky. /jɔː ˈlʌki/ Du bist
ein Glückspilz. 5/A2

You're right. /jɔː ˈraɪt/ Du hast
recht. 5/A2

You're right about that. /jɔː
ˈraɪt‿əˌbaʊt ˈðæt/ Damit hast
du recht. 5/A2

you're wearing /jɔː ˈweərɪŋ/ du
trägst (gerade) Welcome

you've got (= you have got)
/ˈjuːv gɒt, ju ˌhæv ˈgɒt/ du
hast; ihr habt 2/A7

°**young** /jʌŋ/ Junge; jung BS/4

your /jɔː/ dein(e); euer/eure
Welcome

yourself *(pl* **yourselves)**
/jɔːˈself, jɔːˈselvz/ dich 3/B6

youth club /ˈjuːθ ˌklʌb/ Jugendzentrum 5/A7

yummy /ˈjʌmi/ lecker 1/B2

Z

zoo /zuː/ Zoo WB

A

Abend evening
Abendessen dinner
abends *(nur hinter Uhrzeit zwischen 12 Uhr mittags und Mitternacht)* pm (= post meridiem)
aber but
Abfalleimer bin
jemanden abholen pick somebody up
abspülen do the washing up
Affe monkey
alle, jeder everyone, everybody, all
alles everything, all
Alphabet alphabet
alt old
Alter age
am Morgen in the morning
am Telefon on the phone
am Wochenende at the weekend
an at; in
an der Reihe sein be one's turn
andere(r, s) other
anfangen start
anrufen call
ans Telefon gehen answer the phone
ansehen watch
(an)sehen, (an)schauen look (at)
Ansichtskarte postcard
Antwort, antworten answer
Apfel apple
April April
arbeiten work
arbeitsreich busy
Art kind; way
Artikel article
auch too; also
auf on
auf der Straße in the street
auf Deutsch in German
Auf Wiedersehen. Goodbye.
Aufgabe job
Aufkleber sticker

aufräumen tidy
aufstehen get up
Auge eye
August August
aus from
ausleeren; ausräumen empty
ausschalten turn out
aussehen look
nicht ausstehen können hate
aussteigen get out
Auto car

B

Badezimmer bathroom
Bahnhof station
Banane banana
Bauch tummy
Bauernhof farm
Becher mug
Beeile dich! Hurry up!
beenden finish
beginnen start
bei at
Bein leg
bekommen get *(irr)*
benutzen use
beobachten watch
bequem comfortable
Berg mountain
beschäftigt busy
beschreiben describe
beschriften label
besser better
beste (r, s) best
Besuch; besuchen visit
Bett bed
bewölkt, bedeckt cloudy
Bild picture
bis till
Bis bald! See you (soon)!
bitte please
bitten ask
blau blue
Bleistift pencil
Bohnen in Tomatensauce baked beans *(pl)*
brauchen need
braun brown
Brille glasses *(pl)*
bringen take *(irr)*
Bruder brother
Buch book

Bücherei library
buchstabieren spell *(irr)*
bürsten brush
mit dem Bus fahren go by bus

C

Chips crisps *(pl)*
Cousin/e cousin

D

dahin there
danke thanks, thank you
dann then
das that
das ist, das kostet that's
Daunendecke duvet
dein(e) your
denken think *(irr)*
der/die/das the; who *(in Relativsätzen)*
Deutsch German
auf Deutsch in German
Deutschland Germany
Dezember December
dich yourself *(pl* yourselves); you
die U-Bahn nehmen take the tube
Dienstag Tuesday
diese, jene those *(pl of* that)
diese; das these *(pl of* this)
diese(r, s) this
Ding thing
dir you
Donnerstag Thursday
dort there
dort (drüben) over there
dort ist; es gibt there is
dort sind; es gibt there are
dritte (r, s) third
du you
dunkel dark

E

Ei egg
Eichhörnchen squirrel
eigene(r, s) own
ein(e) a/an
einfach easy
einige, ein paar; etwas some

einkaufen do the shopping
Einkaufen; Einkaufs- shopping
einladen invite
einschalten turn on; switch on
Eisbär polar bear
Elefant elephant
Eltern parents *(pl)*
enden finish; end
Englisch English
Enkel grandson
Enkelin granddaughter
Es tut mir leid., Entschuldigung. Sorry.
er he
Erdkunde geography
Erkältung cold
erste (r, s) first
erzählen tell *(irr)*
es it
es kostet it's (= it is)
Essen food
essen eat *(irr)*; have *(irr)*
etwas something
euch you
euer/eure your

F

fahren ride
Fahrrad bike
mit dem Fahrrad by bike
Fahrrad fahren ride a bike
Familie family
fantastisch, super fantastic
Farbe colour
Februar February
Federmäppchen pencil case
Fenster window
Fernsehen gucken watch TV
finden find *(irr)*
Fisch fish
Fledermaus bat
Fliege; fliegen fly *(irr)*
fragen ask
Frau woman *(pl* women); Mrs *(Anrede)*
Freitag Friday
Freizeit free time
Freund/in friend
freundlich friendly
Frosch frog
Frucht, Obst fruit

Frühling spring
Frühstück breakfast
zum Frühstück for
breakfast
frühstücken have
breakfast
Fuchs fox
für for
füttern feed *(irr)*
Fuß foot *(pl* feet)
Fußball football
Fußboden floor

G

Gabel fork
Garten garden
geben give *(irr)*
Geburtstag birthday
Herzlichen Glückwunsch
zum Geburtstag!
Happy birthday!
Gegenstand thing
gehen go *(irr)*; walk
Es geht mir gut, danke.
I'm fine, thanks.
Geist, Gespenst ghost
gelb yellow
Gemüse vegetable
gerade just
etw gern tun like doing
sth
Geschäft, Laden shop
Geschenk present
Geschichte story; history
Gesicht face
gewöhnlich, normaler-
weise usually
Gibt es ...?
Are there ...?
Gibt es ein/e ...?
Is there a ...?
Giraffe giraffe
Gitarre guitar
glauben think *(irr)*
Viel Glück! Good luck!
glücklich happy
Goldfisch goldfish
grau grey
groß big; tall
groß(artig) great
Großelternteil
grandparent
Großmutter
grandmother
Großvater grandfather

grün green
Gummistiefel wellie
gut good
gut aussehend
good-looking
Guten Morgen! Good
morning!

H

Haar hair
haben have got;
have *(irr)*
halb half
hallo hello
Hals neck
Hamster hamster
Handlung action
Handschuh glove
Handy mobile (phone)
hassen hate
Haus house
Hausaufgaben
homework
zu Hause at home
Haustier pet
Heft exercise book
heiß hot
Ich heiße ... My name
is ...; I'm ...
helfen help
Kann ich dir /Ihnen
helfen? Can I help
you?
Hemd shirt
Herbst autumn
Herr *(Anrede)* Mr
Herzlichen Glückwunsch
zum Geburtstag!
Happy birthday!
heute today
heute Abend tonight
Hier, bitte! Here you
are.; Here you go.
hier; hierher here
hinausbringen take out
hinter behind
hoffen hope
Hose (a pair of)
trousers
Huhn chicken
Hund dog
den Hund ausführen
walk the dog
hungrig hungry
Hut hat

ich I; me
ich habe I've got
Igel hedgehog
ihm, ihn him
ihnen *(Pl.)* them
Ihnen *(höfl. Anrede)* you
ihr/ihre her *(3.Pers. Sgl.
weibl.)*; their *(3.Pers. Pl.)*
im Moment at the
moment
immer always
in in; into; to; at; on
in der Mitte von in the
middle of
Informationstechnologie,
IT ICT (= Information
and Communications
Technology)
inlineskaten skate
insgesamt altogether
interessant interesting
(irgend)ein(e) any
irgendetwas anything
irgendjemand;
jede (r, s) anybody
Ist es ...? Is it ...?

ja yes
Jacke jacket
Jahr year
Januar January
jede(r, s) every,
everyone, everybody
jedenfalls anyway
jetzt now
Jetzt bist du dran.
Over to you.
Jugendzentrum
youth club
Juli July
Junge boy
Juni June

(heißer) Kakao hot
chocolate
Käse cheese
Kalender calendar
kalt cold
Kaninchen rabbit
Kann ich dir/Ihnen
helfen? Can I help
you?

Karte map; card
Katze cat
Kaufen buying
kaufen buy *(irr)*
kein(e) no
Keks biscuit
kennen know *(irr)*
Kerze candle
Kind child *(pl* children)
Kino cinema
Kissen pillow
Klasse class
Klassenzimmer
classroom
Kleid dress
Kleider, Kleidung
clothes *(pl)*
klein little, small
klingeln, läuten ring *(irr)*
Klub; AG club
Knie knee
kochen do the cooking
können can
nicht können can't,
cannot
könnte(st, t, n) could
Körper body
komisch funny
kommen come
Komm(t) herein!
Come in.
Komm(t) jetzt! Come
on!
Krawatte tie
Kreide chalk
Krokodil crocodile
Kuchen cake
Küche kitchen
Kuh cow
sich um jdn kümmern
look after sb
Kunde/Kundin
customer
Kunst art
Kurs course
kurz short
Kuscheltier cuddly toy

L

lächeln smile
Lampe lamp
lang long
langweilig boring
lass(t) uns ... let's
(= let us) ...

Lass(t) uns gehen!
Let's go!
laufen run
laut loud
leben, wohnen live
Lehrer/in teacher
leicht easy
lernen learn *(irr)*
lesen read *(irr)*
letzte(r, s) last
Leute people
Lexikon dictionary
Licht light
lieben, sehr mögen love
Ich würde lieber ...
I'd rather ...
Liebling; Lieblings-
favourite
am liebsten mögen
like best
Lineal ruler
Linie; Zeile line
Liste list
Löffel spoon
Löwe lion
Luftballon balloon
lustig funny; fun

 M

machen make *(irr)*;
do *(irr)*
Mach(t) schon! Come on!
Mädchen girl
März March
Mai May
Mama mum
man you
manchmal sometimes
Mann man *(pl* men)
Markt market
Marmelade jam
Maschine, Apparat
machine
Mathe maths
Maus mouse *(pl* mice)
Meerschweinchen
guinea pig
mehr; weitere more
mein(e) my
Menschen people
Messer knife *(pl* knives)
mich me
Milch milk
mir (to) me
mit; bei with

mit dem Bus by bus
mitbringen bring *(irr)*
mitmachen join
MIttagessen lunch
Mittagszeit, Mittags-
pause lunchtime
Mittwoch Wednesday
mögen like
am liebsten mögen
like best
Ich mag ... nicht. I don't
like ...
Montag Monday
Morgen morning
am Morgen in the
morning
Guten Morgen! Good
morning!
morgens, vormittags
*(nur hinter Uhrzeit
zwischen Mitternacht
und 12 Uhr mittags)*
am (= ante meridiem)
Müll rubbish
müssen have to
Mütze cap
Mund mouth
Murmel marble
Muschel seashell
Mutter mother

 N

nach past *(Uhrzeit)*;
after; to
Nachbar/in neighbour
nachdenken über think
about
Nachmittag afternoon
nachmittags *(nur hinter
Uhrzeit zwischen 12 Uhr
mittags und Mitternacht)*
pm (= post meridiem)
nächste(r, s) next
Nacken neck
Nase nose
nass wet
Natürlich! Of course!
Naturwissenschaft
science
neben next to
nehmen take *(irr)*
Ich nehme es. I'll take it.
nein no
nett nice
neu new

nicht not
nie, niemals never
niemand, keiner nobody
noch ein/e another
noch einmal again
noch etwas anything
else
sich Notizen machen
make notes
November November
nun well
nur, bloß only

 O

Obst fruit
oder or
öffnen, aufmachen open
oft, häufig often
Ohr ear
Oktober October
Onkel uncle
Orangensaft orange
juice
ordentlich,
aufgeräumt tidy
Ort place

P

Papa, Vati dad
Papagei parrot
Pause break
Pence p (= penny,
pence)
Pferd horse
Pfütze puddle
Pfund pound
ein Picknick machen
have a picnic
Pinguin penguin
Platz place
Pokalendspiel cup final
Postkarte postcard
präsentieren present (to)
Pullover jumper; sweater
putzen brush
sich die Zähne putzen
brush one's teeth

 R

Ratte rat
Raum room
Du hast recht. You're
right.
reden (mit) talk (to)
Regal shelf *(pl* shelves)

Regen rain
regnerisch rainy
an der Reihe sein be
one's turn
reiten ride (a horse)
Religion RE (= religious
education)
rennen run *(irr)*
richtig right
Rock skirt
rot red
Rücken back

 S

Sänger/in singer
sagen say *(irr)*
sammeln collect
Sammlung collection
Samstag Saturday
sauber machen clean
Schaf sheep *(pl* sheep)
Schal scarf *(pl* scarfs
or* scarves)
schaurig spooky
ein Tor schießen score
a goal
Schinkenspeck bacon
schlafen sleep *(irr)*
schlagen beat *(irr)*
schlank slim
Schnee snow
Schneemann snowman
(pl snowmen)
schnell fast
schön; nett nice
Schön, dich/euch/Sie
zu treffen. Nice to
meet you.
Schön, dich/euch/Sie
zu sehen. Nice to see
you.
Schokolade chocolate
Schrank cupboard
schrecklich terrible
schreiben write *(irr)*
Schreibtisch desk
Schüler/in pupil
(Schüler)versammlung
assembly
Schuh shoe
Schule school
Schulfach subject
Schuljahr, Klasse year
Schultag school day
Schultasche schoolbag

Schulter shoulder
schwarz black
Schwein pig
Schwester sister
Schwimmbad
swimming pool
schwimmen swim (irr)
Schwimmen gehen go
swimming
sehen see (irr)
(an)sehen, (an)schauen
look (at)
sehr very
Seife soap
sein be
sein/seine/seiner/seins
his
September September
setzen, stellen, legen
put (irr)
sich beeilen hurry up
sie she (weibl. Form
Sgl.); they (Plural-
form); her (weibl.
Form des Objekts);
them (Pluralform des
Objekts)
Sie you
singen sing (irr)
sitzen sit (irr)
Ski fahren, Ski laufen
ski
Socke sock
Sohn son
Sommer summer
Sonne sun
Sonnenbrille
sunglasses (pl)
sonnig sunny
Sonntag Sunday
Sonst noch etwas?,
Darf es noch etwas
sein? Anything else?
Sorte kind
Spaß fun
viel Spaß machen
be good fun
Spiegelei fried egg
Spiel match; game
spielen play
Spielplatz playground
Spielzeugauto toy car
Sport sport; (als Schul-
fach:) PE (= physical
education)

Sportcenter sports
centre
Sporthalle sports hall
Sportplatz sports field;
playing field
sprechen, reden
speak (irr)
sprechen (mit) talk (to)
sprechen über
talk about
springen jump
Stadt town
stark strong
staubsaugen vacuum
Stein stone
Steppdecke duvet
Stiefel boot
Stift pen
Straße street
auf der Straße in the
street
Stuhl chair
Stunde (Unterricht)
lesson
Stundenplan timetable
suchen nach look for
Supermarkt
supermarket

Tafel blackboard
Tag day
Tante aunt
tanzen dance
Taschenlampe torch
Tasse cup
Tee tea
teilnehmen an take
part in
am Telefon on the
phone
Teller plate
Tier animal
Tiger tiger
Tisch table
Tischtennis table
tennis
Tochter daughter
Tomate tomato
(pl tomatoes)
ein Tor schießen score
a goal
träumen dream (irr)
tragen wear (irr)
traurig sad

treffen; sich treffen
meet (irr)
trinken drink (irr);
have (irr)
Trinken; Getränk drink
tschüs(s) bye
Tür door
tun do (irr)
etw gern tun like doing
sth
Turnen do gymnastics
Turnhalle gym
(= gymnasium)
Turnschuhe trainers

U-Bahn-Station station
üben practise
Übernachtung
sleepover
Überprüfung der An-
wesenheit registration
Uhr o'clock (bei
Nennung von
Uhrzeiten); clock
um at (Uhrzeit)
umsteigen change
und and
ungefähr about
unheimlich spooky
unordentlich, unauf-
geräumt untidy
unsere(r, s) our
unter under
Unterricht lesson
unterrichten teach

Vater father
Vergiss' nicht .../
Vergesst nicht ...!
Don't forget ...!
Verkäufer/in seller
Verkaufen selling
verlassen; abfahren
leave
verschneit, schnee-
reich snowy
verstehen understand
Ich verstehe es nicht.
I don't understand.
viel much
viel, jede Menge lots of
viele many, a lot (of)
Viertel quarter (Uhrzeit)

Viertel, Nachbarschaft
neighbourhood
violett, lila purple
Vogel bird
von of; from
vor before (zeitlich); to;
in front of (räumlich)

Wand wall
wann when
warm warm
warten auf wait for
warum why
Warum ... du nicht ...?
Why don't you ...?
Was hältst du davon?
What do you think?
Was ist deine Telefon-
nummer? What's your
phone number?
Was ist los? What's on?
Was ist mit ...?/
Wie wäre es mit ...?
What about ...?
was sonst what else
was; welche(r, s) what
(sich) waschen wash
Wasser water
Wechselgeld change
wechseln change
Weg; Art, Weise way
weil, da because
weiß white
weitere more
welche(r, s); was which
Wellensittich budgie
Welt world
wenn; als when
wer; der/die/das who
wessen whose
Wetter weather
wie how; like
Wie alt bist du/sind
Sie? How old are
you?
Wie geht es dir?/
Wie geht es Ihnen?
How are you?
Wie heißt du? What's
your name?
wie man how to
Wie spät ist es? What
time is it?
wie viel how much

Wie viel kostet es?
How much is it?
wie viele how many
Auf Wiedersehen.
Goodbye.
Wind wind
windig windy
Winter winter
wir we
wissen know (irr)
Ich weiß es nicht.
I don't know.

witzig fun
wo; wohin where
Woche week
Wochenende weekend
am Wochenende at the
weekend
Woher kommst du?
Where are you from?
Wohnzimmer living
room
Wolke cloud
wollen want

Wort word
Wurst, Würstchen
sausage

Zahl; Nummer number
Zahn tooth (pl teeth)
sich die Zähne putzen
brush one's teeth
Zahnbürste toothbrush
Zahnpasta toothpaste
zeichnen draw (irr)

Zeit time
Zeitschrift magazine
Zimmer room
Zoo zoo
zuerst first
Zuhause; Haus home
zuhören listen (to)
zum Frühstück for
breakfast
zurück back
zweite (r, s) second
zwischen between

Girls/Women

Abby /'æbi/
Alice /'ælɪs/
Amy /'eɪmi/
Anna /'ænə/
Becky /'beki/
Carol /'kærəl/
Caroline /'kærəlaɪn/
Catherine /'kæθrɪn/
Eleanor /'elənə/
Emily /'eməli/
Emma /'emə/
Eve /i:v/
Fay /feɪ/
Gillian /'dʒɪliən/
Gwen /gwen/
Inka /'ɪŋkə/
Janet /'dʒænɪt/
Jill /dʒɪl/
Josephine /'dʒəʊzɪfi:n/
Judy /'dʒu:di/
Karla /'ka:lə/
Karlotta /ka:'lɒtə/
Katie /'keɪti/
Laura /'lɔ:rə/
Leonie /'li:əni/
Li /'li:/
Lily /'lɪli/
Lisa /'li:sə/
Liz /lɪz/
Lotta /'lɒtə/
Lucy /'lu:si/
Lynn /lɪn/
Milly /'mɪli/
Mo /məʊ/
Ness /nes/
Paula /'pɔ:lə/
Penny /'peni/
Rebecca /ri'bekə/
Rose /rəʊz/
Ruby /'ru:bi/
Sally /'sæli/
Sara, Sarah /'seərə/
Semra /'semrə/
Sharon /'ʃærən/
Sophie /'səʊfi/
Stella /'stelə/
Susan /'su:zn/
TJ /ˌti:'dʒeɪ/
Vanessa /və'nesə/

Boys/Men

Alexander /ˌælɪg'za:ndə/
Amir /ə'mɪə/
Arne /a:n/
Ben /ben/
Berry /'beri/
Bertie /'bɜ:ti/
Bill /bɪl/
Boris /'bɒrɪs/
Brian /'braɪən/
Bruce /bru:s/
Cem /dʒem/
Charlie /'tʃa:li/
Cihan /'dʒɪha:n/
Clive /klaɪv/
Dan, Daniel /dæn, 'dænjəl/
David /'deɪvɪd/
Dennis /'denɪs/
Diego /di'eɪgəʊ/
Duncan /'dʌŋkən/
Hassan /hə'sa:n/
Ishaan /'ɪʃa:n/
Ivor /'aɪvə/
Jack /dʒæk/
Jan /jæn/
Jem /dʒem/
Joe /dʒəʊ/
John /dʒɒn/
Jonty /'dʒɒnti/
Josh /dʒɒʃ/
Justin /'dʒʌstɪn/
Kai /kaɪ/
Karim /kə'ri:m/
Luka /'lu:kə/
Luke /lu:k/
Max /mæks/
Mehmet /'memet/
Morgan /'mɔ:gən/
Nick /nɪk/
Oliver /'ɒlɪvə/
Paul /pɔ:l/
Pete, Peter /pi:t, 'pi:tə/
Phil /fɪl/
Popeye /'pɒpaɪ/
Rajiv /ra:'ʒi:v/
Rhys /ri:s/
Richard /'rɪtʃəd/
Rob, Robert /rɒb, 'rɒbət/
Rosh /rɒʃ/
Roshan /'rɒʃa:n/
Sherlock /'ʃɜ:lɒk/

Skipper /'skɪpə/
Spike /spaɪk/
Tarzan /'ta:zn/
Thomas /'tɒməs/
Tim /tɪm/
Toby /'təʊbi/
Tom /tɒm/

Families

Batson /'bætsən/
Bennett /'benɪt/
Blake /bleɪk/
Collins /'kɒlɪnz/
Fyleman /'faɪlmæn/
Goldman /'gəʊldmæn/
Harnett /'ha:nɪt/
Holmes /'həʊmz/
Howard /'haʊəd/
Jensen /'dʒensən/
King /kɪŋ/
Lalli /'læli/
Lamont /'læmənt/
McDonald /mək'dɒnəld/
McHowl /mək'haʊl/
Miller /'mɪlə/
Milligan /'mɪlɪgən/
Nelson /'nelsən/
Nissen /'nɪsn/
Ross /rɒs/
Smith /smɪθ/
Thorn /θɔ:n/
Timberlake /'tɪmbəleɪk/
Watson /'wɒtsn/
Welch /weltʃ/
White /waɪt/
Williams /'wɪljəmz/

Other Names

Acklam /'ækləm/
Antarctic Elephants /ænˌta:ktɪkˈelɪfənts/
Arsenal /'a:snl/
Bakerloo /ˌbeɪkə'lu:/
BaySixty6 /ˌbeɪ ˌsɪksti 'sɪks/
Billionaire Boy /ˌbɪljə'neə bɔɪ/
bingo /'bɪŋgəʊ/
Blues /blu:z/
Burger Queen /'bɜ:gə ˌkwi:n/
Butterfly /'bʌtəˌflaɪ/

Camden /'kæmdən/
Camden Lock /ˌkæmdən 'lɒk/
Chelsea /'tʃelsi/
Furry Friend /ˌfɜ:ri 'frend/
Hammersmith & City Line /ˌhæməsmɪθ ˌən 'sɪti ˌlaɪn/
Hampton Court /ˌhæmptən 'kɔ:t/
Hendon Central /ˌhendən 'sentrəl/
Hendon Goldfish Club /ˌhendən 'gəʊldfɪʃ klʌb/
Hendon School /ˌhendən 'sku:l/
High Street /'haɪ stri:t/
Hindi /'hɪndi/
Holland Park /ˌhɒlənd 'pa:k/
Hoover /'hu:və/
Hoppity /'hɒpəti/
Ickenham /'ɪkənəm/
Kenny, Kenny Hoover /'keni, ˌkeni 'hu:və/
Kentish Town /ˌkentɪʃ 'taʊn/
Kings Cross /ˌkɪŋz 'krɒs/
Ladbroke Grove /ˌlædbrʊk 'grəʊv/
Magic Boys /ˌmædʒɪk 'bɔɪz/
Mega /'megə/
Northern Line /ˌnɔ:ðn 'laɪn/
Notting Hill /ˌnɒtɪŋ 'hɪl/
Notting Hill Gate /ˌnɒtɪŋ 'hɪl ˌgeɪt/
Portobello Road /ˌpɔ:təˌbeləʊ 'rəʊd/
Punjabi /pʌn'dʒa:bi:/
Purry /'pɜ:ri/
Rainbow /'reɪnbəʊ/
Reds /redz/
Scary Mary /ˌskeəri 'meəri/
Skip /skɪp/
Spot /spɒt/
Tabby /'tæbi/
tabla /'tæblə/

Teentalk /'ti:ntɔ:k/
Teenzone /'ti:nzəʊn/
The Lion King
 /ðə 'laɪən ˌkɪŋ/
Tower Bridge
 /ˌtaʊə 'brɪdʒ/
Victoria /vɪk'tɔ:riə/
Westbourne Park
 /ˌwestbɔ:n 'pa:k/

Westbourne Park
 Station /ˌwestbɔ:n
 ˌpa:k 'steɪʃn/

Geographical Names
Aalborg /'ɔ:l bɔ:g/
Barbados /ba:'beɪdɒs/
Blackpool /'blækpu:l/
Denmark /'denma:k/

Enfield /'enfi:ld/
England /'ɪŋglənd/
Germany /'dʒɜ:məni/
Hastings /'heɪstɪŋz/
Hendon /'hendən/
India /'ɪndiə/
Leeds /li:dz/
Liverpool /'lɪvəpu:l/
London /'lʌndən/

Newcastle /'nju:ˌka:sl/
Norwich /'nɒrɪdʒ/
Ramsgate /'ræmzgeɪt/
Scotland /'skɒtlənd/
Switzerland /'swɪtsələnd/
Tenby /'tenbi/
Thames /temz/
Wales /weɪlz/
York /jɔ:k/

Numbers

0	oh, zero, nil /əʊ, 'zɪərəʊ, nɪl/	78	seventy-eight /ˌsevnti'eɪt/	7th	seventh /sevnθ/
1	one /wʌn/	80	eighty /'eɪti/	8th	eighth /eɪtθ/
2	two /tu:/	89	eighty-nine /ˌeɪti'naɪn/	9th	ninth /naɪnθ/
3	three /θri:/	90	ninety /'naɪnti/	10th	tenth /tenθ/
4	four /fɔ:/	100	a/one hundred /ə/wʌn 'hʌndrəd/	11th	eleventh /ɪ'levnθ/
5	five /faɪv/			12th	twelfth /twelfθ/
6	six /sɪks/	101	one hundred and one /wʌn ˌhʌndrəd ən 'wʌn/	13th	thirteenth /ˌθɜ:'ti:nθ/
7	seven /sevn/	102	one hundred and two /wʌn ˌhʌndrəd ən 'tu:/	14th	fourteenth /ˌfɔ:'ti:nθ/
8	eight /eɪt/			15th	fifteenth /ˌfɪf'ti:nθ/
9	nine /naɪn/	110	one hundred and ten /wʌn ˌhʌndrəd ən 'ten/	16th	sixteenth /ˌsɪks'ti:nθ/
10	ten /ten/	200	two hundred /tu: 'hʌndrəd/	17th	seventeenth /ˌsevn'ti:nθ/
11	eleven /ɪ'levn/			18th	eighteenth /ˌeɪ'ti:nθ/
12	twelve /twelv/	1,000	a/one thousand /ə/wʌn 'θauznd/	19th	nineteenth /ˌnaɪn'ti:nθ/
13	thirteen /ˌθɜ:'ti:n/	1,001	one thousand and one /wʌn ˌθauznd ən 'wʌn/	20th	twentieth /'twentiəθ/
14	fourteen /ˌfɔ:'ti:n/			21st	twenty-first /ˌtwenti'fɜ:st/
15	fifteen /ˌfɪf'ti:n/	1,111	one thousand one hundred and eleven /wʌn ˌθauznd wʌn ˌhʌndrəd ən ɪ'levn/	22nd	twenty-second /ˌtwenti'sekənd/
16	sixteen /ˌsɪks'ti:n/	2,000	two thousand /tu: 'θauznd/	23rd	twenty-third /ˌtwenti'θɜ:d/
17	seventeen /ˌsevn'ti:n/	10,000	ten thousand /ten 'θauznd/		
18	eighteen /ˌeɪ'ti:n/	100,000	a/one hundred thousand /ə/wʌn ˌhʌndrəd 'θauznd/	30th	thirtieth /'θɜ:tiəθ/
19	nineteen /ˌnaɪn'ti:n/			40th	fortieth /'fɔ:tiəθ/
20	twenty /'twenti/	1,000,000	a/one million /ə/wʌn 'mɪljən/	50th	fiftieth /'fɪftiəθ/
21	twenty-one /ˌtwenti'wʌn/	1,000,000,000	a/one billion /ə/wʌn 'bɪljən/	60th	sixtieth /'sɪkstiəθ/
22	twenty-two /ˌtwenti'tu:/			70th	seventieth /'sevntiəθ/
30	thirty /'θɜ:ti/	1st	first /fɜ:st/	80th	eightieth /'eɪtiəθ/
33	thirty-three /ˌθɜ:ti'θri:/	2nd	second /'sekənd/	90th	ninetieth /'naɪntiəθ/
34	thirty-four /ˌθɜ:ti'fɔ:/	3rd	third /θɜ:d/	100th	hundredth /'hʌndrədθ/
40	forty /'fɔ:ti/	4th	fourth /fɔ:θ/		
45	forty-five /ˌfɔ:ti'faɪv/	5th	fifth /fɪfθ/	$\frac{1}{2}$	a/one half /ə/wʌn 'ha:f/
50	fifty /'fɪfti/	6th	sixth /sɪksθ/	$\frac{1}{3}$	a/one third /ə/wʌn 'θɜ:d/
56	fifty-six /ˌfɪfti'sɪks/			$\frac{1}{4}$	a/one quarter /ə/wʌn 'kwɔ:tə/
60	sixty /'sɪksti/			$\frac{1}{8}$	a/one eighth /ə/wʌnˌ'eɪtθ/
67	sixty-seven /ˌsɪksti'sevn/			$\frac{3}{4}$	three quarters /θri: 'kwɔ:təz/
70	seventy /'sevnti/				

infinitive		simple past	infinitive		simple past
be /biː/	sein	was/were /wɒz/wɜː/	leave /liːv/	verlassen; abfahren	left /left/
beat /biːt/	schlagen	beat /biːt/	let /let/	lassen	let /let/
begin /bɪˈgɪn/	anfangen, beginnen	began /bɪˈgæn/	lose /luːz/	verlieren	lost /lɒst/
			make /meɪk/	machen	made /meɪd/
bite /baɪt/	beißen	bit /bɪt/	mean /miːn/	meinen	meant /ment/
bring /brɪŋ/	mitbringen	brought /brɔːt/	meet /miːt/	(sich) treffen	met /met/
build /bɪld/	bauen	built /bɪlt/	put /pʊt/	setzen, stellen, legen	put /pʊt/
buy /baɪ/	kaufen	bought /bɔːt/			
catch /kætʃ/	fangen	caught /kɔːt/	read /riːd/	lesen	read /red/
come /kʌm/	kommen	came /keɪm/	ride /raɪd/	fahren; reiten	rode /rəʊd/
cut /kʌt/	schneiden	cut /kʌt/	ring /rɪŋ/	klingeln, läuten	rang /ræŋ/
choose /tʃuːz/	wählen; sich entscheiden	chose /tʃəʊz/	run /rʌn/	laufen; rennen	ran /ræn/
			say /seɪ/	sagen	said /sed/
do /duː/	machen; tun	did /dɪd/	see /siː/	sehen	saw /sɔː/
draw /drɔː/	zeichnen	drew /druː/	send /send/	schicken	sent /sent/
dream /driːm/	träumen	dreamt /dremt/	shine /ʃaɪn/	scheinen	shone /ʃɒn/
drink /drɪŋk/	trinken	drank /dræŋk/	show /ʃəʊ/	zeigen	showed /ʃəʊd/
eat /iːt/	essen	ate /eɪt/	sing /sɪŋ/	singen	sang /sæŋ/
fall /fɔːl/	fallen	fell /fel/	sit /sɪt/	sitzen	sat /sæt/
feed /fiːd/	füttern	fed /fed/	sleep /sliːp/	schlafen	slept /slept/
feel /fiːl/	sich fühlen	felt /felt/	smell /smel/	riechen	smelt/smelled /smelt/smeld/
find /faɪnd/	finden	found /faʊnd/			
fly /flaɪ/	fliegen	flew /fluː/	speak /spiːk/	sprechen, reden	spoke /spəʊk/
forget /fəˈget/	vergessen	forgot /fəˈgɒt/	spell /spel/	buchstabieren	spelt/spelled /spelt/speld/
get /get/	bekommen	got /gɒt/			
give /gɪv/	geben	gave /geɪv/	stand /stænd/	stehen	stood /stʊd/
go /gəʊ/	gehen	went /went/	steal /stiːl/	stehlen	stole /stəʊl/
grow /grəʊ/	wachsen	grew /gru/	swim /swɪm/	schwimmen	swam /swæm/
hang /hæŋ/	aufhängen	hung /hʌŋ/	take /teɪk/	bringen; nehmen	took /tʊk/
have /hæv/	haben; essen, trinken	had /hæd/	teach /tiːtʃ/	unterrichten	taught /tɔːt/
			tell /tel/	erzählen	told /təʊld/
hear /hɪə/	hören	heard /hɜːd/	think /θɪŋk/	denken; glauben	thought /θɔːt/
hit /hɪt/	treffen, stoßen gegen	hit /hɪt/	throw /θrəʊ/	werfen	threw /θruː/
			understand /ˌʌndəˈstænd/	verstehen	understood /ˌʌndəˈstʊd/
hurt /hɜːt/	wehtun, schmerzen	hurt /hɜːt/	wear /weə/	tragen	wore /wɔː/
know /nəʊ/	kennen; wissen	knew /njuː/	win /wɪn/	gewinnen	won /wʌn/
learn /lɜːn/	lernen	learnt/learned /lɜːnt/lɜːnd/	write /raɪt/	schreiben	wrote /rəʊt/

Tipp:
Einige Verben bilden das simple past nach einem ähnlichen Muster.
Wenn du sie dir in Gruppen sortierst, kannst du dir die Formen vielleicht besser merken.
z. B.: bring – brought, buy – bought, teach – taught, think – thought
oder: cut – cut, let – let, put – put
oder: draw – drew, fly – flew, grow – grew, know – knew

Kannst du noch mehr solche Gruppen bilden?

REPUBLIC
OF
IRELAND

UNITED
KINGDOM

GERMANY

Atlantic Ocean

Shetland
Islands

Orkney
Islands

Outer
Hebrides

Lewis

Skye

▲ Ben Nevis
1344 m

Scotland

Balmoral

Aberdeen

Edinburgh

Tweed

Glasgow

Northern

North Sea